MITHRIDATES
THE GREAT

This is for Derek, who knows that despotic and incompetent governments are not found only in antiquity.

MITHRIDATES THE GREAT

Rome's Indomitable Enemy

Philip Matyszak

Pen & Sword
MILITARY

First published in Great Britain in 2008 by
PEN & SWORD MILITARY
an imprint of
Pen & Sword Books Ltd
47 Church Street
Barnsley
South Yorkshire
S70 2AS

ISBN 978 1 84415 834 8

Printed and bound in Great Britain
By CPI UK

Pen & Sword Books Ltd incorporates the Imprints of
Pen & Sword Aviation, Pen & Sword Family History, Pen & Sword Maritime,
Pen & Sword Military, Wharncliffe Local History,
Pen & Sword Select, Pen & Sword Military Classics, Leo Cooper,
Remember When, Seaforth Publishing and Frontline Publishing

For a complete list of Pen & Sword titles please contact
PEN & SWORD BOOKS LIMITED
47 Church Street, Barnsley, South Yorkshire, S70 2AS, England
E-mail: enquiries@pen-and-sword.co.uk
Website: www.pen-and-sword.co.uk

Contents

Preface

'Mithridates – what a character! I wish Hollywood would realize some true stories are far more interesting than fiction.' So commented one of those whom I approached for help with this project.

And it is true that the life of Mithridates VI Eupator of Pontus reads like an overblown film script of the 1950s. It has palace coups, plots and assassinations. It features incest, fratricide and an unhealthy fascination with poison. There are epic battles, sieges and massacres, kingdoms in turmoil, distressed princesses, corrupt officials and pirates. All that is lacking in the epic drama that was the life of Mithridates is a hero – in this entire saga of battle, double-dealing and betrayal, a good man is indeed hard to find.

Certainly Mithridates does not qualify. The murder of his brother and several of his sons may be forgiveable given the ruthless Darwinism of Hellenistic dynasties, but the massacre of some 80,000 civilians in one day, and the casual execution of prisoners and hostages when it seemed expedient make Mithridates seem at times almost a monster.

Yet at other times, Mithridates is magnificent. Magnificent in his loyalty to his friends (he once refused to accept they they were conspiring against him until he hid under a couch to hear them plot his betrayal), in his physical courage, and above all, magnificent in his indomitable refusal to admit defeat or contemplate surrender. This is a character who left a sinking ship when a pirate vessel came alongside and by sheer force of personality not only persuaded the pirates to take him to safe harbour, but also to salvage his ship. Mithridates was a man who, as an aged refugee, could flee into an uncharted and barbaric wilderness with a handful of followers, and come out of the other side with an army. He was ruthless, Machiavellian and bloodthirsty, but, most certainly, he was a King. Well he deserves his title of 'the Great'.

Yet for all this, Mithridates is little known, even to scholars of antiquity. The trends of modern research have led more toward sociological and economic studies, and the biography of great men, even those who trod the central stage of antiquity, has fallen somewhat by the wayside. The most recent studies of Mithridates are those of A N Sherwin-White in his magisterial *Roman Foreign Policy in the East*, and the more eclectic yet immaculately researched *The Foreign Policy of Mithridates Eupator* by B C McGing. Even these two books were written almost a quarter of a century ago, and for an academic audience.

This volume aims to make Mithridates accessible to a more general readership, and I take the opportunity to thank those – from Oxford scholars to Turkish travel guides – for the enthusiasm which they showed in helping to bring this story to life. No understanding of Cappadocian dynasties is required to enjoy this book, and the convoluted politics of the region have been subordinated in what is primarily the history of a war where the front line moved from Athens to the Euphrates and a good way back again. If this book has heroes, it is the Pontic soldiery who took on the killing machine of the Roman army and came closer to breaking it than is generally realized. To a large degree, this is primarily their story.

The loyalty of these men to their king through decades of warfare, through heady triumphs and crushing defeats is a remarkable testament to their stubbornness and to the charisma of the man who led them. Chronicling the life of Mithridates has been a fascinating exercise, and I strongly suspect that, even after two millennia, the defiant Pontic battle king will still attract new followers.

Innsbruck, 2008

Acknowledgements

As always, this book has partly been the result of discussions with others in the ancient world. I'd particularly like to thank Adrian Goldsworthy for reading and commenting on some of the battles, and Barbara Levick for her encouragement. My thanks also go to those who generously contributed pictures for this project, and to the members of the UNRV forum who pointed me to some interesting sources on Mithridatic poisons. I also owe thanks to Denise Cles and her husband Mark for their hospitality and, above all, to my wife Malgosia, who fed, watered and occasionally dusted me whilst I spent 2007 immersed in books and journals.

List of Plates

Maps

List of Maps

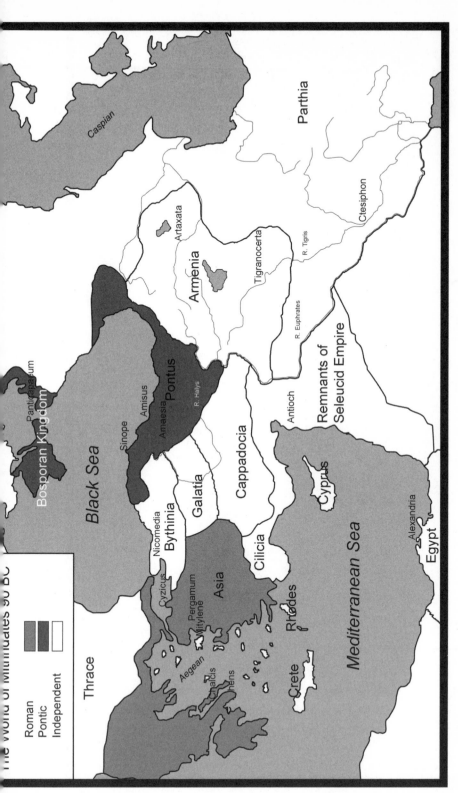

The world of Mithridates. The date of 90 BC is only an approximate guide; for example, the Armenian empire is shown at its (later) greatest extent.

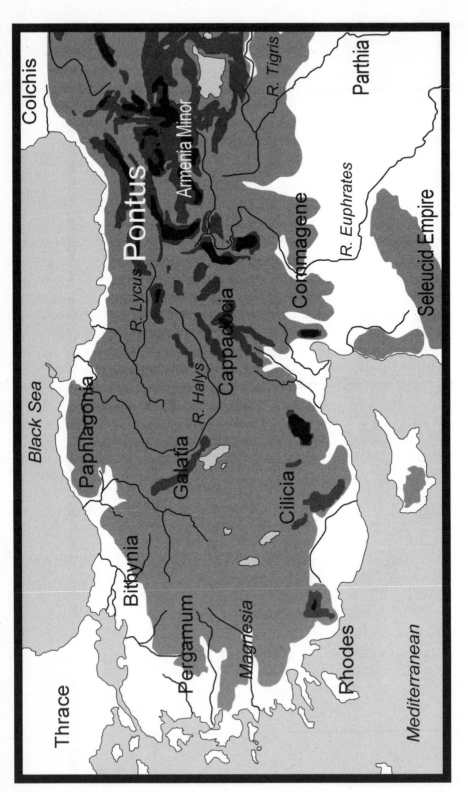

Asia Minor, showing major regions and physical geography.

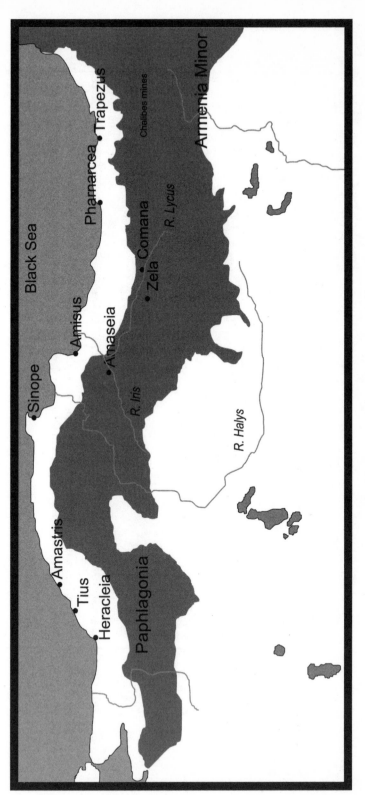

Physical geography of Pontus showing the approximate positions of the main cities, uplands and river systems.

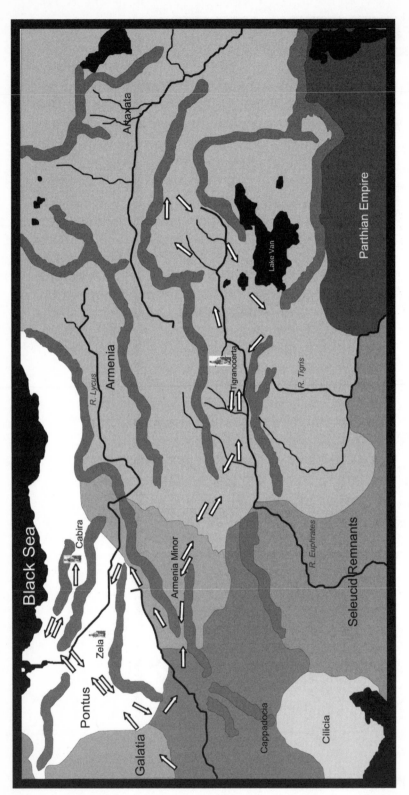

There and back again. Map depicting the possible approximate route of the Fimbrian legions during their final campaign under Lucullus. In reality their travels to the north of Lake Van were considerably more convoluted and extensive.

Introduction

The World of Mithridates

When Mithridates VI of Pontus was born in 120 BC, his homeland of Asia Minor was at the centre of the world. To the south and east, beyond the mountains of Armenia, lay Mesopotamia, the land between the Tigris and Euphrates rivers. This was the fabled cradle of civilization, home of cities such as Ur and Assur, where man had first learned the arts of building and writing – and organized warfare.

Just west of Mesopotamia lay Syria and Palestine, home of the Semitic peoples who had taught writing to the Greeks. Damascus, today the oldest continuously inhabited city in the world, was already four millennia into its six thousand years of history. The Jewish people had their kingdom centred around Jerusalem, whilst Syria was the heartland of the failing but powerful Hellenic empire of Alexander the Great's successors, the Seleucids. Even in Mithridates' time these eastern cultures were ancient – the Assyrian and Babylonian empires had risen and fallen, as had the Achaemenid empire of Cyrus the Persian, whose realm had encompassed all of Asia Minor and had even threatened Greece until the Persian myriads were defeated at Marathon and Salamis.

Further south and west again, Egypt, like Syria, was under Hellenic rule. After the death of Alexander, Egypt had been claimed by his general Ptolemy, and his dynasty ruled there still. Just as the Nile met the Mediterranean, the Greek and Egyptian worlds met at Alexandria, at this time the world's unrivalled centre of culture and learning, home of two of the great wonders of the ancient world – the lighthouse at the city's harbour of Pharos and the Great Library.

The Greek historian Herodotus claimed that his homeland owed much to the culture of Egypt. Though younger than the great civilizations of the east, Greece had already given much to the world in theatre, art, architecture, and above all in the restless inquiring spirit of its peoples. Just as the Greeks had pushed forward the boundaries of learning in philosophy, mathematics, and literature, they had also pushed back the borders of the known world. They had founded colonies across the Mediterranean, from Marseilles in the west to the eastern shores of the Black Sea in Colchis, the fabled land to which Jason and his Argonauts had travelled in their search for the golden fleece (and the

Greeks had also planted their colonies on the shores of Pontus itself). Beyond the Greek cities to the north and west, extending as far as the Crimea were the lands of the nomad horse warriors known as the Scythians. Further north yet was the land of the Sarmatians; aristocratic warriors in heavy armour, cavalry perhaps superior to any in the world at that time – superb horsemen, tough and well-equipped, the Sarmatians were the perfect foil to the armoured infantrymen favoured by the Hellenistic states.

The wild lands bordering the Black Sea to the east of Macedon were home to the people of Thrace. The Thracians were an ancient people, skilled in metalwork and horse training, yet their home on the western plains was constantly troubled by invaders and the dissensions of their feuding tribes.

And far to the west, beyond Greece, on the borders of the civilized world (or as others argued, just beyond them), was the nascent power of Rome. Rome was a new and terrifying phenomenon, with its almost unbeatable legions, its crude and unsophisticated grasp of diplomacy, and the vagaries of its politics, which depended on whom the fickle masses of that city voted into power each year. Rome had already defeated Macedon, the homeland of Alexander the Great, and now the Hellenic kingdoms in Syria and Asia Minor watched Rome's growing power with fully-justified foreboding.

The Shadow of Rome

Yet when the Greek world had first become aware of Rome over a century before, it had been with the awareness of a predator seeing a large and tempting quarry wander into view. At that time Rome had just gained the upper hand in a long drawn-out series of wars with the mountain peoples of south central Italy. Not that the hillmen had yet admitted defeat – their stubborn refusal to submit to Rome would still provide a welcome distraction for Rome's armies in Mithridates' day. However, by 290 BC the Romans had at least temporarily beaten their foes into sullen submission, leaving Rome the dominant state in Italy.

It might occur to a general with an ambitiously expansionist viewpoint that an army which defeated Rome could easily mop up the rest of Italy, use Italy's massive reserves of manpower to absorb Sicily, and from there sweep east once more and conquer the rest of the world. That, roughly, was the master plan of Pyrrhus of Epirus, another of the successors of Alexander the Great, and generally agreed to be the best general of his day. Claiming that he was supporting the Greek cities of southern Italy against Roman aggression, Pyrrhus and his army of 25,000 men invaded the peninsula during the 280s BC and tried repeatedly to master Rome.

It was the first clash of the Greek and Roman worlds, and from the Roman perspective this passage of arms ended as a winning draw. Pyrrhus was unable to wear down the stubborn resistance of Rome, despite repeatedly beating its citizens in the series of bloody battles which have given the modern world the expression 'a pyrrhic victory', meaning a win which costs more than it is worth. The battles left both armies exhausted, but the Romans, fighting on their native soil, had greater stamina in terms of money and manpower. Belatedly, Pyrrhus concluded that he had bitten off more than he could chew. He withdrew, possibly to marshal his forces for a further attempt. However, Pyrrhus died before he could resume his assault, and his failure handed the Romans hegemony of the Italian peninsula.

Graeco–Roman relations remained in a state of armed non–aggression for the remainder of the third century BC. This is not to say that the world was at peace – far from it. The empire of Alexander the Great had fractured into the kingdoms of Macedonia, which also dominated Greece, the Seleucids, with their rambling, semi–shambolic empire that stretched from the Mediterranean coast almost to the Himalayas, and the Ptolemies who dominated Egypt. These states, each large enough to be considered empires in their own right, engaged in continual and largely-pointless warfare which produced little change apart from mercenaries becoming wealthy and border peasants perpetually confused as to which empire they were currently part of.

Rome too had been engaged in non-stop warfare. However, by the time Rome had finished, a large number of North Africans, Gauls and Spaniards, Corsicans and Sicilians were left in no doubt at all as to which empire was in charge. Many of Rome's new possessions were acquired at the cost of Carthage, Rome's great rival in the west. By 202 BC Carthage had been reduced to a shadow of its former glory, and Hannibal, the general who had almost brought Rome to its knees with his epic invasion across the Alps, had fled to the Hellenic kingdoms of Asia.

Roman eyes followed Hannibal east. It would be wrong to claim that Pyrrhus' master plan was dusted down and rewritten for Roman protagonists, but it is also certain that the Roman senate considered that it had unfinished business with the heirs of Alexander.

Rome itself was changing. By and large the Greeks had heretofore regarded the Romans as uncivilized, simply because the Romans had no art of their own, no literature, and indeed, barely any pretension to literacy. That the greatest Roman historians were currently alive was only because they were the first ones that Rome had ever had. However, Rome was beginning to acquire culture –

admittedly this culture had been looted wholesale from other cities, but it was culture nevertheless. Matters such as the theatre were beginning to stir interest, and once Rome got over its bemusement at the first Greek philosophers to arrive in the city, intellectual inquiry became socially acceptable among the warrior elite that ruled Rome under the name of 'the Senate'. Over the next two generations Greek culture was to make the same sort of headway in Rome as Roman legions were making in Greece – 'Conquering her rough conqueror' as one poet put it. By the 140s BC even Cato the Elder, a misanthropic anti-Hellenic reactionary, saw nothing incongruous in erecting Rome's first basilica – a Greek-style building for use in public affairs. Even Roman religion began to merge with the Greek version, until only the names of the gods and goddesses differed. But sharing much of the same culture did not make the Romans more Greek – they called contemporary Greeks 'Graeculi ' ('Greeklings' or 'little Greeks') - diminished descendants of their great forebears. And as for the peoples who shared Asia Minor with the Greeks, well, they were Asiatics – decadent, cowardly, servile, and generally beneath contempt. It never seemed to occur to the Romans, in all the decades that followed, that their contempt and lack of understanding were just as heartily reciprocated by the peoples of Asia Minor.

Philip V of Macedon, the Hellenistic ruler nearest to Rome, had long been uncomfortable with Roman interference on the western shores of the Greek peninsula. Consequently, although Greek and Carthaginian usually got along like cat and dog, Philip had allied himself with Hannibal in the war against Rome. True, Philip's actual contribution to the war effort had been negligible, but Rome had reasons for being unforgiving. After sixteen desperate years of warfare against Hannibal, Rome needed slaves to work her depopulated fields, money for her depleted treasury, and money also to pay for the increasingly luxurious tastes of her upper classes. Like any shrewd business concern, Rome chose to leverage her prime asset to clear her liabilities. And Rome's prime asset was a very, very good army, honed to perfection by a decade and a half of fighting Hannibal, the greatest tactician until Napoleon.

Furthermore, Philip was then allied with the Seleucid king Antiochus III, and the pair were picking off those small Greek city states which attempted to maintain a degree of independence. For the imperial power which Rome now rightly considered herself to be, these small states were potential stepping stones into mainland Greece, so the senate was none too pleased to see the Hellenic empires consolidating the region under their control. Rome hastened to ally herself with such of these small states as remained. Sooner or later, the senate reasoned (sooner, as it happened), Philip's territorial ambitions in Greece would bring him into collision with their new allies, and thus Philip would provoke war with Rome itself.

Philip did not go down without a fight – he fought with skill and tenacity, but still was driven out of Greece. In 197 BC his phalanx and his determination to resist were broken in the Battle of Cynoscephalae. Philip paid over a thousand talents of bullion, and sullenly yielded hegemony of Greece. The Romans, conscious of Macedon's value as a bulwark against the wild tribes further north, let his kingdom of Macedonia be – for the present.

The Greek cities had largely supported the Romans against Philip in return for their 'freedom'. They remained passive, leaving the Romans with secure lines of communication as they went on to challenge the greatest of the Hellenistic realms – the Seleucids. Antiochus III had been warned by the Romans that he should confine his activities to the east of the Aegean Sea, a warning which the Seleucid king blithely ignored. Taking advantage of Philip's discomfiture at the hands of the Roman legions, Antiochus blatantly interfered in the affairs of Thrace, right next door to Macedon on the coast of the Black Sea.

Rome may have defeated Macedon close to home, but Antiochus appears to have been convinced that the upstart power would receive a brutal reality check if it was foolish enough to challenge the Seleucids on their own ground. This conviction was soon put to the test as Rome was not slow to pick up the gauntlet. An army arrived, led by Lucius Scipio, who in turn was accompanied by his brother, the famous Scipio Africanus, the conqueror of Hannibal. The decisive confrontation between two sides occurred in 190 BC at the Battle of Magnesia. Partly through the help of the army of Pergamum, Roman allies in Asia Minor, the Romans were victorious. This was a decisive moment in the history of the eastern Mediterranean, for though the Romans had no intention of occupying Seleucid territory (though gold and slaves would still do nicely, both as tribute and booty), Seleucid power was irrevocably weakened by defeat. Antiochus was forced to restrict his sphere of influence again, this time to the Syrian side of the Taurus Mountains, leaving Rome the dominant power in Asia Minor.

The Seleucid empire, always a somewhat ramshackle affair, now began the generations-long process of slowly falling apart at the seams. When Antiochus IV attempted to restore his dynasty's fortunes in 168 BC with an invasion of Egypt, he and his army were stopped by a single Roman envoy. The envoy bluntly ordered the king and his army to turn back. When Antiochus asked for time to consider his options, the Roman used his stick of office to draw a line in the sand around the king. He informed Antiochus that he was not to step over that line until he had decided on his course of action. That course of action, when Antiochus eventually got over his indignation, turned out to be the cancellation of the invasion, and a retreat back to Asia with whatever shreds of dignity could be retrieved from the situation. It was a chilling demonstration, both of the power of the Romans and of their arrogant ignorance of how to behave in civilized society.

If the Seleucids were content to allow their empire to moulder slowly away, the Macedonians chose to go out with a bang. Their agents were constantly fomenting problems for the Romans in Greece, whilst in any case, the Romans found themselves driven to distraction by the petty feuds and small wars with which the Greek cities celebrated their new freedom. In 167 BC the Romans deposed the Macedonian king, and when even that proved insufficient to control his irrepressible nation, they finally occupied Macedon and made it a province in 147 BC.

At the same time the Romans bluntly informed the Greeks of the limits of their freedom by making an example of the city of Corinth. For taking Macedon's part in the recent troubles, the Romans attacked the city, sacked it, enslaved every man, woman and child in the place, and burned its buildings to the ground so comprehensively that this great Greek city was deserted for over a century. The civilized world was appalled. Whilst it was accepted that the Romans had an unhealthily zealous approach to warfare, and the diplomatic finesse of country bumpkins, the utter destruction of one of the pearls of Greek culture (and over a minor military disagreement!) was an act of horrifying barbarity. The destruction of Corinth, the humiliation of Antiochus and the subjugation of Macedonia signalled clearly that the age of the Hellenic empires was nearing its end.

The Successors of Seleucia

As with a forest when a mighty tree collapses, young saplings spring up in the clearing and begin to compete for their place in the sun. East of the Euphrates a race of warrior tribesmen claimed descent from the Achaemenid Persians who had once ruled all of the region and who had twice invaded the Greek mainland. They took their name from the province of Parthava, their homeland just southwest of the Caspian Sea, and called themselves Parthians. They fought with a mixture of light, highly-mobile bowmen and heavily armoured cavalry. Like the Romans who attempted to defeat them in later years, the Seleucid phalanx found that this mixed ability to strike from a distance with missile weapons before getting up close and personal with lancers made the Parthians formidable foes on their home ground.

The Seleucid yoke was thrown off even before the coming of the Romans, but after Magnesia there was little to limit the Parthian state's expansion. Parthia sat astride the 'Silk Road'; a trade route that reached across the Mediterranean and central Asia to China and even to the spice islands beyond. It has been speculated that the chaos in Syria and Judaea diverted the flow of trade from the orient so that it now ran northwest through Armenia to the Black Sea ports, and this was one of the sources of the unexpected prosperity of both Armenia and Pontus in this period. (And the survival of the trade route explains how the Roman elite could obtain luxuries such as silk underwear, which their recent conquests now allowed them to afford.)

Trade did not harm the Parthians either. It helped to fund an army which defeated the Seleucid army of Demetrias II in 139 BC, and took the king himself prisoner. The leader of the Parthians at this time was Mithridates I. The name 'Mithridates' means 'given by Mithras', Mithras being an Indo-European god who, somewhat ironically, became a favourite of the Roman legions in later years.

This Mithridates was no relation of Mithridates of Pontus, nor indeed of the various other royal Mithridati who were about at this time. Fortunately, even the kings themselves realized that to avert an identity crisis caused by too many like-named monarchs some further identifying tag was required. Consequently each king chose for himself a fine, upstanding quality with which he wanted to be associated. The Parthian Mithridates called himself Mithridates Philhellene in order to soothe the fears of the Greeks who had a valuable economic role in the cities which he conquered. Under Mithridates Philhellene, Parthia conquered Babylonia in 144 BC, and the ancient empire of the Medes and Persians within the following decade.

The Seleucid king, Demetrias II, was eventually released by the Parthians in 129 BC, and to show that there were no hard feelings, he married the Parthian king's daughter – a match that symbolized to those few who still needed convincing that Parthia was now a fully-fledged regional superpower.

Between Parthia and Asia Minor lay the mountain kingdom of Armenia. Originally a part of the empire of Alexander the Great, Armenia enjoyed a brief independence before it was conquered by the Seleucids under Antiochus III. The kingdom, which legend claimed had long been ruled by the Orontid dynasty, was then governed directly by satraps. Access to the kingdom for

Parthian armies was restricted to the defensible choke points of the city of Sophene and the crossings of the upper Euphrates. Armenia was more accessible from the west, so the satraps maintained their loyalty for as long as Selucia remained a threat. With the weakening of Seleucid rule after Magnesia, the Armenian satraps unilaterally declared independence, secure in the knowledge that their superb cavalry was a match for the horsemen of Parthia, who were in any case more at home on the lowland plains. Armenia at this point was formed from two small kingdoms, respectively west and east of the Euphrates. The western kingdom was known as Lesser Armenia and the former satrap took the name of King Zariadris. The eastern kingdom was called Greater Armenia and came to be ruled by Zariadris' son Artaxias. It was Artaxias who rebuilt the ancient city at Yerevan and called it Artaxata, after the custom of rulers to name after themselves cities they founded or totally rebuilt.

Like the Parthians, the Armenians determined to make the most of the fluid political situation, and adopted an expansionist stance, snapping up weaker border states, and expanding northward and westward along the eastern shore of the Black Sea. However, once the Parthian King Mithridates II (also known as Arsaces IX), had finished mopping up resistance in Mesopotamia, he led his forces against Armenia. He defeated the current king, Artavasdes I, and took as a hostage his young son Tigranes, the man who was later to be known to history as Tigranes the Great. The Parthians seem to have been content to rule mainly by proxy, and Armenia remained a quasi-independent state, ready to expand once more as soon as the time seemed right.

Asia Minor

This then, was the world that the father of Mithridates knew. In the middle of that world was the great mass of Asia Minor, thrusting over the northern Mediterranean to divide it from the Black Sea. Surrounded by water on three sides, Asia Minor was a world in itself, containing widely varied geographical features, micro-climates, and diverse peoples; from the sophisticated and Hellenized kingdoms in the west, to the mountainous princedoms abutting Armenia in the east. Diverse as it was (the sources tell us that twenty-two languages were spoken in Pontus alone), Asia Minor had been settled and civilized, home of the Hittite civilization, long before the Greeks fought before the walls of Troy. Indeed, it was here, the ancient sources tell us, that the first iron swords were forged.

Both history and geography had combined to prevent Asia Minor from becoming a single political or ethnic unit. The major feature of the land mass is a huge upland plateau that dominates the interior. Here the winters are harsh and the rivers are few. Water is found in brackish pools, and most peasant farmers content themselves with a pastoral existence with herds of sheep, goats, and occasional cattle. During the opening years of the third century, a tribe of Gauls had forced their way into the region. They had fought a bruising series of campaigns against the armies of various states but these had stubbornly refused to be parted from their desirable lands. Therefore, after pinballing from one kingdom to another, the Gauls finally ensconced themselves on the upland plateau, from where none of the neighbours considered it worthwhile to force them off. These peoples were known as the Galatians, the same people to whom St Paul was to write his biblical epistle two centuries later.

At this time, the Galatians were divided into groups called tetrarchies, though there were often more than four leaders of the nation, which was itself divided into three tribes. Whilst they maintained a lively series of internecine wars among themselves (as was generally the case), the Galatians were incapable of being more than a general nuisance to the neighbours. However, when they did manage to pull together for more than a few months the Galatians could become a menace serious enough to require a major military response. Fortunately the poverty of their upland home meant that Galatians were always ready to accept employment as mercenaries, even if the job entailed keeping their fellow countrymen on the right side of the border.

South and east of Galatia, perched on the edge of the Anatolian plateau, was the kingdom of Cappadocia. Cappadocia was a relatively poor land, cut off from the northern Mediterranean by the mountains of Cilicia, and with the powerful and predatory kingdom of Armenia to the east. Before the plains in the west dried out into the barren fastnesses of Lycaonia, the land supported the herds of horses which were the basis of Cappadocia's famed cavalry. There were no real cities in Cappadocia as the Greeks would understand the term. Instead there were villages of peasants often sheltering near a reassuring hilltop fortress held by the local dynast. As elsewhere in Asia Minor, much of the country was temple land, for the religions of the region were both ancient and powerful, and the priests held land and did service to their king just as did his other barons. Ruled by a failing dynasty, it seemed inevitable that Cappadocia would soon fall into the clutches of a neighbouring kingdom, and few states were better placed to do that clutching than Pontus to the north, just over the River Halys. On the other hand, Rome was determined that the status quo in Asia Minor should remain just so, and kept a jealously protective eye on the vulnerable state.

South of Cappadocia, the mountains stretch right to the sea. In a long sweep from Caria to Tarsus the land is almost impassable. Where the mountains open into valleys, these valleys are cut off from each other, and are only occasionally linked by the sea. This area, too anarchic to be considered a kingdom, and too diverse to be called a nation, was known as Cilicia. Here, the people naturally formed themselves into close-knit feudal societies, difficult to reach from outside, and even harder to govern, though several local minor kingdoms gave it a sporting try. Lately, a new phenomenon had been observed, with harbours being fortified and fortresses built on rocky headlands. The builders were not an army, though they might have been mistaken for a navy - their fleet was as large and as well-equipped as any in the Mediterranean at that time. These were pirates. Not the sort of pirates which ambushed lonely merchantmen far from the main trade routes, but the sort of pirates who took entire cities by storm and dominated the seas as far west as Spain. Cilicia, with its rough coastline and impassable hinterland, was just the sort of retreat the pirates needed, especially as the advance of Rome had made their bases in Crete too vulnerable for comfort.

Piracy had been a menace in the Mediterranean since the discovery of sailing, and usually it was the job of the dominant naval power to keep that menace in check. Until recently that task had fallen to the island merchant traders of Rhodes. Hanging like a teardrop south of the landmass of Asia Minor, the island of Rhodes had a long history as a naval power, and had even built its famous Colossus to celebrate the Seleucid failure to add the island to their empire, despite a fierce invasion and siege. (The Colossus overlooked the harbour, and did not, as popular legend has it, bestride the entrance.) The growing power of Rome had made itself felt in Rhodes as well. The island city-state was constantly riven by strife between pro- and anti-Roman factions, and what was sometimes a loyal ally of Rome could suddenly swing to a hostile neutral, depending on which faction had the upper hand. The Romans regarded this Rhodian fickleness with deep suspicion. They had crippled Rhodes' trading base by making Delos a free port, and from there Rome annually shipped slaves by the tens of thousands to Italy, something which the peoples of the region deeply resented.

Furthermore, the Romans had decided that the Rhodians were not to be trusted with their fleet, and had ordered its numbers sharply reduced. So brutally was the fleet pruned that it was more in danger from pirates than able to suppress them. This meant that piracy flourished unchecked, for the Romans were famously reluctant to take to the water, and congenitally incapable of staying afloat when they did so. (The first war with Carthage was fought mainly at sea, and the Romans lost far more men through drowning than they did to enemy action.) From the Pontic viewpoint, Rhodes merited careful attention, as the island was still a naval power, and it held a considerable chunk of mainland southwest Asia Minor in Caria and Lycia. Cilicia too was of considerable interest, both because the Pontic kings and the pirates had long maintained cordial relations with each other, and because the Romans, unable to take on the pirates at sea, had a legion in Cilicia which was trying rather fruitlessly to root out pirate bases on the coast.

In the central northwest, between the religious centre of Ephesus and the ruins of Troy, was the kingdom of Pergamum. With its capital on the fertile plains of the river Caicus, Pergamum was rich, settled and stable. Under the rule of the Hellenized Attalid kings, Pergamum had developed libraries, gymnasiums and all the trappings of Greek culture. It was here that it was discovered that by carefully curing the inner part of a sheepskin, a writing surface could be created that was as light as papyrus, yet more flexible, but could still hold writing without damage or fading. This material was once called *pergaminum*, a name which has today mutated to 'parchment'. Pergamum had long seen the value of allying itself with Rome, and in return for protection and support against Pergamum's rivals Rome was allowed the pleasure of constantly interfering in Pergamum's affairs. (Nor indeed were the rulers of Pergamum, and of neighbouring kingdoms, slow to invite that interference by sending envoys rushing to Rome to justify or protest their conduct in the constant border wars, incursions, and downright invasions which enlivened life in the region.)

It may have been this interference which inspired the last of the Attalids, Attalus II to make the state of Rome heir to his kingdom. Since Rome had been laying down the law by embassy and decree for decades, Attalus may have (mistakenly) thought it would benefit his kingdom to be ruled directly by Rome, as Rome's interest would then be clearly aligned with that of his former subjects. On the other hand, Attalus would have been keenly aware that death by successor was the usual form of mortality among Hellenistic monarchs, whose courts had brought palace intrigue to a refined and deadly art form. Attalus might have (correctly) assumed that by making Rome his heir it was in no-one's interest to see him die. In fact, his death in 132 BC was so sincerely regretted by the feudal baronies of the Pergamene interior that they rose in revolt against Roman rule and, under their leader Aristonicus, briefly threatened to expel the Romans from Asia.

Rome responded with her famous technique of 'divide and conquer'. Secure in the support of the Greek cities of the coast, they invited Pergamum's neighbours to join in taking on Aristonicus in the interior. The subsequent spoils of war saw Cappadocia picking up Lycaonia, and Pontus getting a chunk of Phrygia and part of Paphlagonia (of which more later). Though somewhat reduced in size, Rome's bridgehead in Asia Minor was secured.

Bithynia was Pontus' neighbour to the west. It had started as one of the many tiny kingdoms into which Asia Minor had splintered with the weakening of Seleucid control. Under the competent and energetic control of King Prusias the First it had become a well-appointed domain, with fertile lowlands in the Propontis, and a handy buffer zone between itself and Pontus in the form of the mountainous region of Paphlagonia, which it held jointly with its neighbour. Adept diplomacy, by which the Bithynians had sided first with Macedon and then, just at the right moment for the switch, with Rome, had gained Bithynia an ever-increasing territory. Her kings were not shy in using force to grab more still whenever they could, at one time even employing the great Hannibal for this purpose whilst he was on the run from the Romans.

Like Pergamum, Bithynia was a very Hellenized kingdom, though family relations between the two were fraught, with the Bithynians constantly attempting to seize desirable bits of their neighbour's kingdom, even as they fended off the attempts of the Galatians to grab bits of theirs.

Yet, despite the constant warfare, usurpations and civil wars, Asia Minor was a generally prosperous and civilized place. Most campaigns were fought with mercenaries who were careful not to badly damage the assets of what might be next year's employer, and it was understood that cities which rolled over without a fight could be allowed to carry on business as usual under new ownership. When people actually took their warfare seriously, this often involved the absorption or attempted succession of a Greek city from a kingdom of which they wanted no part. Like the Greeks of mainland Greece, the Greeks of Asia Minor were proud of their heritage of the *polis*, the small, independent city-state, and such was their eagerness to live in this condition that they persisted in credulously allying themselves with whomever promised them 'freedom', no matter how harsh the disillusionment which inevitably followed.

As well as Greek city-states which might or might not be independent at any given moment, there were numerous principalities such as Commagene, Priene, and Sarmagene (the '-ene' ending indicates a former Seleucid administrative area). The larger of these maintained a precarious independence, others changed hands depending on the vagaries of war, royal marriages and diplomacy.

Overall, the situation was not unlike that in Europe in the early sixteenth century. There were established powers which could be sure of retaining their national identity no matter what, new nation-states in the process of being forged, and a mass of free cities, transient leagues and tiny kingdoms and principalities struggling to avoid being swallowed or becoming pawns of their larger neighbours. There was no certainty that a single power would rise to become suzerain of the entire region, and if one power did come to rule them all, there was no certainty that power would be Rome.

Chapter 1

Winning Pontus

The Mithridatid kingdom

The history of Pontus is the history of its ruling family, the Mithridatid kings. It was their tenacity, military skill and ability to out-double-cross, betray and backstab their rivals that built the Pontic kingdom from scratch, and it was their economic nous that developed it into a profitable concern.

The propaganda of the Mithridatids proclaimed their descent from the Achaemenid Persian kings, and modern historians have rather surprised themselves by discovering indications that this was so.[1] The evidence for these early ancestors of Mithridates VI is sketchy and in places contradictory. Depending on how we read the sources, the early Mithridatids were minor nobility based around the town of Cius in Propontis, or wealthy Persian noblemen who dominated the much larger area of Mysia. But however one reads the evidence, the family certainly existed well before its future kingdom.

The family history becomes clearer soon after the death of Alexander the Great, ruler of all Asia Minor and much else besides. On Alexander's death, one of his generals called Antigonus forcibly took charge of the region. Whilst consolidating his rule, he put to death a man called Mithridates of Cius, the first unmistakeably identifiable ancestor of Mithridates VI.[2] The executed Mithridates had a relative of the same name (referred to by the historian Appian as 'a scion of the royal house of Persia'). He was probably a nephew of Mithridates of Cius, and was at that time staying in the court of Antigonus. One night (so the legend goes) Antigonus dreamed that he had sown a harvest of gold dust, and the crop was reaped by the young Mithridates. Accordingly the superstitious Antigonus planned to have this Mithridates executed. He confided this fact to his son Demetrius (the same Demetrius who later in life famously failed to capture Rhodes), notwithstanding the fact that Demetrius and Mithridates were close friends. Demetrius was sworn to silence, but overcame the conflict between filial loyalty and comradeship by mutely sketching the word 'flee' in the sand whilst the pair were walking along the beach. Asiatic nobility survived by picking up on hints far more subtle than this, and within hours Mithridates was on the run.[3]

The year 300 BC saw the fugitive dug into the mountains of Paphlagonia, on the westernmost border of his family's future kingdom. With the fortress town of Cimiata as his base, Mithridates took advantage of the confusion elsewhere in Asia Minor to begin gouging himself a little kingdom out of the inland river valleys to the east. The next time Mithridates appears in the historical record is as an ambitious upstart with predatory designs on the town of Amastris on the Black Sea coast. Amastris, founded by a Greek noblewoman, was also claimed by the Greek city of Heraclea, on the grounds that Amastris' founder had been a Heracliot. However, Heraclea had fallen out with the current Seleucid king, who, partly to spite the Heracliots, handed Amastris to Ariobarzanes, son of Mithridates. The dynasty thus won its first Greek city, a handsome establishment with two good harbours, and a thriving business in exporting boxwood from the immediate interior.

In 281 BC the Seleucids made an effort to bring the embryonic Pontic kingdom back under their control, but Mithridates fought them off with the help of the newly-arrived Galatians. It is probable that he issued his first coins at this point, defiantly asserting the independence that his kingdom had just so conclusively proven. By the time this Mithridates died in 266 BC, he well deserved his nickname of Ctesias ('founder'). He left his heir a small but well-appointed realm with considerable potential for expansion.

All that is known of the heir, Ariobarzanes, once he changed from ruling Amastris to Pontus as a whole, is that the kingdom was so weak that the Galatians successfully ravaged the place on his death. However, this does not mean that Ariobarzanes had not been busy during his reign. One of the distinguishing features of the area that was to become Pontus is a range of mountains created by the earthquake-prone Anatolian fault line. These mountains, home of almost the only temperate rainforests on the Eurasian landmass, separate a coastal plain only a few miles wide from the interior of Asia Minor. The drier, warmer interior of this area is dominated by the systems of the Halys and the Lycus rivers. It is quite possible that Ariobarzanes followed his father's example and spent his time busily expanding up these river valleys, out of sight of the Greek cities of the coast on whom our historical record relies.

Certainly by the time Mithridates II came to the throne in about 250 BC he was considered suitable to marry a daughter of the Seleucid royal house, and the proud Seleucids did not marry off their offspring to just anybody. Bloodlines were very important to the royalty of Asia Minor, mainly because kingdoms were very seldom inherited by those outside a rambling network of relatives by marriage. This was certainly not due to family affection, but because the powerful landowners on whom the kings relied for financial and military support preferred that this was so. For Mithridates II to be admitted to the ranks of the Seleucid family suggests both that the Mithridatid claim to Persian royal blood was credible, and that Ariobarzanes had indeed built a good-sized extension on to the family property. Later, Mithridates VI was to claim Phrygia as part of the Pontic kingdom on the basis that Mithridates II had received it as part of his wife's dowry.

Lying just to the southeast of Pontus, Phrygia was not a particularly good fit with the then-existing borders of the kingdom. A mountainous area, it was both where Alexander had cut the Gordian knot and where Midas had his golden touch. However, Phrygia had suffered badly at the hands of the Galatians, and the nascent power of Pergamum had a firm grip on what was left. Mithridates II chose instead to concentrate on the northeastern seaboard, where citizens of the wealthy Greek city of Sinope suddenly became aware that the power beyond the mountains had a deep and personal interest in them. It is not known whether Mithridates II actually made a military grab for the city, but if he did he was unsuccessful, since Sinope remained independent for another generation and Pontus vanishes off the pages of history; apart that is, from mention of Mithridates II scoring a further diplomatic coup by marrying his daughter to the Seleucid king – the first time that a Seleucid monarch had taken a wife outside Macedonian royalty.[4]

One has to assume the period of 220 -190 BC as the reign of Mithridates III, simply because he has to be fitted into the record somewhere. The only evidence for the existence of Pontus at this time is the coinage which archaeologists are still unearthing in the region. They show a distinctly Asiatic-looking Mithridates (presumably III) on the obverse, together with the crescent moon and star which was to become a symbol of Pontus and the Mithridatids (a symbol which has since become a bone of heated contention both as to its origins and its relationship with the star and crescent symbol of the Turks). However, it is probable that Mithridates III tightened the Pontic noose around Sinope by bringing Amisus (a coastal city to Sinope's east), into his hegemony.

If Mithridates III was content to keep a low profile, the next ruler, Pharnarces I, was not. He immediately became involved in a messy war between Pergamum and Bithynia, and when the Romans forced a ceasefire in about 183 BC, he did not stand down his army but instead pounced on and captured Sinope.[5] This was a crucial acquisition. With a splendid harbour, once used by the Hittites, Sinope was the Black Sea terminus for trade caravans from Mesopotamia, and thus another stop on the Silk Road which so enriched all the countries which it passed through. Pharnarces brought Sinope's colonies of Cerasus and Cotyora into his kingdom at the same time, and shifted the populations of these colonies to a site near Cerasus. There he established an omnibus edition of the two colonies which he named Pharnarcia. At about the same time the rich mines of the Chalybes region are recorded as belonging to the Mithridatids, though Mithridates III may have acquired these late in his reign rather than Pharnarces early in his. In any case, this area, in the east of the kingdom, was immensely rich in iron, but also boasted substantial silver and copper deposits. With control of this area came Trapezus, a city on the coast which specialized in refining the metals from the Chalybes mines and exporting them to the Mediterranean world. Pharnarces also made the first ventures into the Chersonese; the start of a family project aimed at turning the entire Black Sea into a Pontic lake.

This vigorous empire builder also moved aggressively into Cappadocia and Paphlagonia, and even attempted to steal the town of Tium from Bithynia in the west. This was too much for the neighbours, and Pharnarces was brought to heel by an armed coalition which forced him to withdraw from many of his conquests (Though he kept Sinope and most of the Pontic gains to the east). Pharnarces died about 170 BC, leaving the finances of the kingdom in some disorder, testimony to the fact that his ambition had outstripped his resources. Yet Pharnarces also bequeathed his heirs the infrastructure to make those resources considerably more extensive.

Mithridates IV nicknamed himself Philadelphus, which suggests he was probably the brother of Pharnarces (the name Philadelphus suggests fraternal love). Love of a sister was also involved, as Mithridates IV adopted a practice not uncommon among Hellenistic kings and married his sister, Laodice (one of the many Laodices who crop up in the history of the region). Laodice appears on the coins of Mithridates IV associated with Hera, queen of the gods, a portrayal which, like his Greek nickname, shows that this Mithridates was trying hard to make his new Greek subjects like him. Under Mithridates IV, Pontus also tried the rare foreign policy of getting on well with the neighbours and there were no major wars in his reign.

It is probable that Mithridates IV was ruling on behalf of his nephew, the son of Pharnarces. This young man became king when Mithridates IV died (or was disposed of) around 150 BC, and he took the name of Mithridates V Euergetes (Benefactor). Mithridates V seems to have adopted a pro-Roman policy. He gave nominal assistance to the Romans in the final war against Carthage in 149 BC, and his support for Rome in the rebellion of Aristonicus meant that Rome acquiesced in his partial occupation of Phrygia. That Pontus was able to extend its reach to Phrygia means that by now the state must have been dominant in Paphlagonia, as well as in Cappadocia. Control of Cappadocia was achieved by blatant invasion. Aware that this would offend Roman sensibilities, Mithridates V stayed in occupation only long enough to marry his daughter (another Laodice) to the king, effectively making Cappadocia a client state. It is possible that at some point in his diplomatic dealings Mithridates V met a man called Cornelius Sulla, since the sons of the two were to meet in later years and the paternal 'friendship' was a topic of discussion.[6]

Mithridates V set another precedent for his son in his aggressive recruitment of Greek mercenaries. There had probably always been an element of these soldiers in the Pontic armies, but Mithridates V is on record as actively recruiting across the entire Aegean island chain and on the Greek mainland. It is probable that Mithridates V also invested in Cretan archers, whose bows were superior to those of his own hillmen.

By now Pontus was a well-established kingdom stretching across most of the southern shore of the Black Sea, and deep into the interior of Asia Minor. It had mineral wealth, good crops, and useful supplies of timber, not to mention a healthy trade with Mesopotamia and onward from there to Rome. Their coinage shows that the later Mithridatid kings chose to defiantly proclaim their Iranian origins in the face of the current fashion for Hellenization, yet they nevertheless took care to be seen as benevolent rulers who had the best interests of their Greek subjects at heart. Indeed, it was one of the major achievements of the Mithridatid kings that they ruled their kingdom with apparently very little friction between the half-dozen or so major ethnic groups of which it was composed.

To the mercantilist, cosmopolitan Greeks of the Black Sea ports, the Mithridatids were civilized monarchs with a Hellenistic court, who sent embassies to Rome, and who made donations and sacrifices to the gods at the Greek sanctuaries. Yet to the people of the interior, many of whom knew little of life outside their own valleys, the Mithridatids were the ancient heirs of the Persian kings, to whom their priests and barons owed unswerving loyalty.

To the outside world, Pontus was an energetic, expansionist power, ready to try diplomacy or armed force as the occasion suited. Every rebuff sent the

Pontic rulers into a period of consolidation from which they emerged, richer, stronger, and as fixed on their target as before. Mithridates V had every reason to feel pleased with his contribution. Pontus had hegemony in Paphlagonia and Cappadocia, Galatia was cowed, and relations with Rome were good. The kingdom was rich and getting richer. His wife had given him two sons and there were possibilities for his heirs to further expand into the Chersonese and the eastern shores of the Black Sea. In short, by 120 BC everything was going swimmingly for Mithridates V, right up to the moment when his wife had him assassinated.

Mithridates VI Eupator

At the time of his father's death, Mithridates VI was in his early teens. He was well aware that it would suit many at court if he got no older. His untimely death would enable his mother to continue as regent until his younger brother was old enough to assume the throne, and undoubtedly this situation would also suit the younger brother and his supporters.

It was also apparent that the new regent of Pontus intended to continue her husband's policy of friendship with Rome, even though the Romans, worried by the growing power of Pontus, took every opportunity of chiselling away at the kingdom's borders. The gains of the war with Aristonicus were reversed, with the senate refusing to allow Pontus control of Phrygia, and supporting the claims of the Bithynians to disputed parts of Paphlagonia. Given the spirited character of Mithridates and his later determination to expand the kingdom at every opportunity, it is unlikely that he took this Roman interference patiently. Therefore it might well be that the Roman governor in Pergamum quietly let it be known that Rome would not be unhappy if the charismatic young Mithridates never came to power.

It was probably at this point that Mithridates, aware of his numerous and powerful enemies, earned his nomination as the world's first experimental toxicologist. He started taking small doses of poison on a regular basis; both to accustom himself to the taste, and his system to the effects. After a while he had put together a small pharmacopoeia of poisons and antidotes that were known for generations afterwards as 'Mithridatic potions'. Pliny the Elder gives one such antidote claiming that it was found by Pompey among Mithridates' private papers in his own hand-writing. The ingredients were two dried walnuts, two figs, and twenty leaves of rue (a bitter aromatic plant), pounded together with a grain of salt. This might not have conferred immunity to poison as claimed, but would certainly have given the poison swift enough passage through the victim's system to limit any damage. Other potions described by Pliny and the later writer Celsus have literally dozens of ingredients, and are also described as the fruit of Mithridates' relentless investigations.[7] Mithridates' alleged immunity to poison might well have saved his life on several occasions, not least because it persuaded potential assassins that poison was not even worth trying.

While accepting that Mithridates had powerful ill-wishers, we should be wary of the romantic myth that the young king took himself off into hiding in the Pontic wilderness like an early version of Robin Hood. Hunting and horse riding were normal parts of a Persian prince's upbringing. No doubt Mithridates enjoyed these enthusiastically, but it is unlikely that he was engaged in them for seven years in the wilderness as was later reported. Someone, at least, was certainly ruling as Mithridates VI, as coins appear bearing his image, and dedications on statues refer to him as king of Pontus.

It is probable that young Mithridates, who was as aware as anyone of the mortality rate among the royalty of the region, abandoned Sinope in favour of extended tours of his kingdom. This both removed him from his mother's court (and his mother's cooks) and gave him the chance to gather personal support among the provincial governors of the kingdom's provinces (called *eparchies*). This support would be needed for the power struggle with his immediate family which Mithridates must have known was imminent. That these tours later gave his biographers the chance to link a period in the wilderness with a similar legend about the great Persian king Cyrus, was something of a bonus.

With Mithridates, those responsible for promoting his image had promising material to work with. The young king was handsome enough to bear comparison with Alexander the Great; if only Alexander had been able to handle a sixteen-horse chariot as Mithridates could. The Romans, who considered Asiatic monarchs effete and decadent, readily made an exception for Mithridates. Naturally robust, he regularly exercised and took part in sporting events. This gave him exceptional stamina, and he was said to have been able to ride 1,000 *stades* (about 110 miles) in a day, wearing out a chain of horses in the process. He was also a keen bowman, and alleged that it was his passion for archery which led him to keep a bow handy at all times (one never knows when having a long-range weapon about might come in handy). His fondness for exercise gave Mithridates a formidable physical presence, which as a skilled propagandist he exploited – for example by sending copies of his armour to Delphi, ostensibly as a gift to the gods, but in reality to show that the ruler of Pontus was powerful in every respect.

The writer Justin also reports that when Mithridates was born in Sinope, the skies above his birthplace were illuminated by 'a comet which burned with great splendour, so that for seventy days in succession, the whole sky appeared to be on fire with a brightness that seemed to obscure even the sun. The tail of the comet covered a quarter of the sky, and its rising and setting took a whole four hours'.[8] Justin was quoting a historian called Trogus. Though Trogus' father had probably fought against Mithridates, the son was definitely a fan. Mithridates was for him a king 'whose greatness was afterwards such that he surpassed all kings in glory – not only those kings of his own times, but of preceding ages too'.

Mithridates was well aware of the advantages of what would today be called a personality cult. He deliberately portrayed himself as a fusion of Greek and Persian culture, giving himself the Greek nickname of Eupator, 'loving father', and also adopting the title of Dionysius, a god associated with liberty, peace and law; on the other hand, Mithridates habitually dressed in the robes of a Persian noble. He explicitly boasted to his troops that they found in him the best of both worlds. 'I count my ancestors, on my father's side, from Cyrus and Darius, the founders of the Persian empire, and on my mother's side Alexander the Great and Seleucus Nicator, who established the Macedonian empire'.[9]

Sadly, at this point Mithridates' mother was not present to hear her lineage so proudly recounted. Some time before 116 BC the lady departs from the scene. Some historians believe that Mithridates had her killed, others assert that she was merely thrown into a dungeon and forgotten. It appears that the palace coup by which Mithridates removed his mother from power was a largely bloodless affair. Basically, having survived to an age when he could rule the country, Mithridates simply started to do so. His orders were obeyed, and politically his mother became irrelevant.

The younger brother was disposed of. He was executed. The nature of the charge was largely irrelevant, since everyone knew that his true crime was that he had been born of the same parents as the king, and (to paraphrase the later Roman emperor, Augustus) one can have too many Mithridatids. Perhaps working on the principle that one kept one's friends close, and one's enemies closer, Mithridates took his younger sister (Laodice, naturally) as his wife. His older sister (Laodice) was already married to the king of Cappadocia as a result of a foreign policy adventure on the part of Mithridates V. His remaining sisters he kept in luxurious seclusion, unwilling to marry them to possible rivals, yet reserving them for a suitable diplomatic match should the need arise.

Now firmly in the saddle, Mithridates could take stock of his kingdom. The heart of Pontus was the royal capital of Amaseia, where the Pontic kings were traditionally buried. High in the hills, yet only 82km from the Black Sea coast, Amaseia was a highly defensible site, protected on one side by the river Iris, and on the other by steep cliffs. The great citadel contained both the royal palace and a huge altar to Zeus Stratios, whom the Mithridatids identified with Ahura-Mazda, the Iranian fire god and official protector of the dynasty. Originally founded by the ancient Hittite civilization, Amaseia gained its name from Amasis, the legendary queen of the Amazons who was said to have ruled from there. The cool climate and fertile soil of the area produced crops such as the apples for which the region is famous even today.

Mithridates knew that the true strength of his kingdom lay here and in the lands of the interior, especially along the Lycus and Iris river valleys. These areas often comprised huge tracts of temple land such as those at Comana and Zela (the temple complex at Comana was large enough to support 6,000 sacred slaves, reports the geographer Strabo).[10] Comana was also a rare city in the Pontic interior; a lively trade centre with a famously cosmopolitan and decadent lifestyle. These provinces of the interior gave Mithridates unquestioning loyalty almost to the last. It was here, in the many highly-defensible royal strongholds which dotted the area, that Mithridates was later to keep his reserves of treasure, and from here that he raised levy after levy of troops.

The interior provided support and manpower, and these in turn gave Pontus dominance of the fertile coastal plain, and the wealthy Greek cities of (from west to east) Amastris, Sinope, Amisus, Pharnarcia and Trapezus. These not only provided trading outlets for the Pontic interior and beyond but were also useful bases from which Mithridates intended to fulfil the ancestral ambition of expanding across the Black Sea. Between the interior and the coastal plain, the thickly forested mountains had the timber for the ships which could make this ambition possible. From the borders of Armenia to the mountains of Paphlagonia the kingdom was about a thousand miles across, and with a population estimated as being over two million strong.

A large population and reserves of money and metal meant a strong army. We do not know as much as we would like about the Pontic army, the composition of which certainly changed as Mithridates' empire grew and shrank. Certainly even the core levies of the kingdom would have been a mixture which varied from Greek cities with the latest in military technology to semi-barbarian tribes such as the Leucosyrians from the deep interior. It is an interesting reflection of Mithridates ability as a leader that he was able to keep this cosmopolitan army largely intact and coordinated, not to mention that for decades he kept it considerably more loyal and disciplined than the forces of his Roman opponents.

It might be assumed that the core of the army was the phalanx, a unit of close-formation pikemen who used long pikes as their primary weapon. Because a pike could be up to twenty-one feet long, this meant that several ranks could present their pikes to the enemy at once, forming a veritable hedge of spears. (The Roman general Aemilius Paullus faced the phalanx in 168 BC during the third Macedonian war, and admitted that just the memory of it bearing down on him was enough to bring him out in a cold sweat.) Horrible as the phalanx was when advancing head-on, it was pathetically vulnerable on the flanks. Three ranks of men with their pikes levelled cannot be easily turned to face a threat on the left or right, and since the forward progress of the phalanx required everyone to move forward in time, even a few rabbit holes in the wrong place could severely impair its progress.

However, given the right conditions, and adequate cover for the flanks, the phalanx could keep an enemy army pinned whilst cavalry swept down to take them from the sides and rear. It was a technique which Alexander had used time and again to conquer huge swathes of Asia, and it was still the preferred form of warfare among his successors. The Greek cities of Pontus provided a good supply of phalangites (as members of a phalanx are called), and the interminable wars of the Seleucids and their successors meant that there was always a large pool of mercenaries to draw upon, as the Mithridatids often did. Often only the front ranks of the phalanx wore armour, but Pontus, with its wealth and large iron reserves could afford to be generous in this regard.

On rough ground, where the phalanx feared to tread, it was the job of the *peltast* to rush in. Because they required rather less training than the rigorously drilled phalanx, peltasts were often recruited from semi-Hellenized tribes, or newly levied citizens. Because their mobility was the peltasts' prime asset, it was also easy for the peltasts to rush out again if they encountered opposition stronger than they could handle. They wore minimal armour, and carried a spear twice as tall as themselves (so about 11 feet), the better to deal with cavalry. (Cavalry, though useless against formed troops, was death on hooves to skirmishers and troops which had broken ranks.) The prevalence of bowmen in oriental armies meant that peltasts also needed large, light shields and metal helmets. By contrast, the phalangites had discovered that raising their pikes to between forty-five degrees and vertical managed to deflect a surprising amount of incoming arrows, and they therefore coped with just a minimal shield strapped to a forearm.

Dealing with enemy bowmen, as opposed to enduring them, was the job of *psiloi*. These were very lightly-armed, highly mobile troops, often armed with missile weapons themselves. The close ties between the Mithridatids and Crete meant that Pontus always had a good supply of Crete's famous mercenary archers on tap, and within Pontus itself, it was a rare shepherd who was not proficient with a sling.

A special class of mercenaries were the Galatians. Thanks to their warrior culture, the Galatians were usually happy to fight against anyone, and between themselves if no-one else was available. The wealth of Pontus meant that the Galatians could combine business with pleasure, and large numbers of them were usually available to fight under the Mithridatid standard. It appears that the Galatians still fought in traditional Gallic style. Though skilled metal workers, all but tribal leaders generally fought naked. This is less silly than it seems when one considers that many deaths in ancient battles resulted from dirty clothing being forced into the bloodstreams of the wounded. Slashers to a man, every Gaul who could afford it wielded a long sword which some did not even bother putting a pointy end on to. The Gauls made excellent shock troops, as it took experienced opponents to stand firm against a headlong charge by hundreds of large sword-wielding warriors who wore nothing but spiky lime hairstyles and ferocious expressions. The bad news was that the Galatians had only a rudimentary grasp of military discipline, and tended to regard setbacks as an invitation to go home.

The perfect mixture for an ancient army was generally regarded as about fifty-five percent heavy infantry, twenty percent light infantry and skirmishers and twenty-five to thirty percent cavalry. Not many ancient armies managed to get to the thirty percent cavalry mark, but thanks in part to the south Pontic Cappadocian plains and the plains of Lycaonia, the Pontic army managed this without difficulty. Because horsemen in the ancient world fought without stirrups, any attempt to charge at high speed with a couched lance would have propelled the lancer backward over his horse's buttocks on impact. Therefore cavalrymen fought with swords or with long spears which they wielded at shoulder height. The exceptions were heavily-protected horsemen known as cataphracts (literally 'covered-overs'), who were virtually an armoured phalanx on hooves. However, Mithridates seems not to have made much use of this innovation in warfare.

His cavalrymen still varied as much as did the infantry. From the very east of the country, Armenia Minor provided both armoured heavy cavalry able to stand and fight all but heavy infantry, and light horse archers, capable of emulating their Parthian cousins and firing over the rumps of their horses even as they galloped away from their attackers.

The Galatians made use of the fact that they occupied some fine horse country, and were considerably better horsed than their compatriots in Europe. Because the horsemen tended to be from among the aristocracy, they were armoured, and usually carried sword and shield. In this they were similar to Cappadocian cavalry who seem to have been kitted out as were the average Greek horsemen, on unarmoured horses with riders wearing cuirass or mail, and carrying javelins and/or *xyston* (a kind of long thrusting spear). As will be seen, Mithridates expansion of his kingdom was to increase the variety of the cavalry arm even further.

Finally, Mithridates seems to have been the first of his line to give serious consideration to a navy, although the raw material in the form of well-forested hillsides and Greek expertise had been available for decades. In part, Pontus had not needed a fleet, because the kingdom made a point of being friendly with the pirates who infested the coast of Crete, and more recently, Cilicia. Now, with mastery of the Black Sea in mind, Mithridates began to recruit shipbuilders. It might also have occurred to him that if the questions of Phrygia and Paphlagonia could not be amicably resolved, Pontus and the Romans were probably going to have a serious falling out at some point.

Given that the Roman navy was as bad as the Roman army was good, and that the only practical way of getting an army to face Mithridates in Asia Minor was to bring it by sea, it would be a good idea to face the Romans on the water rather than on land. The problem was what to do about the Romans and their allies already in Asia Minor. From the later evidence, it appears that the young Mithridates spent a substantial part of his early reign considering this question.

Chapter 2

Building a Kingdom

The North and Northeast

It would have been extraordinary if the young Mithridates had not given considerable thought before he came to power as to what sort of kingdom he wanted Pontus to be. He had before him the examples of his two immediate predecessors, the reign of his father and the regency of his mother. The foreign policy of both was based on friendship with Rome. Mithridates V had actively assisted the Romans during the rebellion of Aristonicus, and his mother had complacently acquiesced whilst Rome stripped the kingdom of the rewards it had received for that help. On the other hand, Pontus had kept its conquests to the east, and retained hegemony over Cappadocia – gains acquired without, and in the case of Cappadocia, despite, Rome. Mithridates seems to have drawn the obvious conclusion. Whilst enmity with Rome was unproductive, and possibly fatal, the friendship of Rome was not worth having either. A further example of this fact was the former kingdom of Pergamum, which had once been Rome's most loyal ally in the region, and was now a Roman province being methodically raped by tax-collectors.[1]

Mithridates would also have noted that Rome was an aggressively expansionist power which had moved in less than two generations from the shores of Italy to those of Africa, Spain and Greece. There was nothing in Rome's recent history to suggest it was going to stop there, and being too hard to conquer was the best defence that Pontus could have. In short, Mithridates seems to have concluded that Pontus had to get big, and become strong, or die. Such a policy would in any case have appealed to young Mithridates, who was refreshingly free from a victim mentality. His view appears to have been that the Romans were doing what he would have done in the same situation; the same, in fact, as he intended to do once he had budged the Romans from the picture. As the Romans themselves were later to note with a large degree of respect, Mithridates saw himself not as a victim of Rome but as a rival for mastery; certainly in Asia Minor, and after that, who knows?

Yet the question remained. If Pontus was going to build itself an empire, where was the new territory going to come from? The Romans, whilst helping themselves to the spoils of Asia (as they termed their new acquisition of Pergamum), kept a jealous eye on the balance of power amongst their new neighbours. From the Roman point of view, the westernmost borders of over-powerful Pontus had been trimmed back, and the kingdom had borne the humiliation with commendable fortitude. A major war in the west was only going to happen over strong Roman objections, and with Rome itself taking sides against the aggressor. Perhaps a coalition of all the powers in Asia Minor might have been able to deprive Rome of its possessions in the region, but for a herd of country bumpkins the Romans were proving annoyingly good at diplomacy. Anyone attempting to take on Rome would almost certainly suffer the fate of Aristonicus, with the other powers of Asia Minor piling in on the Roman side for whatever rewards they could get. Mithridates was probably sophisticated enough to recognize tactics of divide and conquer when he saw them in operation, but he was neither militarily strong enough in his own kingdom nor diplomatically trusted enough among his neighbours to be able to do anything about it.

The only alternative was to take advantage of the Roman obsession with the status quo. If Rome would not permit Pontus' rivals to attack him from the west, Mithridates could rely on the *Pax Romana* to secure that flank of the kingdom while the military power of Pontus was deployed elsewhere. South was Cappadocia, satisfactorily cowed at present, and anyway, another area where Rome frowned on explicit interference. East was Armenia. Mithridates and his advisers probably contemplated this rich and growing kingdom with predatory interest. But Armenia was hard to invade and easy to defend, closely linked with Parthia, and currently a useful buffer between Pontus and the expansionist Parthian empire.

However, if Armenia was a sleeping dog best left to lie, there was still Armenia Minor. For generations Armenia Minor had been subject to Pontus without really being part of it. It lay snuggled between northeast Cappadocia, Armenia proper and southeast Pontus. Not only was it a rich area with an excellent supply of cavalry, but it offered access to the lands on the eastern shores of the Black Sea, especially the legendary lands of Colchis, north of Armenia. And it had probably occurred to Mithridates that if Pontus did not get established in Colchis, then the Armenians would probably get around to doing so, either by themselves or at the prompting of their Parthian suzerains.

In consequence, probably some time around 115 BC, Mithridates sent a large army to the borders of Armenia Minor, and politely asked Antipater, the current ruler, to hand over the kingdom.[2] Antipater wisely did so without fighting. In later years Armenia Minor was to become a Mithridatid redoubt, a fortress-studded corner of the kingdom to which Mithridates fell back when life became too perilous in the west. Probably with the same expedition and the same army with which he annexed Armenia Minor, Mithridates next descended on the port of Trapezus, of which Pontus had long been suzerain and protector. It was suggested that the citizens of Trapezus could be better protected (for example, from large armies camped nearby) if they were fully enrolled citizens of Pontus and, unsurprisingly, the citizens agreed.

Having tidied up his southeastern and eastern borders, Mithridates found that the north literally demanded his attention. Those doing the demanding were Greeks from the Tauric Chersonese, the area known today as the Crimea. The Greeks had been in the Crimea for a long time, as indeed they had been in the whole Black Sea region (they called the Black Sea 'Pontus Euxinus' – 'the friendly sea'). For many years, the cities of the Chersonese had played a valuable role in the ancient economy. Not sharing the same Mediterranean climate as many other Greek cities and their colonies, they were often able to export grain to famine-blighted areas when crops failed, and (more seldom) imported grain in times of surplus elsewhere. They always provided a ready market for olive oil and wine. Fishing and bee-keeping were also major industries in the region.

However, life on the Black Sea shores was not always easy. The Greeks liked their city-state social model and did not (unlike the Macedonians) go in for large-scale kingdoms. Therefore almost every colony was perched on the coast ('like frogs around a pond' said Plato) and had a large and wild hinterland. Some accommodation had to be reached with the tribes of the interior, and this usually involved paying some form of tribute in return for protection. This was not a particularly stable form of peace, and recently things had become much worse. The sources for what was happening in the Crimea at this time are fragmentary and scarce, but it appears that social order in what is now southern Russia had broken down due to large-scale tribal movements and, as a result, the Scythians of the Crimean interior were under pressure.

The Scythians responded to this pressure by transferring it to the Greek cities, both in raids for booty, and demands for ever-greater sums for protection that was often not given. The Greeks fought back, sometimes militarily, sometimes politically by forming alliances between themselves or with the Sarmatians, another tribe of horse-warriors who specialized in heavy cavalry. However, the Scythians were extraordinarily well organized under a capable king, and is seems probable that at least one Greek city, Olbia, vulnerable through its northern location, surrendered itself to the direct control of the Scythians. The two most powerful city-states of the area, Chersonesus and the Bosphoran kingdom, had their backs to the wall and seemed doomed to fall. Indeed, Chersonesus was probably sacked by barbarians from the interior some time just after 120 BC. In desperation the Greeks turned to their trading partners on the other side of the Black Sea; Sinope, Trapezus, and Amisus, and asked for help. These cities passed on the request to their ruler Mithridates, who happened to have an army available at that moment.[3]

It is fair to say that Mithridates was delighted by this request, since his ancestor Pharnarces I had tried and failed to establish Pontic hegemony in the Chersonese, and now the very people who had led the resistance were begging for him to take charge. Pharnarces had ended his Crimean adventure by signing a treaty in which he promised to help Chersonesus in time of peril, and now his descendant cheerfully delivered on that promise. He sent his army under the command of one Diophantus of Sinope, a competent general, and, as events proved, also a capable diplomat. Diophantus might have been even more talented yet, but the literary work by a Diophantus from this period, called the *Pontica*, cannot be said to be his.

The first challenge was the Scythians and Diophantus beat them convincingly. After subduing the local tribes around Chersonesus, Diophantus marched east, where he did not so much conquer the Bosphoran kingdom as have it pressed into his possession by a beleaguered king deeply grateful to be rid of it. With the south and east secure, Diophantus marched against the Scythians once more, and forced them into reluctant surrender. Mithridates later boasted that in defeating the Scythians he had achieved what Cyrus the Great and Alexander the Great had failed to do (though he failed to mention that these two had not actually tried very hard).

Nor did the Scythians remain subdued very long. They waited until Diophantus, and probably his army, had returned to Sinope, and rose in revolt. Though the Greeks alternately mocked them for their backwardness or praised their simple lifestyle, the Scythians were not ignorant barbarians. True, they wore trousers (which settled the matter as far as the Greeks were concerned), but they were skilled metal-workers, who seem (from archaeological grave finds) to have had a rich cultural tradition. The average Scythian fought on horseback, and his primary weapon was the bow (Scythian archers served as mercenary policemen in fifth-century Athens). Scythian nobles fought in armour rather in the Sarmatian tradition. Most of their cavalry were also bowmen, who carried arrows and bow in a case called the *gorytas* which held both together. These bows were composites, a mixture of horn, wood and metal with a range and penetration which was all the more disconcerting for being delivered by fast-moving light cavalry.

Some Scythian infantrymen used javelins, but it seems that their shock troops preferred a double-handed axe about a metre long. Secondary weapons consisted of either another smaller axe, or a belt dagger not much smaller than a short sword. Fortunately for the Chersonese Greeks, the Scythian cavalry-based army was not well adapted for storming cities. The prudent Diophantus had left a citadel (possibly called Eupatorion) to defend Chersonesus, and this held off the Scythians until Diophantus returned. The chronology of this period is hopelessly confused but it appears that the Scythians, with retribution looming, allied themselves with tribes further to the north and tried to overwhelm the Pontic army by sheer force of numbers. The geographer Strabo (who was from Pontus) relates that 50,000 Scythians and their allies took on a Pontic army one tenth of the size, and were defeated with great slaughter. A final Scythian attempt was made to take control of the Bosphoran kingdom by treachery. The plot came into operation whilst Diophantus was there, finalizing the handover of the kingdom to Pontus. The Bosphoran king was assassinated, but Diophantus escaped in a boat sent by the Chersonese. The Pontic general returned at the start of the next campaigning season with his veteran army, and a one-sided reconquest followed. Thereafter, the Crimea and its peoples was, with varying degrees of relief and reluctance among the inhabitants, made into a newly integrated part of the Pontic kingdom.[4]

Though not stated explicitly by our historical sources, it is almost certain that Olbia was conquered. Coinage with Mithridatic themes appears in large quantities in the archaeological record; it seems that Mithridates did as he had done outside Chersonesus and built a fortress outside Olbia which served both as a bulwark for the town against barbarian attack, and as a reminder to the citizens that their military destiny was no longer in their own hands.

It can be inferred from later events that with the Crimea as a base, Mithridates began to spread his power east and westwards around the Black Sea. Since he had gone to the effort of acquiring Trapezus as a way-station to Colchis, it can be assumed that this region fell to him soon after. Mithridatid apologists claimed that their king inherited the region from its previous sovereign. Other sources are explicit that he conquered it, so it seems probable that this 'inheritance' was as voluntary as those by which Pontus gained Armenia Minor and the Bosphoran kingdom. Colchis was then put under the command of a governor who ruled the region on his behalf, whilst

Panticapaeum, former capital of the Bosphoran kingdom, became the seat of Mithridates government in the north.

Pontus also expanded on to the Asian side of the Bosporus, taking in those tribes and cities traditionally subject to the kingdom. Strabo describes a particularly epic battle fought on the ice of the frozen straits which brought the eastern peninsula under Pontic control. This left only a small portion of the eastern Black Sea coast out of Pontic control. This was occupied by a tribe called the Achaeans, assumed, because of the linguistic similarity with the Homeric Greeks, to be descendants of soldiers returning home from the Trojan wars who had, like Odysseus, lost their way. In fact the Achaeans were more backward and barbaric than was the norm for Black Sea tribes, and the effort-to-reward ratio of conquering them meant that Mithridates never got around to it.

Evidence for Pontic expansion to the west is lacking, but as Mithridates is recorded as fighting the Bastarnae, a tribe in the region of Byzantium, and as that tribe later fought in his army as allies, it can be assumed that Pontic arms also enjoyed considerable success in the west. This is confirmed by coinage from nominally independent cities which bore Mithridatic themes, and the boasts of Pontic propaganda, which proclaimed Mithridates as master of all the tribes and cities around the Black Sea. One reason why it is hard to determine whether cities came under Pontic control is that Mithridates did not attempt to change the system of government at the local level. Petty kings remained in charge of their kingdoms; those Greek cities ruled by oligarchies continued to be so ruled, whilst in democratic cities, the peoples assemblies met and voted as before. The principal difference was that tribute was no longer paid to an unpredictable barbarian chieftain. Instead, that barbarian chieftain, like themselves, paid tribute to Pontus.

The tribute from the Crimea alone came to 200 talents of silver and 180,000 *medimni* of corn. Since a *medimnus* could keep a man fed for a month and a half, and 200 talents of silver would support an entire army for considerably longer, it can be seen that Mithridates' Black Sea campaigns greatly increased the military power of his kingdom, even before the very valuable reserves of manpower are taken into account. Yet in the long run, the greatest gain yielded by these early conquests was not measurable in concrete terms. By his salvation of Greek cities from barbarian peril, Mithridates came to be seen as the protector of the Greek cities of Asia Minor. This provided him with immense help in his later campaigns, and allowed him to garner support long after his later behaviour had ceased to merit it.

Bithynia, Cappadocia and Rome

As king of Pontus, Mithridates was expected to follow the conventions set by his royal predecessors. One of these was that a king did not go to war in person, but sent his generals to do the actual fighting. It was one of Mithridates' strengths that he selected highly competent subordinates, and another that he seems to have been one of the few ancient commanders with a genuine appreciation of the value of military intelligence.

In the case of Asia Minor, Mithridates seems to have decided that the best way to get the lie of the land was to see for himself. His kingdom was stable, his army was constructively engaged elsewhere, so Mithridates took himself on a tour or the region. He travelled incognito, with just a few friends, and would have been encouraged by what he found.[5] Bithynia was under the rule of Nicomedes III, and though Bithynia was a strong and well-organized kingdom which had grown from the wreck of the Seleucid empire much as had Pontus, Bithynia's greater proximity to Pergamum and consequently-greater exposure to Roman culture had left both king and people seething over the arrogance and greed of Roman debt-collectors.* Despite a history of rivalry between their kingdoms, Mithridates would have marked Nicomedes as a potential ally, and an important one, as Bithynia controlled naval access to the Black Sea. Both Nicomedes and Mithridates were worried and angered by the Roman decision to rule Phrygia directly, using the excuse that Phrygia had once been part of the kingdom of Pergamum. Mithridates felt he had at least as good a claim to the place as the Romans had, on the basis that one ancestor had received it as part of a marriage settlement, and Mithridates V, father of the current Mithridates, had received it again as a reward for helping the Romans to defeat Aristonicus. To add insult to injury, Pontus had paid a substantial bribe for possession of Phrygia to the Roman commission which had settled affairs after the revolt of Aristonicus.

Galatia was quiet, its people subdued by a series of defeats against the better-organized kingdoms of the region, and the state itself demoralized and disorganized. Cappadocia was more of a problem. The kingdom was nominally under the rule of Ariarathes VI, but Ariarathes had been married to the elder sister of Mithridates - with the Pontic army in attendance to ensure that the wedding went ahead. At the time Ariarathes had been younger and easily controlled. But Roman ambassadors made it clear to Ariarathes that they would support a Cappadocian bid for independence in fact as well as in name, and Ariarathes was becoming increasingly self-assertive. Prompt action was required if Pontic control of Cappadocia was to not to slip away. Another invasion was out of the question as it would antagonize Rome and, in any case,

---

* Nicomedes was later to reply tartly to a Roman request for military help by saying that he had no population left to help with – Roman debt collectors had hauled the lot off into slavery

the people of Cappadocia (as Mithridates would have established) showed little taste for direct rule from Pontus. Nevertheless, appropriate steps were taken. The independent-minded Ariarathes was assassinated, and whilst his sister continued to rule in the name of her son, Ariarathes VII, Mithridates ensured that true power lay with the tool through whom the assassination was accomplished, a courtier named Gordias.[6]

Looking further afield, Mithridates would have been encouraged to note that Rome was looking less invincible than usual. Jugurtha, an African usurper, had made a career of defying Roman settlements of his kingdom, and usually managed to bribe his way past any Roman objections. When he went too far by killing Italian traders, he withstood a Roman invasion in 111 BC, and comprehensively defeated another sent against him in 109 BC. In the same year, Rome suffered a string of defeats at the hands of German invaders who looked as though they might succeed in eliminating Rome altogether.

With much to ponder, Mithridates returned home some time in 108 BC. He discovered that his wife had been busy in his absence. Not only had she produced a son, but, inspired by her mother's example, had plans of ruling Pontus as regent in that son's name. She had irrevocably committed some courtiers to her side by the simple technique of sleeping with them, and was understandably eager to remove Mithridates before he caught up on the news from home. Either Mithridates had sensibly neglected to inform his sister-wife of his acquired immunity to poison or he was tipped off in advance. In either case a poisoning attempt failed, with fatal consequences for the would-be poisoners.

The new rapport between Bithynia and Pontus manifested itself soon after Mithridates returned home, when, in a spirit of international cooperation, the pair invaded and occupied Paphlagonia. The excuse was probably the traditional Pontic allegation that Paphlagonia had been given to Pontus by the previous king (as with Colchis, Armenia Minor and the Bosphoran kingdom). However, Bithynia had always maintained a grip on a part of Paphlagonia, and probably took the lion's share of possession. Certainly it fell to Nicomedes to install the puppet king, who took the name Pylaemenes. This was the name of the traditional ruling house of Paphlagonia. Though it is probable that the new king was in fact related to Nicomedes, giving him a traditional family name reassured his subjects – a trick that Mithridates filed away for future use.

The expected growl of protest came from the Roman wolf, in the form of a delegation ordering both kingdoms to quit their new conquest forthwith. The delegates were blandly informed of the fullest friendship and regard which the two kingdoms had for the Romans, and their orders were totally ignored. Whilst he was at it, Mithridates ignored a demand to 'return the Scythian princes to their kingdoms', which the Romans apparently made at the same time. Rome was preoccupied with Jugurtha to their south and preparing to fight for survival against the Germanic invasion from their north, so had precious little time or resources to defend the interests of faraway minor statelets about which the voters knew little and cared less. Encouraged by the lack of vigour in the Roman response, Mithridates calmly helped himself to a large slice of that part of Galatia adjoining his borders. There he repeated the policy used in the Crimea and built a fortress, Mithridateum, to hold down the local populace.[7]

Also apparently inspired by the success of his Paphlagonian adventure, Nicomedes attempted a yet more ambitious project. Probably some time in 103 BC, he made a daring march across northern Galatia, right against the Pontic border, and swooped on Cappadocia. It is probable that the Galatians, being highly peeved with Mithridates at that point, made no objection to the Bithynian army crossing their territory. Nor was Mithridates particularly popular in Cappadocia. Laodice took the opportunity to make plain how she felt about her brother Mithridates having organized the murder of her husband. She welcomed the Bithynian invasion with such enthusiasm that she immediately married Nicomedes. Indeed, it may well have been at Laodice's invitation that Nicomedes came in the first place.

There was no way that the proud Mithridates would calmly accept a diplomatic slap in the face of this magnitude. Perhaps Nicomedes assumed that he, as the husband of Laodice, had a claim to the kingdom which Rome would recognize as legitimate, especially as the Romans were none too keen on Pontic influence in Cappadocia in the first place. If he hoped that such considerations would at least cause Mithridates to hesitate, he was disappointed. Mithridates gathered an army and briskly bundled the newly-weds out of the country, setting his nephew, the son in whose name Laodice had been ruling, as king in his own right. It would then have occurred to Mithridates that the Romans needed bringing up to speed on the latest developments. Accordingly, he dispatched an embassy to Rome to explain his side of the story. This seems to be the most probable cause of the embassy which arrived in Rome in 101 BC; an embassy which the Romans treated with such undiplomatic contempt that the senate tried to bring capital charges against the tribune mainly responsible for this.[8] That the senate were so sympathetic is partly explained by their extreme antipathy to the tribune concerned. But also Mithridates had followed the career of Jugurtha with careful attention, and realized the value of equipping his embassy with a goodly sum of money with which to bribe senators.

Either the bribes worked, the Romans were sufficiently embarrassed by their treatment of the Pontic embassy, or they were just too preoccupied with the problems of their failing Republic to worry much about Cappadocia at that point. In any case, Mithridates was temporarily left with a free hand. Which he needed. The new, young Cappadocian king was not prepared to return to the status quo and adamantly refused to let his kingdom be ruled by Gordias, the man who had assassinated his father.

Possibly with the help of Armenia, and almost certainly with covert assistance from Nicomedes and Laodice, the young king managed to assemble an army in remarkably short time. With this at his back, he boldly asserted his independence and that of his kingdom. Mithridates accepted the challenge. Nevertheless, he professed his admiration for the skill and energy of his relative, and asked for a chance for the two to meet in person, and see if the diplomatic crisis could not be sorted out by uncle and nephew talking face-to-face.

Ariarathes agreed, but knowing his family well, added the provisos that neither was to be accompanied by a bodyguard, and his uncle should undergo a thorough body search before the meeting. So comprehensive was this body search that it verged upon the intimate, and only ended when Mithridates irritably asked exactly what kind of 'weapon' his searcher was hoping to discover in the king's trousers. In fact, as the unfortunate Ariarathes was to discover, the correct answer should have been 'the short, but quite adequately effective knife which his majesty has strapped to his private parts'. Given that Mithridates was a physically powerful individual even when unarmed, it can be assumed that the family meeting was brief, brutal and bloody. Afterwards Mithridates informed the opposing army that they no longer had a king to lead them, and the enemy melted away without a fight.[9]

All this left a vacancy for the throne of Cappadocia. Mithridates chose to fill the post with his eight-year-old son, perhaps hoping that his own child might be inspired by the family loyalty so lacking in his mother, sister/wife, brother and nephew. Taking a leaf from Nicomedes' book, he gave the child the name Ariarathes IX. Undeterred, Nicomedes produced another Ariarathes of his own, the brother of the murdered king who had been hoping to live out his life peacefully in Asia. For a while the two kings each 'ruled' Cappadocia, issuing coins as though sole monarch – a situation which lasted as long as it took the generals of Mithridates to find and defeat the Bithynian claimant. With this man's death the line of genuine Ariarathid kings came to an end, though this did not stop the enterprising Nicomedes from producing another 'Ariarathes', albeit one of patently synthetic pedigree and setting him up in opposition to the (equally false) Pontic Ariarathes.

It was inevitable that once the German menace had been seen off, the Romans would return their attention to the shenanigans in Cappadocia. The general principally responsible for defeating the Germans was Marius, and some time in 99 or 98 BC Marius travelled to Asia Minor, allegedly to fulfil a vow made during the German war. More probably, Marius either correctly divined that Asia Minor would be the scene of Rome's next major war, or he was assessing the chances of discreetly provoking that war himself and so earning greater wealth and glory as the commander who won it. Plutarch says that when Marius met with Mithridates, though Mithridates treated him with all deference and respect, the king was bluntly warned by the Roman that Pontus would come to grief 'unless it became greater than Rome, or did as it was commanded in silence'.[10]

Shortly thereafter came news that the Romans were thoroughly unimpressed by the fake genealogies with which both Mithridates and Nicomedes had equipped the embassies sent to Rome to argue the case for their different versions of Ariarathes. Mithridates was to get out of Cappadocia at once, and take his puppet king with him. Bithynia was to stop interfering with the succession, leaving the Cappadocians free to be ruled as they pleased. And while they were about it, Nicomedes and Mithridates could get out of Paphlagonia and allow self-rule to that region as well.

With their customary tactlessness, the Romans made it plain that this was not a matter for discussion or prevarication. They had a large veteran army available, and nothing pressing for it to do at that moment. Mithridates considered his options, and the advice of Marius, and did as he was commanded in silence. The Cappadocian nobility, unaccustomed to any other form of government, chose to remain a monarchy. They selected a king from their own number: Ariobarzanes, the first of his line. It is unknown how Ariobarzanes felt about his elevation, but he would have been very unwise to assume that he would be left to rule his new kingdom in peace. In fact Mithridates was already working to depose him, and had elected to do so by invoking a force heretofore quiescent in the affairs of the region – Armenia.

Armenia

Armenia had been quiet because it had been thoroughly under the thumb of the Parthians, and the Parthians had enough problems with digesting their new conquests without looking for trouble with the well-organized, militarily competent and relatively inaccessible kingdoms of Asia Minor.

Though virtually a client kingdom, Armenia still required a king, and so, about 100 BC, the Parthians released the heir to the Armenian kingdom, who had grown up in Parthia as a hostage to his future realm's good behaviour. This was Tigranes II, son of the previous ruler, the first Tigranes. In return for coming into his kingdom, Tigranes II had to yield to Parthia the rule of 'seventy valleys', though it is uncertain where these valleys were and how much of a loss they represented to Armenia.

By now aged about forty, Tigranes almost immediately started to make up for lost time. His first task was to take his kingdom in hand and wrest control from the powerful barons who were virtually kings in their own fiefdoms. Demonstrating the ability and ambition which was to earn him the suffix of 'the Great', Tigranes quickly rallied the kingdom behind him. He boosted his military credibility and compensated for the loss of the seventy valleys by conquering the principality of Sophene on the southeastern border of Cappadocia. It was probably this which brought him to the attention of Mithridates, whose kingdom abutted Armenia in Armenia minor, east Pontus and Colchis. The two kings recognized one another as kindred spirits and, soon after, Tigranes married Mithridates' daughter. This lass was called Cleopatra, a name to be made famous by a later queen of Egypt, but at the time recalling a sister of Alexander the Great – an interesting pointer to how Mithridates portrayed himself in his early propaganda.

Tigranes was deeply interested in affairs to the south of his borders, where the collapse of the Seleucid empire seemed to offer considerable potential for expansion. At the same time, Tigranes' contacts in the Parthian court would have brought him word of Parthian distraction on their eastern borders due to invading tribes of horsemen (the ancestors of Atilla the Hun). Yet for all this wealth of opportunity, one was conspicuous in its temptation. That was for Tigranes to accept the invitation of his new father-in-law to invade and conquer Cappadocia. There can be little doubt that this invasion was paid for with Pontic silver. Three years after Ariobarzanes accepted the Cappadocian throne, he was on the run and Gordias, henchman of Mithridates, was back in charge.[11]

Mithridates had scrupulously obeyed Roman orders. He had kept out of Cappadocia while Armenia invaded it and placed a Pontic puppet in power, and he could disingenuously claim total innocence for the actions of his son-in-law. In short, Mithridates had contrived to simultaneously obey Roman orders and make Rome look foolish to its allies and subjects in the region. This was a dangerous game to play, and Mithridates must have been aware that Roman patience was wearing very thin.

Chapter 3

The First Clash with Rome

Early Skirmishes

As it happened, the right man was on hand to deal with the Cappadocian situation. This was Lucius Cornelius Sulla, propraetor of Rome, who was already on his way to Asia Minor to have a go at sorting out the perennial pirate problem in Cilicia. Sulla was from an ancient family of Roman aristocrats which had fallen on hard times. At first Sulla had shown little sign of wanting to change the family fortune, having spent his youth as a hard-drinking wastrel with a taste for the uninhibited life of the theatre folk with whom he often caroused. Yet, once he received a large inheritance from a wealthy mistress, Sulla suddenly reconsidered his place in the world and embarked on a political career. Serving with the army (as did almost every Roman with political aspirations), Sulla played a key role in ending the war with Jugurtha in Africa. He was charged with extracting the renegade king from the court of Bocchus of Mauritania, where Jugurtha had taken refuge. For a while it was touch and go whether Sulla would be handed over to Jugurtha or the other way around, but Sulla's diplomacy and the implicit backing of the Roman legions carried the day.

Sulla's success was not received with total enthusiasm by his envious commander, the glory-hungry Marius. When Rome turned to cope with the threat of the German invasion, Sulla found himself so firmly sidelined by Marius that he abandoned his former commander, and served with considerable distinction under another general. The Asian command on which Sulla was now embarked was partly his reward for his earlier conduct.

The senate's changed orders instructed Sulla to restore Ariobarzanes to his throne, but gave him no additional resources with which to do this. In fact, apart from a legion fruitlessly toiling away against the pirates in Cilicia, Rome had only a minimal military presence in Asia Minor at this time. Roman diplomacy was based on the principle, universally understood after a century of hard lessons taught to a variety of Mediterranean states, that if Rome did have to get to the point of sending a major military force, diplomatic relations would only be resumed once the legions were encamped in the capital of the offending kingdom – and normally after installing the successor of the ruler who had caused the problem in the first place.

As a means of projecting military power at minimal cost this was highly effective, but it meant that in low-intensity warfare, Roman commanders were often left to make bricks without straw; having to enforce the will of Rome without troops to do the job. This was the situation in which Sulla found himself. Most of the troops he eventually assembled into a small army were supporters of Ariobarzanes, Bithynian levies and auxiliaries from Pergamum. Meanwhile, Mithridates had seconded Archelaus, one of his most competent generals, to the assistance of Gordias.

At least once, this got Sulla into considerable difficulty. Struggling to get to grips with unfamiliar terrain, the 'Roman' force suddenly found itself in a weak position, facing a large number of enemies who knew the land intimately. Sulla resorted to a trick he was to use again in later years. He asked for a truce and negotiations. With the enemy relaxed, he quietly pulled his troops back to safer ground. Thereafter Sulla's biographer, Plutarch, assures us that Sulla hit his stride and with 'considerable slaughter of Cappadocians, and even more of their Armenian allies' restored Ariobarzanes and expelled Gordias. Interestingly, Plutarch explicitly tells us that although the operation was ostensibly against the Armenian occupation of Cappadocia, the real objective of the senate was to check the growing power of Mithridates.[1] His immediate objective achieved, Sulla – with Ariobarzanes in tow – proceeded to the banks of the Euphrates, where he established Rome's first formal diplomatic ties with the Parthian empire.

Meanwhile, back in Bithynia, Nicomedes III had died. It was too much to expect his successor, Nicomedes IV, to lose interest in Cappadocia as he had married a niece of Mithridates (a daughter whom Mithridates' older sister had managed to conceive by Ariarathes VI before Mithridates had him assassinated). In fact, it is highly probable that Nicomedes IV contributed to the Pontic disappointment in Cappadocia by lending troops to support Sulla, and if we are to believe the later charges laid against Mithridates by Nicomedes, the Pontic king reciprocated by sending an assassin to deal with Nicomedes in the same way as his father-in-law had been disposed of. The assassin failed.

Yet every change of monarch in a Hellenistic kingdom created disappointed supporters of failed candidates, and adherents of the old regime displaced by those of the new. The same situation was true of Bithynia, where the biggest loser after the death of Nicomedes III was Socrates, bastard brother of the king, who had become so indispensable during the last years of Nicomedes' rule as to have been virtually a co-monarch. Displaced by Nicomedes IV, Socrates appealed to Rome for support, but was turned down by the senate. Instead he found a ready backer in Mithridates. In purely nominal deference to Rome, the Pontic king stood ostentatiously clear of the action as Socrates mysteriously acquired money and a Pontic army, thinly disguised as 'mercenaries', which swept him to power. Unable to resist the overwhelming force which Socrates had at his disposal, Nicomedes fled to the Romans. The Romans offered political support, loans of money (at interest), but at that point still had nothing like the military muscle in the region to match Pontus.

The Road to War

In the years approaching 90 BC, Mithridates appears to have become steadily more assertive and aggressive. His confrontations with Rome now took place behind ever more threadbare proxies, and he made almost no attempt to disguise his motivation. Given that Rome was considerably less than popular in the Greek East, this attitude of near-outright defiance gained Mithridates ever-increasing support from the cities and peoples of the region, as numerous pro-Pontic inscriptions and dedications attest.[2] The Romans noted with concern that Pontus was levying large numbers of troops and also actively recruiting allies from among the Sarmatian and Thracian tribes. Meanwhile, a large-scale ship-building programme had given Pontus naval supremacy in the Black Sea, and potentially much further afield. It was unlikely that Armenia, a steadfast Pontic ally, was targeted for conquest. Further east was also unlikely and Pontus had expanded as far as was sensible to the north and northeast.

There seemed little doubt, therefore, that the intended recipients of this military build-up were Rome and her allies in Asia Minor, and it came at the worst possible time for Rome. It was not just Rome's possessions in the East which suffered from Roman arrogance and corruption. Even Rome's allies in Italy had felt the force of senatorial misgovernment. The anger of the allies was all the fiercer because the Italians lived in close proximity to Roman citizens who enjoyed considerable legal protection from abuse of power by Roman officials. Furthermore, these same Roman citizens had the vote with which to punish those who offended them, and election to high office was fervently sought by the Roman elite. Yet the obvious solution to tensions in Italy –

Roman citizenship for the Italians - was blocked by self-interested parties in Rome. When the Roman who had done most to support their cause was murdered, Italian fury boiled over. At the end of 91 BC, the Italian cities banded together and went to war. It was, in fact, the opposite of a war of independence. If they could not become Romans, then the Italians would destroy Rome. Since the Italians had fought alongside the Roman legions and had the same discipline, weapons and tactics, the danger to Rome was in many ways even greater than the near-mortal peril of the German invasion. Mithridates took the opportunity to once more boot Ariobarzanes out of Cappadocia and re-install his own son, but with their backs to the wall, the Romans hardly noticed.

So extreme was the danger that the Romans did something almost unthinkable for that iron-willed nation. They gave way. It was conceded that the Italians had emphatically made their point, and any city that stopped fighting against the Romans could have the citizenship. This was classic Roman divide and rule tactics, which split those fighting for the citizenship from those, like the Samnites, who would settle for nothing less than turning Rome into smoking cinders.

By the end of 90 BC, their enemies were far from crushed, but the Romans could see light at the end of the tunnel. Foreign policy specialists turned their attention back to Asia Minor, and were far from impressed by the conduct of Mithridates. It is probable that Mithridates himself was feeling some embarrassment. He probably had not expected the Romans to recover as swiftly as they had, nor had he expected the recovery to be so complete. An Italy divided into hostile camps, preferably with an uneasy peace between them, would have meant that neither side could commit the kind of resources needed to separate Mithridates from his new acquisitions.

As it was, Mithridates could just about cover himself in the shreds of a legal defence. Armenian generals had once again led the Cappadocian invasion, and Socrates had no formal ties with Pontus. True, Paphlagonia had probably been occupied by Pontic forces again, but with so minor a kingdom, surely a modest bribe disguised as a 'fine' might cover any inconvenience? Especially if Pontus withdrew, apologised, and promised never to do it again?

Mithridates was about to find out. The Romans sent a commission to sort out matters in Asia Minor, and the man leading the commission was Manius Aquillius. At first sight, Aquillius would have been a welcome choice for Mithridates. This was not the first Manius Aquillius to grace the shores of Asia Minor, for the father of the present commissioner, the consul of 129 BC, had left on friendly terms with the father of Mithridates. Aquillius senior had been sent to finish off the war against Aristonicus which had followed the transfer of Pergamum to Roman control. Mithridates V had contributed to the Roman war effort as an ally, and had paid in solid cash for the award of Phrygia which he received for his efforts.

Sadly, despite his military achievements, the road-building and his constitutional efforts on behalf of the Pergamese, this ungrateful people had protested about Aquillius senior's corruption so bitterly that he was hauled before the courts in Rome. Fortunately, the courts were no less corrupt than Aquillius himself and he got off, despite widespread acknowledgement that the charges against him were totally accurate. The bad news for Pontus was that, as a result of the scandal, the settlement of Phrygia was never ratified by the senate, despite Pontic protestations that the place had been fairly brought and paid for.

Now the son was on his way and showing signs of the same refreshing venality which had made his father so congenial to do business with. Aquillius minor had been consul in 101 BC, and had crushed a slave revolt in Sicily soon afterwards. He had helped himself to the spoils of victory so liberally that he was prosecuted for it, but, like his father, had been found innocent despite some convincing evidence to the contrary. So far, from the Pontic point of view, so good. Rome could not possibly want a war in Asia Minor with Italy so unsettled, and the man who was coming out to settle matters seemed to be someone with whom Mithridates could do business.

Manius Aquillius was not the only player with whom Mithridates had to contend. There was also Cassius in Pergamum, a competent administrator and, unusually for a Roman, almost honest. There was a further Roman official called Oppius, who seems to have been appointed as a result of the incipient crisis with Pontus. This allowed one official to concentrate upon the military situation, particularly in Cappadocia, whilst the other got on with the manifold administrative responsibilities of provincial government. Also with Aquillius were two other commissioners, though these were apparently so lacking in influence that History has neglected to make proper note of their names.

What is not known, but is of vast significance, is what briefing Aquillius had received from the senate. That he was instructed to restore Ariobarzanes and Nicomedes IV is beyond question, but had he also received instructions that the wings of Mithridates were to be clipped? Was the intention simply to restore the kings that Mithridates had usurped, or was it intended that there should also be some form of demonstration that the Romans took a very dim view of the attempt to kick them whilst they were down?[3]

It was also interesting that Manius was very much a creature of Marius. He had served under Marius in the German war, and it was primarily the influence of Marius that had saved him from being convicted for corruption. Marius had not had a good war during the Italian revolt. Feeling that his efforts were unappreciated after a few mediocre wins against the enemy, Marius had virtually withdrawn from the fray, bitterly indignant at the plaudits being heaped on the achievements of Sulla. Could Marius, even at this early stage, have been looking at a war in Asia to redeem his reputation?

Whatever their motivation, the commissioners took a solidly uncompromising line with Mithridates. Nicomedes IV and Ariobarzanes were to be restored, immediately and without quibbling, and Pontus was to get out of Phrygia forthwith. The Romans had never stripped Pontus of the title of 'friend and ally of Rome', and now, in a neat diplomatic twist, they ordered their 'friend' to provide the troops to make these expulsions possible. It was a moment of acute political tension, and Mithridates was the first to blink. With surly reluctance, and prodded by troops the Romans had raised from Galatia and among the Phrygians, he withdrew his puppets from Cappadocia and his army from Phrygia. Socrates was assassinated, which meant that Nicomedes IV became king by default, without Mithridates needing to back down in Bithynia.

Once more Rome had enforced its will in Asia Minor. But Aquillius wanted more than this. Time and again Mithridates had defied Rome through his proxies. He was due a measure of his own medicine, and a dose which, not coincidentally, would prove highly profitable to Aquillius and his colleagues.[4]

Ariobarzanes and Nicomedes were ordered to mount plundering raids on Pontus. Ariobarzanes, already a hardened survivor of regional geopolitics, excused himself from the enterprise, probably informing his Roman sponsors that there were easier ways to commit suicide. Nicomedes had no such option. He was deeply in debt to the Romans who had bailed him out financially whilst he was in exile, and his closer proximity to the Roman province made it possible for his assistance to be requested more forcefully. Accordingly, late in 90 BC, Bithynian forces made an armed incursion into Pontus, plundering maritime Paphlagonia almost as far as Amisus. Nor was economic warfare neglected, as the Hellespont was closed to Pontic shipping.

Though the Pontic army was more than capable of wiping out the invaders, Mithridates held back whilst he tried to establish exactly what was happening. He sent an ambassador called Pelopidas to the Romans, and played the same card that Aquillius had earlier. As Rome's 'friend and ally', Mithridates claimed the protection of the Romans, and the return of the spoils looted from his territory. If the Romans were not prepared to intervene, then Mithridates would be content also with that, so long as they stood aside whilst he and Nicomedes fought it out, king to king. Much as it embarrassed Aquillius and the Romans to acknowledge it, Mithridates had a valid point. In their own defence, the Bithynians pointed out that Mithridates had hardly acted in good faith in the past, and that his vast army was hardly compatible with peaceful intentions. Pelopidas countered that what Mithridates had done in the past he had answered for, and his intentions were open to discussion. What was not in dispute was that Pontus had been blatantly wronged, and reparations were due.

The diplomatic solution would have been for Nicomedes to pay an insultingly small sum in damages, and for the delegates to discreetly make it plain that further misbehaviour by Pontus would see more harassment indirectly sponsored by Rome. But Aquillius seems to have felt doing even that amounted to a concession which would cause Rome to lose face in Asia Minor. Consequently, Pelopidas was fobbed off with a vague statement that 'Rome wished no harm to come to either the king of Bithynia or the king of Pontus'.[5] In other words, Mithridates was to take his punishment, and part of that punishment was the humiliation of his kingdom before the peoples and cities of Asia Minor. The Romans seem not to have realized, or not to have cared, that their actions put them publicly in the wrong. Mithridatic propaganda could now argue that the Romans were starting a war out of pure greed for plunder, and argue their case so convincingly that even Roman historians such as Appian were inclined to agree.

The next move lay with Mithridates. He did not declare war on Bithynia, which would have been tantamount to declaring war on Rome. Instead he reoccupied Cappadocia, and blandly informed the Romans that if they would sort out Nicomedes, he would reciprocate by helping them with their troubles in Italy – a none-too-subtle hint that Rome hardly needed to add to its current problems by starting a major war in Asia Minor. From the point of view of Aquillius the question did not arise – by reoccupying Cappadocia in defiance of Roman orders, Pontus had effectively declared war.

At the very least, Mithridates must have been aware that it was probable that Aquillius would react in this way. So why did he decide to challenge what was already the most formidable military power the world had ever known? To answer this question, we must consider the Rome of 89 BC, not what Rome was to become. What Mithridates saw was a state which had grown like a weed across the Mediterranean basin, and which now, like a weed which has outgrown its strength, was toppling under its own weight. Besides the heavy weather that Rome had made against Jugurtha, Rome was also struggling in Spain where the natives were busily handing out painful lessons in guerrilla warfare. Mithridates could always hope that peoples such as the Germanic tribes would make another assault across the Alps, and in any case, Rome was heartily loathed in Greece, Asia Minor, and, as the natives were even now making clear, in Italy. A series of oracular 'visions' were circulating in the East at this time, prophesying the fall of Rome. There could be no doubt that many of the cities of the Greek West were waiting only for leadership before they threw their weight behind making these visions a reality. Mithridates could convince himself and his allies that he was the new Alexander, and as Alexander had pushed aside the vast, yet decadent and corrupt Persian empire, so the cleansing fury of Pontus would light a fire which would annihilate Roman power east of the Adriatic Sea, and after that, who knows? As events were to show, this was a flawed yet far from unrealistic vision.

On the other side of the coin, if Rome was so vulnerable, why choose 90 BC as the time to take on so well-prepared and competent an enemy? Even aside from the Italian war, which was still in full swing, Aquillius must have known that Rome was already over-committed in Spain, whilst in Africa, northern Italy and Macedonia the legions were urgently needed to hold down Rome's bad-tempered and rebellious subjects. It was because he knew this weakness that Mithridates had been prepared to push as hard as he had, and this was why, when the Romans challenged him, he was quite prepared to show that he was not bluffing.

The origin for the first war with Mithridates almost certainly lies in Rome's deep preoccupation with the still intensely dangerous war in Italy. Because of this they allowed a dispute about the restoration of two petty kings in Asia Minor to escalate to a full-blown war without their considering the consequences of each step their representatives were taking. It is repeatedly alleged that Rome's men on the ground in Asia Minor did not consult the senate before they committed their nation to war, but Rome certainly had plenty of time to reign in her representatives during the long build-up before the actual campaigning kicked off.[6] Greed may have played a part, for Pontus was very wealthy, but arrogance is at least as likely. It is certain that, despite comprehensive Bithynian warnings, the strength of Pontus was underestimated. Aquillius might have considered this a matter well within his competence to handle, and perhaps the senate took him at his word. Certainly there would have been considerable irritation with Mithridates in Rome. In

Asia Minor, the will of Rome had repeatedly been defied. Therefore, those defying Rome would pay. After all, they were only Asiatics.

The legions were unavailable, but Sulla had coped well enough in Cappadocia with only native levies. Therefore it appears that the Roman commanders in Asia Minor decided that what they needed was more, much more, of the same. Out of a sense of sheer self-preservation, Nicomedes contributed as many troops as he could raise. The Galatians also contributed a good number, both because they were still furious with the Pontic occupation of part of their territory, and because it was out of the question that a major regional war should leave them sitting on the sidelines. However, such was the nature of Galatian politics that the very act of declaring against Pontus by one part of Galatia brought another section of that bellicose nation within the Pontic camp. Likewise, Cappadocia contributed all the troops that Ariobarzanes could raise, but matching levies were raised by the supporters of Gordias and Mithridates. It is highly probable (the chronology at this point is confused) that both sides started the year 89 BC by gathering their resources – further proof that neither side had really expected matters to come to such a pass so soon. Mithridates was probably best placed to get the war under way, but he was playing a long game, being keenly aware that (as his predecessor Pharnarces had discovered) he could not win a major regional war without allies in other states. Therefore he had to be seen as defending against aggression, however tempting it must have been to get his defending in first whilst his enemies were not fully prepared.

The Battle of Amnias

Asia Minor at this time was still very wealthy, and able to support armies of considerable magnitude. Whilst we have very precise figures from the ancient sources, these are by no means consistent. Exactly how many men were actually present must always be a matter of speculation. Appian reckons that the Romans mustered 120,000 men between them. Cassius put himself on the border of Bithynia and Galatia, whilst Aquillius moved into the most dangerous position, ready to intercept and defeat Mithridates along his line of march if, as expected, he took the initiative and invaded Bithynia. Oppius meanwhile was in Cappadocia positioning himself for an attack on the Pontic underbelly, perhaps considering a strike up the valley of the Iris at the Pontic capital of Amaseia.

Nicomedes was aiming for the same destination as Oppius, but by a different route. He had taken 50,000 foot and 6,000 cavalry, and was making his way up the valley of the River Amnias, through the highlands of Paphlagonia. From there, once over the Halys, a good road led through the fertile olive groves of the Pontic heartland, past Lake Stiphane (modern Ladik Gyul), and then there was a gentle descent to the Iris river valley. Here, all going well, Nicomedes would unite with Oppius, and the pair would swoop on Amaseia (possibly detouring slightly en route to plunder Sinope) and claim victory. Such, at least, seems to have been the plan. As Wellington was later to observe, it is a rare plan that survives contact with the enemy, and Mithridates was following a different agenda entirely.

His army was mustering at Chiliokomon, between the Iris and the Amnias. This army was supposedly between 150,000 and a quarter of a million strong, though it is quite likely that the Roman historians greatly magnified the numbers so as to make their subsequent performance look better. For generals, Mithridates had chosen two brothers, Neoptolemus and Archelaus, whilst Arcathias, the son of one of Mithridates' concubines, was in charge of 10,000 horse from Armenia.[7] When news reached the Pontic camp that Nicomedes was on the move, Arcathias was sent to determine whether this was a full-scale invasion or a feint. Neoptolemus and Archelaus accompanied him with light infantry and some chariots, but the overall impression is of a reconnaissance in force rather than a full-scale counter-invasion.

The Pontic chariots – Mithridates is said to have had six hundred of these – were something of a throwback. As a platform for missile troops the chariot had over the centuries been replaced by horsemen, both because selective breeding had made horses steadily larger and more easily able to bear riders in combat, and because there were few areas in Asia Minor that lent themselves readily to chariot warfare. Yet Mithridates had chosen not merely chariots, but scythed chariots – heavy chariots with huge curved blades affixed to the wheels. These chariots could be devastating against enemies inexperienced with coping with them, assuming that somewhere suitable could be found for their deployment.

Such a place was the wide flat plain bordering the River Amnias, into which Nicomedes obligingly led his army, confident that his greatly-superior numbers and more heavily-armoured infantry would force the enemy to give ground. To avoid that very eventuality, the Pontic generals sent a force ahead to seize a rocky outcrop between the two armies which would make an excellent defensive bastion. Nicomedes anticipated the move and deployed his own forces so rapidly that the Pontic advance force was in danger of being enveloped. Neoptolemus advanced to their rescue, with the cavalry of

Arcathius keeping the enemy off his flanks. Meanwhile, Archelaus and his highly-mobile light infantry scooted around the edge of the enemy army to distract them with a flank attack should the need arise, as it probably would, given the greater strength and numbers of the Bithynians. Accordingly, once the Pontic centre started to crumble under the mauling its troops were receiving, Archelaus launched his attack to distract the enemy, whilst Neoptolemus' men fell back and reorganized themselves.

Having established that Pontus had superiority in cavalry, Arcathius looped back to try to get behind the enemy lines, which were in some disarray after fighting on two different fronts. It was time for the scythed chariots. These, as Appian relates

> were driven at high speed into the Bithynian ranks. Some men were sliced in two within an eyeblink, others were practically shredded. The army of Nicomedes saw men in two halves, yet still alive and breathing, others sliced to pieces, their mangled organs still hanging from the scythes. They had by no means lost the battle, yet the sight was so hideous that they were overcome with confusion, and fear disordered their ranks.[8]

The Pontic troops pressed their advantage. Archelaus and Neoptolemus returned to the attack, each from a different angle. This was disconcerting enough for the Bithynian phalangites, since the entire principle of the phalanx was that the entire army should fight pointing in the same direction. But the problem became immeasurably worse when Arcathius turned up again and hit them in the rear with his cavalry. Though now at a disadvantage, the Bithynians fought on grimly. Yet in the back of their minds there must have been the knowledge that if this was only the advance guard of the Pontic army, the Bithynians were surely doomed once the main Pontic force turned up, as it might do at any minute. Eventually, with his men dying in large numbers, and the battle turning steadily in favour of his enemies, Nicomedes decided that it was time to cut his losses, leave his army to its fate, and get himself off the plain whilst he still had the chance.

The departure of their king was the signal for the Bithynian army to call it a day. Fighting to the death was not a local tradition, and dying for one's king became less appealing when that same king was a rapidly diminishing dot heading for safety on the horizon.

Battle of the River Amnias

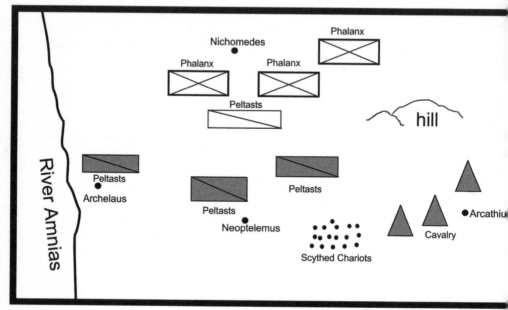

Phase I

Phase II

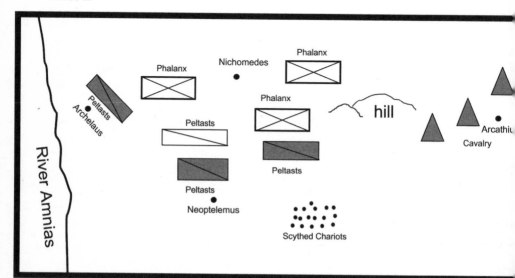

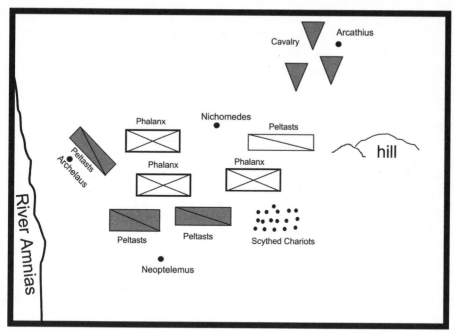

Phase III

Phase IV

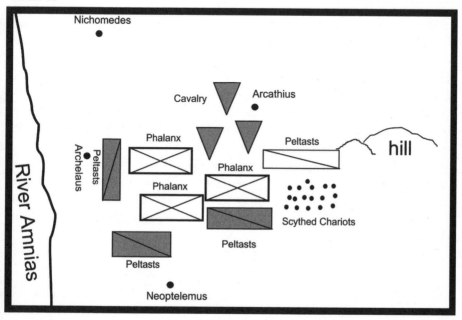

For Pontus this was a highly rewarding battle in every sense. It was certainly won through the skill of the commanders who had used the mobility of their troops to maximum advantage, and had played the trump card of the scythe chariots at the best possible moment. Yet this would not have been possible without the discipline of soldiers who could manoeuvre quickly in discrete units, and retain their formation in the face of enemies who were more numerous and better-equipped. Almost certainly, the experience gained in fighting Scythians was now paying dividends – this was the performance of a veteran army, confident in its ability and that of its commanders, even against uncomfortable odds. Not only was Pontic morale greatly boosted (since a major enemy army had been knocked out without even engaging the main Pontic force) but Pontic coffers received a commensurate boost, as Nicomedes' camp was captured and his war-chest along with it.

Mithridates made the most of the propaganda value of his victory, explaining to the remnants of the Bithynian army now in his power that his quarrel was with Rome rather than themselves. He not only allowed anyone who wanted to go home to do so, but even gave each funds and provisions for the journey. But not everyone would have wanted to go home. The loyalty of Nicomedes' mercenaries was to Nicomedes' pay-chest, and if that was under Pontic control, then so were the mercenaries. Consequently, it is probable that the manpower of the Pontic forces actually increased despite the casualties incurred in the battle.

The campaign in Asia Minor

The Romans may have been disconcerted by the defeat of Nicomedes, but hardly surprised. Their deployment along the major lines of communication into Pontus suggests that they were ready to pile into Pontus if things went well, and to stop Mithridates from getting out if things went badly. What threw this plan out of kilter was that things turned out worse than the Roman worst-case scenario. What Rome had to face was not a Pontic army limping from a bruising encounter with Bithynia's finest, but a Pontic army roaring over the passes with sky-high morale, eager for the next confrontation. Evidence of this, and of the demoralization of their enemies, is apparent from the next engagement, when 100 Sarmatian horse came across eight times their number of Bithynian cavalry, and promptly attacked. Those Bithynians who were not killed or scattered were taken as prisoners to Mithridates, who, as before, freed them and sent them to their homes.

At the time the Pontic army was moving to Mount Scoroba, on the border between Bithynia and Pontus, which meant that Mithridates now had Aquillius squarely in his sights. The Roman was fully aware of this, and of the fact that the forces at his disposal were inadequate under these new circumstances. He had by now been joined by Nicomedes, who would have briefed him comprehensively on the gravity of the military situation. Accordingly, Aquillius decided that it was no longer possible to stop Mithridates at the fortress of Protopachium, as he had intended. Instead he ordered Nicomedes to join Cassius, and pulled his own troops back toward the River Sangarius.[9]

It is not known whether he intended to defend the river crossing or retreat to Pergamum, but the question became irrelevant as the Pontic army caught up with him on the way and forced him to give battle. As Aquillius had feared, his smaller army was overwhelmed, and some 10,000 foot and 4000 cavalry were lost to the enemy. Along with a substantial amount of prestige (this was a Roman general who was defeated, after all) came another financial windfall, as Mithridates helped himself to the booty of another enemy camp and its pay-chest. Aquillius personally escaped to Pergamum, perhaps making a mental note of the defects in Rome's original deployment. By scattering the Roman and allied forces about the periphery of western Pontus, they had allowed Mithridates, who had the advantage of internal lines of communication, to move swiftly to defeat each of their armies individually. Though in total the Roman and allied armies had outnumbered Mithridates, his army was larger than any one of theirs – and it was certainly larger even than the armies left to Cassius and Oppius combined.

Quite possibly the army of Oppius did the same arithmetic. When we last heard of him, Oppius was master of an army of 40,000 men. He next appears in the historical record with a small band of cavalry and some mercenaries, and with these he was rather optimistically trying to hold the town of Laodocia on the River Lycus. What happened to his army is unknown. It is possible, but unlikely, that there had been another major battle in which Oppius was defeated, or more probably, those who had signed up for a quick and easy looting expedition into Pontus deserted as soon as they discovered that this war was going to be no such thing. This left the Roman forces looking even thinner, which caused the realists to carefully reconsider their options and depart, until finally the only soldiers remaining were those with personal loyalty to Oppius, or mercenaries determined to take their wages until the last moment that it was safe to do so.

In recent years, new evidence has come to light of Oppius' frantic troop-raising activity whilst he was in Laodocia. This is in the form of a letter from

Oppius to a Greek city (Aphrodisias), thanking them for raising auxiliary troops, a letter which the Greeks carefully committed to stone in case they needed to prove their good intentions to the Romans later.[10] Sadly, it appears that these and other troops unaccountably failed to turn up.

To defeat Oppius, Mithridates merely needed to send an envoy. When promised that if they handed over the Roman commander they would receive the same beneficent terms as the numerous Greek cities which had already surrendered, the Laodocians jumped at the offer. Thenceforth, the retinue of Mithridates included one captured Roman magistrate, convincing proof for doubters of the power of Pontus and the vulnerability of Rome.

And then there was one. Cassius was in Phrygia, but uneasily aware that Pontus was now fully in control of Bithynia, and that Mithridates, once he had reorganized that kingdom, would turn his attention to the last bastion of Roman resistance. Desperately trying to recoup lost numbers, Cassius recruited or press-ganged as much of the local population as he could persuade to carry a spear; but, probably when he received news of the capture of Oppius and the loss of his army, he disbanded his rag-tag force of artisans and yokels in disgust and pulled back to Apameia. Mithridates followed at his leisure, folding Phrygia into his expanding empire, and pointedly staying at the same inn as that in which Alexander the Great had lodged on his journey eastward. Like Phrygia, Apameia surrendered without a fight, and Cassius, who had received substantial help and funding from the wealthy citizens of the town, hurried off to find shelter further west, eventually ending up in Rhodes.[11]

With the loss of Rome's last effective field army in Asia Minor, the trickle of defections to Pontus became a flood as cities and provinces hastened to ingratiate themselves with the region's new master. Mithridates had already shown what he could do for his new friends by landing a large sum of cash on Apameia to help them rebuild after earthquake damage. It occurred to one and all that handing over Aquillius would endear whoever did so to Mithridates. The Roman commissioner was trying to get to Rhodes, the nearest point which had unambiguously declared for Rome, but the distance was too great, and the countryside too hostile. Aquillius was captured and added to Mithridates' collection of captured Roman officials. By some reports Mithridates also captured Cassius at Apameia and thus briefly had the full set, though he released Cassius on the grounds that he had no quarrel with the man. Certainly Oppius was later released, and allowed to avail himself of the famous medical facilities on the island of Cos whilst he recovered from the shock of his ordeal (though Cos, too, later fell to Mithridates).

For Aquillius there was no relief. Mithridates needed a scapegoat, and he really was very disappointed in Aquillius and the uncompromising stand he had taken at the start of their relationship. The unfortunate commissioner was paraded through each town that Mithridates visited, often tied backwards on the back of a donkey; his humiliation symbolizing that of the power he represented. Aquillius' suffering reached a dramatic end at Pergamum, where Mithridates had him killed with molten gold poured down his throat.[12] This brutally-effective propaganda gesture showed all Asia Minor both Mithridates' contempt of Roman money-grubbing ways and the fact that Mithridates had no intention of negotiating with Rome once he had made his point, for everyone knew that the senate would not readily forgive such mistreatment of one of its own.

As 89 BC drew to a close, Mithridates could look back on a year well spent. Pontus and his lands across the Black Sea were secure, Cappadocia was finally and unambiguously his, and his flanks to the south and east were secured by the bulwark of Armenia. Bithynia and Pergamum were now as much the possessions of Pontus as Pergamum had once been of Rome. Once deprived of their land base, the small Roman squadron of ships blocking the Hellespont had been easily pushed aside, and commerce was flowing through the Black Sea ports again. Yet more to the point, the large Pontic navy of some three hundred decked ships now guarded the seaboard of Asia Minor, and there was no friendly ally to provide the Romans with the kind of bridgehead which they had been given for the campaign of Magnesia against the Seleucids.

The nearest Rome had to an ally was Rhodes in the southwest, and resistance to Pontus increased the nearer one came to that island. Some cities of Caria held out – some surrendering after a prolonged siege, others maintaining their resistance through the whole of the war. Some cities, such as Magnesia-ad-Sipylum, put up more than a token resistance (Archelaus was wounded there). However, many others were like Ephesus, where the citizens helped the Romans as long as they could, providing many with safe passage to Rhodes, but, when the Pontic army turned up, they opened the gates and outdid themselves in finding ingenious ways of demonstrating how fervently anti-Roman they had been all along. Mithridates gave the loyalty of his new allies a further boost by proclaiming a five-year amnesty from tribute. Perhaps he was feeling particularly benevolent as he was a husband again, having married Monima, a pretty girl who caught his eye at Stratonice, a recalcitrant town which he personally brought to heel on the way back from Ionia (Ionia was the general term for the historically-Greek western seaboard.)

Having won and secured Asia Minor, Mithridates waited with some confidence for the Roman counter-strike. Having undoubtedly studied Roman history, Mithridates knew that the Roman response to the loss of a medium-sized army in one year was to gather forces, elect a commander, and return the next year with a considerably larger army. Rather to his surprise, this did not happen.

Chapter 4

Imperial Pontus

Meanwhile, back in Rome ...

If Mithridates had been encouraged to launch his military adventure in Asia Minor by the belief that Rome was failing as a social and political entity, the year 88 BC provided dramatic support for the theory. Because much of what happened in Asia Minor and Greece over subsequent years was determined by events in the forum of Rome, it is worth considering these events in some depth.

Although the war against the recalcitrant Italians was still a work in progress, Rome's response to the victories of Mithridates had until this point been going as expected. Interestingly, for those uncertain of the extent to which Aquillius had been acting on orders from back home, it was only now that the senate formally declared war on Pontus. Given Rome's straitened circumstances, raising money for war on this new front was very difficult. Eventually it was decided to sell off ancient treasures reserved for sacrifices to the gods. Since these treasures had been preserved from the very earliest years of Rome's existence, the sale demonstrated, as Appian says, both 'how limited were Rome's resources at this time, and how unlimited Roman ambition'.[1] A very considerable army of six legions had been raised from these funds, and was waiting at Nola in Campania for a commander. This commander was presumably going to be Sulla who had been rewarded with the consulship for his outstanding performance against the Italian rebels in the preceding years, and who was in any case an obvious choice as he had campaigned in Asia Minor successfully in the past.

However, Rome's veteran commander, Marius, had long had an eye on the possibility of war in Asia Minor, and was desperately keen on getting the command for himself, despite the fact that he was going on seventy years old. Oblivious to the embarrassment it caused fellow Romans, he insisted on doing military exercises on the Campus Martius as a none-too-subtle hint that he was still up for the job. It did not help that he was frantically jealous of Sulla, and the supporters of each had nearly come to blows shortly before the Italian rebellion.

Marius found an ally in Sulpicius Rufus, tribune and unofficial leader of those Italians who had made their peace with Rome. Sulpicius Rufus had a radical legislative programme that he wanted to push through despite a senate which opposed radical legislative programmes on principle. The political support of Marius, an ex-consul and a man who had proposed a number of sensible reforms when himself a tribune, went a long way toward reconciling the equestrians (those Romans of aristocratic rank who were not senators) to Sulpicius' proposals. In return, Marius demanded that Sulpicius call an extraordinary meeting of the people, and transfer command of the war against Mithridates to himself. The move was not quite unconstitutional, for Rome was a democracy, and the will of the people trumped that of the senate. However, it was almost unprecedented that a senatorial appointment should be over-ruled in this way, not least because it would replace an eminently suitable candidate for the job with one less so.

Sulla and his fellow consul responded, as they were entitled to do, by declaring a suspension of public business, which meant that Sulpicius could not immediately go ahead with his proposals. This gave Sulla and his allies a chance of talking the people round before they voted, and Sulpicius was determined to have none of it. He raised a riot (in which the son of Sulla's fellow consul was killed) and brought about the lifting of the suspension of public business by *force majeure*. Sulla fled to his army and Sulpicius proceeded to push his proposals through, including the replacement of Sulla with Marius as commander of the war against Mithridates.

It was the glory and the tragedy of the Roman people that they possessed no reverse gear. Just as backing down against a foreign enemy was inconceivable, so it never seems to have occurred to Sulla to accept the *fait accompli*. He was a consul of Rome who had been driven out of the city by a violent and subversive mob. It was his intention – nay, his duty – to return to Rome and restore order. Fortunately he happened to have an army handy to do just that.

The 'Asian Vespers'

Exactly what Mithridates thought when he heard that Rome was attacking itself with the army that had been raised to defeat him can only be imagined. Certainly events in Rome did little to encourage Roman allies, and much to inspire their enemies. Nevertheless, it was probable that the legions would arrive eventually, and the loyalty of Mithridates' allies would be tested. Mithridates had thought of a solution which would bind the Greek cities irrevocably to him. This solution would damn him forever in Roman eyes, but after his treatment of Aquillius, Mithridates had little to lose on that score in any case. Essentially what he planned was to extend his treatment of Aquillius to the entire Roman population of Asia Minor, and to make his new allies accomplices in the deed.

There were several thousand Romans in Asia Minor, only a small minority of them military. Most were traders and businessmen, men who fervently hoped that Mithridates would follow the usual convention of war in the region and accept the surrender of a city as a simple transfer of ownership that had little effect on those who paid the taxes and kept the wheels of commerce turning. Whilst a foreign accent and Latin speech was hard to conceal, not all who spoke Latin were Romans. It is highly probable that many who had boasted of their Roman citizenship now earnestly assured their neighbours that they were in fact Italian, and in fact Italians who deeply sympathized with the efforts of their fellow-countrymen to destroy Rome. Nevertheless, these people were a security threat. If and when the legions came, could these people be trusted not to throw open city gates at a crucial moment, not to supply the Romans with intelligence about Pontic forces and dispositions, and not, when the going got tough, to seduce the city fathers with honeyed promises of special treatment to those who surrendered in a timely manner?

It is uncertain to what extent the peoples of the region distinguished between those Latin speakers who had come to despoil their land as Romans and those who did so as Italians. There seems no reason to believe that the Italians of Asia Minor did not use what Roman connections they had to gain an advantage over their local rivals in business, or use their greater affinity with Roman culture to gain favourable judgements where the writ of Roman law ran. In short, for many of the peoples of Asia Minor, Italians and Romans were merely different flavours of barbarian, equally insensitive, grasping and exploitative. If it was difficult to distinguish between them, Mithridates' solution was straightforward and breathtakingly inhumane. He would kill them all, Romans and Italians, men women and children, all 80,000 of them.[2]

Mithridates dispatched secret letters to the city councils and provincial governors, telling them that in thirty days from the sending of the letters all Romans and Italians, without exception, were to be massacred. By way of encouragement, he offered the city councils a share in the property of those they were about to kill (the rest going to the crown). It was to be proclaimed that any slaves who killed their Roman masters and their families were to receive freedom, but even freed slaves were to be killed if they were of Italian origin. Debtors were invited to kill off their Roman creditors. This would relieve them of half their debts; the rest still needed to be paid, but to the Pontic treasury. It is evident that Pontus would obtain a massive financial windfall from this mass murder, not least because the Romans and Italians were in Asia Minor to get money out of the place, and by and large they had been doing so very successfully. However, it was about more than money, as is shown by the instruction that the bodies were to be thrown out of town and left unburied. The Latin peoples placed great importance on the reverent interment of the dead, so this insult meant that those following Mithridates' orders could expect the full vindictive wrath of Rome should Asia Minor ever fall under its control.

So bitterly were the Roman peoples hated throughout the region that not a single city council appears to have even quietly tipped off a favoured few about these terrible orders until the day ordained for the massacre. In fact, the zeal with which the orders were obeyed when the time came shows that hatred of Rome, rather than fear of Mithridates, was the driving force. In one city in southwest Asia Minor, the Romans fled to their goddess of Vesta for protection. Those clinging to the statue were pulled forcibly away, and then the parents were forced to watch as their children were killed. Then husbands had to watch the murder of their wives, and then they were killed themselves.

At the coastal city of Adramyttium, some Romans tried to escape into the sea, but their killers followed them out and drowned them. Most Romans did as people in their situation traditionally did, fleeing to the temples for sanctuary. At Pergamum, they used archers to shoot down their victims even as they clung to the statues of the gods. The citizens of Tralles were more scrupulous about avoiding blood-guilt, and hired a Paphlagonian thug to do the dirty work for them. Rather than drag those clinging to the statues away to be slain, as the Ephesians and many others did, he simply lopped off their hands on the spot. The example of Tralles shows clearly that what was happening in this massacre was not simply the work of a blood-crazed rabble; the deed here shows careful planning and (literal) execution by the city authorities. This massacre is known to modern historians as the 'Asian Vespers' (or 'Ephesian Vespers' after the city where Roman casualties were the highest). Casualties have been estimated at between 50,000 and 150,000 Romans, Italians and their families.[3]

The effects of the massacre were highly significant. Firstly, it removed any doubts in Rome and Italy that Mithridates was to be destroyed. His crime was literally unforgivable. Secondly, if any cities had been wavering in their support of Mithridates, the Pontic colours were now nailed to their collective masthead.

More insidiously, the peoples of the region were aware that the sanctity of their temples had in many cases been violated, and in their tens of thousands the spirits of the deceased, with justice squarely on their side, were currently presenting their petitions for revenge to the gods. When these same allies of Pontus came to face Rome in battle, this knowledge – on the part of soldiers facing imminent sudden death – acted as a drag on morale.

The siege of Rhodes

With the mainland of Asia Minor securely in his possession, Mithridates moved on to the Greek islands of the Aegean. It is probable that at this point he was still working on the principle that the first stages of the coming campaign would be fought at sea, and that therefore he might as well make the Romans fight for any naval bases they could use as a springboard for attacking Asia Minor proper.

Cos was his first target, and a lucrative one too. The Ptolemies of Egypt, like any good Hellenistic royal family, were wracked by internecine in-fighting. The mother of the current monarch had stashed her insurance policy, in the form of a grandson and a large dollop of the royal treasure on Cos. Mithridates was received on that island with the same enthusiasm which made many of his conquests simple triumphal processions into whatever place he was occupying. The Ptolemaic princeling was adopted into the Pontic royal household, and the Ptolemaic gold, rare art and precious stones were adopted into the bulging coffers of the Pontic treasury (Mithridates also helped himself to some money which the Jews had left there fore safe-keeping). The people of Cos distinguished themselves by insisting that they should honour the sanctuary sought by the Romans on the island, who thus escaped the general massacre of their fellow-countrymen on the mainland. By then Mithridates had moved on to Mytilene on the island of Lesbos, which cheerfully surrendered without a fight.

The next target was Rhodes, now the lone outpost of Roman power. To here the Roman provincial governor, Lucius Cassius, had already found his way, and now was grimly marshalling a defence. The surviving Italians and Romans were gathered here, and they assisted the Rhodians in strengthening the walls and harbours, and in constructing and carefully positioning catapults and other siege weapons. When word came that Mithridates was on his way, the Rhodians destroyed those houses that were outside their walls, and braced themselves for the assault.

The city, however, was not relying on a purely passive defence. Rhodes had been the dominant sea power in the region until the Romans (probably to their present regret) had jealously ordered the reduction of the fleet. National pride demanded that the islanders put up at least a show of resistance at sea, and accordingly their fleet sailed out to meet that of Pontus.

The ships of the two opposing fleets would have been much alike, for the art of shipbuilding was shared among Hellenistic artisans across the eastern Mediterranean. Warships were based on the trireme, which as the name implies (tri – 'three'; reme- 'oars') had three banks of oars. Under the Ptolemaic and Seleucid kings, warships had reached a level of sophistication that was not to be re-attained for centuries. The trireme remained the basic fleet vessel, but larger ships, including *quinquiremes* and even 'sixteeners', now existed. Despite the names, it is unlikely that these referred to extra banks of oars, but instead to different arrangements of the rowers who propelled these ships in battle.

Accustomed to the gentle tides of the Mediterranean, ancient warships were not particularly seaworthy. Some ships had complete decks, and were known as *cataphract* (covered over) ships, and even a basic trireme had a gangway running down the middle and a platform at the back for the captain and the steering oarsman. It was their habit to remain near the coast, and run for shore when faced with inclement weather (it has been estimated that swells more than a metre high would get a trireme into severe difficulty). Even ships built mostly out of pine tended to have oak keels, and ancillary keels on the sides so that these keels could support the weight of the ships when they were run up the sand onto a beach, which was the usual method of parking a ship in the absence of a harbour.

Under sail, a warship was a slow and cumbersome beast capable of making an average speed of two knots on a typical journey. Sails were useless in combat, and usually left ashore. Battle speed was provided by rowers who could get their machines up to seven knots. The more skilled a crew the faster the ship could go, and the better it could manoeuvre. This was important, because warships had a huge and cumbersome ram on the front just below the waterline, and every captain's dream was to hit an enemy dead amidships with the ram, thus finishing the combat with a single blow. Cruising down the side of an enemy ship, snapping its oars and causing chaos among the rowers within, was generally considered a satisfactory prelude, but both manoeuvres required the attacking ship to get into the right position in the first place, so sailing ability was at least as important as the size and number of the ships in the fleet.

Pontus, blessed by the abundant forests on the southern seaboard of the Black Sea, had a huge number of vessels, some three hundred warships and a host of minor craft and transports as well. The abundance of timber meant that these ships were triremes and above, whilst the wealth of Pontus meant that such a fleet could be sustained for long periods. Maintaining an ancient fleet was not cheap. Even a basic trireme had a crew of between two and three hundred men, and for most of antiquity rowing was a skilled art. The slave ship with rowers sweating under the lash belonged to a later era – Mithridates' rowers expected to be paid, and at times like these good rowers came at a premium.

From the first encounter it became plain that the contest at sea would be between Rhodian naval experience and the Pontic advantages of larger and more numerous ships. Fortunately, Appian has given us a good description of what followed, and it is from his report that this account of events is largely drawn.

Mithridates was in personal charge of the Pontic attack, having made one of the quinquiremes his flagship. On seeing the Rhodian fleet moving out to meet him, he ordered his fleet to extend its line of battle, and for the ships on the wings to row faster. However, the Rhodian sailors were canny enough to understand the meaning of the manoeuvre and backed off quickly enough to avoid being surrounded. The opposing ships slowly approached the main harbour of Rhodes. Eventually, unable to discern any weakness in the Pontic line, the Greeks fell back into the harbour itself, though keeping themselves and their ships ready for any opportunity which presented itself.

This was probably all that Mithridates has wanted at this point, for with the Rhodian fleet safely penned in, it was safe for him to order his highly-vulnerable transports to take to sea with his main force of assault infantry. In the meantime he set up camp near the city, and set his forces to probing the defences and skirmishing with the Rhodians on the walls.

At this point there occurred one of those opportunities the Rhodian fleet had been waiting for. Secure in the belief that the enemy warships were safely caged by the Pontic fleet, a royal supply ship came close enough to the harbour for a fast bireme to streak out and capture it. The indignant Pontic fleet hurried to retrieve the situation, but they were met with Rhodian ships that reinforced their own side as fast as the Pontics could arrive. As Appian reports:

> A severe engagement followed. Both in his fury and in the size of his fleet, Mithridates was superior to his opponents, but the Rhodians circled skilfully and rammed his ships to such effect that the battle ended with the Rhodians retiring into harbour with a captured trireme in tow and other spoils besides.[4]

Soon after, the Pontic forces got their revenge by bagging a Rhodian quinquireme. They kept this minor triumph to themselves, perhaps in the hope that the Rhodians would venture out to find their missing ship. When, in due course, a search party of six ships emerged from the harbour, Mithridates sent twenty-six ships after them, perhaps trusting that odds of over four to one would more than compensate for any lack of seamanship. Maybe in daylight this would have been the case, but the wily Rhodian admiral used the superior speed of his ships to avoid action until sunset. Then, when the Pontic ships wearied of their fruitless chase and turned in disgust to rejoin the main fleet, the Rhodians suddenly wheeled and hit them hard from behind.

In the near-total chaos which followed, the Rhodians sank two Pontic ships, scattered others, and slipped back into port almost unscathed. Not so Mithridates, who had sent his ship scurrying to and fro trying to organize the fleet against this sudden attack. In the darkness and confusion an allied ship from Chios slammed into the side of his flagship. The incident shook both Mithridates' confidence in his navy and his confidence in the loyalty of his allies, for though he made light of the incident at the time, a festering suspicion began to take root regarding the loyalty of the Greeks in general and the Chians in particular.

After these alarms and excursions, the morale of the Rhodian fleet was sky-high, and that of the Pontics at a correspondingly low ebb. Therefore when the large and vulnerable Pontic troop transports appeared on the horizon, the Rhodian fleet raced out to meet them, exactly as Mithridates had feared. The transports had arrived sooner than planned, and in considerable disorder, as they had been swept to Rhodes on the back of a strong storm – something which Mithridates might have expected as it was getting late in the sailing season.

Before they had time to pull themselves together, the Rhodians were in among them, burning some ships, ramming others and taking hundreds of Mithridates' men prisoner. The overwhelming weight of the Pontic fleet eventually brought order to the chaos, and the Rhodians, who knew exactly how far to push their luck, retired into harbour whilst they were still well ahead.

Despite enduring this further setback, Mithridates now at least had his army, albeit a somewhat bruised and shaken one. With the persistence which was later to become legendary, he pushed on. He constructed a *sambucca* for an assault on the harbour. As far as can be established, the *sambucca* was a sort of pontoon built between two ships on which a siege tower was mounted.* Other soldiers were given ladders and ordered to make their assault from smaller

---

* The device got its name from a contemporary musical instrument, but the design of the instrument is also uncertain.

boats. Meanwhile, a further attack would take place on the landward side, where deserters had shown the king a suitable spot for attack. The plan was to hit the Rhodians at night, attacking from both land and sea, and to swarm over the walls before the enemy could coordinate a defence. The signal for the attack was to be a fire lit on nearby Mount Atabyrius.

Unfortunately, a fire was also the signal which the Rhodians had decided upon as a warning of attack. When they perceived the Pontics sneaking upon them, the Rhodians lit their warning fire, whereupon the Pontic army rushed forward noisily, assuming they had been given the signal to attack. Since no-one was properly in position, and the Rhodians were thoroughly alerted anyway, Mithridates sensibly pulled his army back before it was committed. It took until the next morning to get everything sorted out. Though the assault went ahead anyway for form's sake, there was no chance of the Rhodians being even slightly surprised, and they rebuffed the landward attack with ease.

The *sambucca* was a problem for the defenders though. By their nature, city walls are remarkably static, whilst being mounted on a ship gave the Pontic siege tower considerable mobility. Armed with a formidable array of siege weapons, the *sambucca* was backed up by a mass of soldiers in small boats, who stood ready to defend the tower against a sally, and being equipped with their ladders, these soldiers were equally ready to follow up any breach the *sambucca* might make in the Rhodian defences. The chosen site of the *sambucca*'s assault was against the temple of Isis, which was apparently built into the walls. Later the Rhodians were to swear that the goddess took the Pontic assault personally, and herself appeared on the walls to heave a massive fireball at the attackers. Evidently this did the trick. Either that, or the rough seas left over from the storm meant that the pontoon supporting the tower was none too stable, and the sambucca started to collapse under its own weight as it approached the walls and encountered the higher waves near shore. Either way, Mithridates' assault collapsed as comprehensively as his floating siege tower.

This was the last straw. Leaving a flotilla to keep the Rhodian fleet out of mischief, Mithridates returned home. He had found personal command of his army a none-too-encouraging experience, and he was determined, for the present at least, to return to his core competencies of raising troops and money. This task had become particularly pressing, for a new vista of opportunity had suddenly opened up in Greece.

Athens

Mithridates was a man who liked to know how things were going beyond his borders, and even before the start of the war with Rome his agents were active in Greece. For example, the Roman governor of Macedonia had his hands full coping with a sudden spate of Thracian incursions, and there is no reason to disbelieve the Roman suspicion that these were encouraged and sponsored by Mithridates. It is unlikely that Mithridates had any immediate plans for the area, but he was aware that any Roman attack on his lands would probably start from there, and it was his intention to make things as uncomfortable for the Romans as he could.

Athens had finished the 90s BC in the grip of a tyranny. In the ancient world 'tyrant' did not mean a cruel and oppressive ruler, but rather a dictator who had seized power to which he had neither a constitutional nor hereditary right. This tyrant was called Medeius. He followed a pro-Roman policy, almost certainly because he hoped that this would encourage the Romans to recognize his rule and thus give it some legitimacy. Consequently, almost by reflex, the party opposed to Medeius took an anti-Roman stance, which in those times was by definition a pro-Pontic stance.

Since Rome in 90 BC had other preoccupations than supporting Athenian usurpers, Medeius slips quietly off the pages of history, his fate unknown, when the pro-Pontic party became ascendant. A philosopher called Athenion was sent on a diplomatic embassy to Mithridates, and after his meeting sent back word to his countrymen that Mithridates was proposing to restore democracy, cancel debts, and spread largesse generously among one and all.

Athenion immediately became a local hero. When the ship bringing him home was blown off course, he was given a flotilla of warships to escort him home. Cheering crowds turned out to see Athenion carried into the city in a silver-gilded litter, to be received by the priests of Dionysius who claimed that Athenion had met with the reincarnated spirit of their God. The aristocracy, who had probably been supporters of Medeius, tried to make the best of it, and seem to have agreed to make Mithridates the eponymous archon of the year. The Athenians named their years after one of the city's elected leaders – archons – and later made desperate efforts to persuade the Romans that the year had in fact been an *anarchia*, a year in which no archon was selected.

Athenion rode a wave of popularity to put himself into a position of power. He was a firm democrat, not to say a demagogue, and rapidly alienated the Athenian elite. The claim that Athenion himself was the son of an Egyptian slave dancer is standard political rhetoric of the time, and it cannot be established now whether he was as corrupt and larcenous as the sources claim.[6] It is certain that the Athenian upper classes fled to the nearest Roman authorities for support, which made it equally certain that Athenion would swear loyalty to Mithridates.

The days of the Athenian empire were long gone, and the military support of Athens was hardly worth having. But the harbour of Athens, the Piraeus, was perhaps the finest anchorage east of Brundisium. Athens itself served as a gateway to the rest of Greece, both physically and morally, because the endorsement of Mithridates by Athens, the spiritual home of Hellenism, was a propaganda gift beyond price and one that swayed the sentiments of many other Greek cities in Mithridates' favour. All this the intricacies of Greek politics had handed to Pontus on a plate, without Mithridates having to send a single soldier to win it.

Strategically, Greece presented Mithridates with a dilemma. His original intention had almost certainly been to fight the Romans on the beaches of Asia Minor, assuming the Roman landing force made it past his fleet in the first place. It was to make this task harder that Mithridates had tried to subjugate Rhodes, and why his general Archelaus was currently mopping up the rest of the Cyclades with a large fleet and larger army. Occupying Greece meant tying up these forces and probably more beside, and also taking on the veteran Roman army currently holding down Macedonia as soon as that army had disentangled itself from the Thracians.

On the other hand, how could the self-proclaimed leader of Hellenism shy away from the task of liberating the motherland? More cynically, since it was necessary to fight the Romans somewhere, why not in Greece? A hard-fought war in antiquity was devastating to the local countryside (southern Italy had still not fully recovered from the war against Hannibal three generations before) and a devastated Greece was far preferable to a devastated Asia Minor; even if Pontus was pushed out of Greece, Rome would have still lost a productive province. Also there was the question of momentum. Rome had been hard hit by the Italian rebellion and the loss of its lands and influence in Asia Minor had followed. Now the Greek isles were falling like dominoes. If Greece went too, who knows what might be next? Rome's power seemed to be unravelling. Sulla's coup had already delayed the expected Roman army of reconquest by a year. The pressure had to be kept up; it would surely be foolish to give Rome space to pull itself back together.

Athens launched an enterprising assault on Delos (another major naval trading centre), but was given a bloody nose by the island's Roman defenders.

This hardly mattered in one way, because Archelaus took the place soon afterwards in any case, but it is possible that the defeat caused Athenion to be replaced in Athens. Hereafter, Athens was led by one Ariston - another allegedly low-born philosopher, who may, however, simply be Athenion under a different spelling (by now most upper class Athenians - the only people who wrote local history - had either abandoned the city or been killed, and internal events in Athens are very unclear).

Boeotia, the state next to Attica, collapsed quickly, with only the little city-state of Thespis holding out. Pontic troops poured into Athens, and easily took Euboea. When Sparta fell into Pontic hands, it seemed as though the tide that had swept across Asia Minor and the Aegean was about to claim all of Greece as well.

The Greek campaign of 88-87 BC

The Roman governor of Macedonia, Caius Sentius Saturninus, already had a lot on his plate, but he could hardly allow Greece to fall to Mithridates by default. Fortunately for Rome, the very competent Q[uintus] Bruttius Sera was on Sentius' staff, and this man was sent south with whatever troops could be spared. Bruttius' brief was almost certainly to remind the locals that there was a Roman military presence in Greece and to make as much of a nuisance of himself as he could.

He started well, with a brisk naval engagement which pitted his tiny flotilla against an equally-small arm of the Pontic fleet. Bruttius used his temporary victory at sea to seize the island of Sciathos, which the Pontics were using as a storehouse for their booty from Euboea. Those escaped slaves whom Bruttius caught on the island were crucified as a reminder to slaves elsewhere in Greece that freedom under Pontus was not a risk-free option. Free men had their hands cut off. This action showed how Rome intended to counter Mithridates' propaganda measure of allowing those Greeks who opposed him to go home unpunished. If opposing Rome involved severe penalties, and opposing Mithridates did not, then all other things being equal, choosing a side became easier for the undecided.

Now reinforced by a further 1,000 horse and foot from Macedonia, Bruttius pushed into Boeotia, perhaps hoping to take the pressure off Thespis, which Mithridates' general Archelaus was besieging. Ariston and Archelaus took the bait and a military action followed which lasted for the next three days. Bruttius took care not to become fully committed and to keep his lines of retreat open. When, as expected, the Greek cities committed to the Pontic cause were coerced into adding their weight to the forces opposing him, he pulled back.[7]

Bruttius had done his job, which was to keep Pontic forces busy and out of northern Greece. It must have been with immense relief that he received messengers from Sulla's subordinate, Lucullus, who announced that the Roman advance guard had arrived and that Sulla himself was following with five full legions. Bruttius was thanked for his efforts and ordered to take his small army post-haste back to Macedonia, where Sentius needed every man available to prepare for a second Pontic army which was reported to be closing in on Macedonia via the north shore of the Black Sea.

Sulla's five Roman legions represented a massive reality check for those heady dreams of Greek freedom. With eighty thousand dead Romans and Italians and a brutal war in Italy still smouldering, no-one expected Sulla to try diplomacy or clemency to bring the Greek cities to his side. Sulla was currently levying auxiliaries and cavalry from the cities of northern Greece which Bruttius had saved for him. As soon as he had adequate numbers, especially of cavalry, he would head south, and Mithridates' new allies would have to decide whether they were prepared to sacrifice themselves for his cause. Thebes was among the first cities to surrender the moment it was given the option, and soon little Thespis found that its pro-Roman stance suddenly reflected the new majority opinion in Greece.

Until now, Rome had fought its war through allied proxies. The encounter with Bruttius had been enough to show Archelaus that fighting actual Romans was a different game altogether. Furthermore, Sulla had battle-hardened veterans of the Italian war among his legionaries, making his army one of the most frightening propositions in the known world. It appears that, after a single bruising encounter (if even that – only one source, Pausanius, reports this clash), Archelaus decided to fall back on Athens, and let Sulla's army beat itself to death against that city's walls.

Certainly, Roman legions in the field changed the odds for the worse, but the Pontic situation was far from desperate. The Pontic army was large, well-commanded, experienced and loyal. Greece had shown itself a weathercock, ready to side with whoever could muster the greatest force at a given moment, and would therefore drop back into Pontic hands once Sulla had been dealt with.

Athens was strong defensively and Pontic naval supremacy meant that it, or at least its port of Piraeus, could be supplied from the sea. Sulla's own supply lines were far from secure and his political situation in Rome could hardly have been worse; as soon as he had left Italy, Sulla's enemies in Rome had assumed power and declared Sulla an outlaw and leader of a renegade army. Sulla could be certain that neither money nor reinforcements were on the way from Rome, whilst Mithridates was busily raising large amounts of both in Asia Minor. For the moment Pontus was checked, but no-one yet knew whether Sulla's arrival represented a temporary setback or the turn of the tide.

Chapter 5

Battleground Greece

Greece was something of an impromptu venue for the clash between Rome and Pontus, a theatre of war which both sides entered before they were fully prepared to do so. Certainly, if Archelaus had arrived in Greece with anything resembling the strength which he later had at his disposal, then Sura would have been brushed aside, and Sulla would have found the Pontic army challenging him as soon as he landed in Illyria.

As is clear from later developments, Mithridates intended his main blow to be a right hook over the top of the Black Sea to Macedonia, whilst Archelaus' descent on Athens and Boeotia was more of an ad hoc response to an irresistible opportunity. Therefore, even as Sulla mustered his strength in Thessaly, Archelaus was doing the same further south. However, as a cautious and competent general, Archelaus was not prepared to keep all his eggs in the basket of Athens. Instead, he made his main supply base on Euboea, the long island which runs parallel to Attica to the east. This hardly affected the Pontic supply chain, for only a short strait separates Euboea from Marathon, which is itself, as any long-distance runner knows, about 25 miles from Athens. But for the Romans, who were totally outmatched at sea, that strait might as well have been the Atlantic Ocean.

Even in Attica, Archelaus was reluctant to lose contact with the sea. He made his main base at the harbour of Athens, Piraeus, rather than in the city itself. With his supply lines secure, the walls strengthened, and reinforcements on the way, Archelaus hunkered down to weather the Roman storm.

This left Sulla with something of a quandary. He was master of most of Greece, but in order to remain master, he had to stay on the premises. He could not fight the Pontics, because there were none to fight. One lot were dug in behind the walls of the Piraeus, and the second army was currently somewhere in western Thrace, preparing to meet the two legions which the Roman governor of Macedonia was nervously bracing for the defence of his province.

Yet time was not on Sulla's side. His army was at its best and eager for action but it expected to be paid regularly, even when it was simply sitting around. With the purse-strings in Rome firmly in the grip of Sulla's enemies, pay had to come from booty, and booty had to come from enemies, who were currently in short supply. Furthermore, Sulla's *imperium*, his official period of command, was only for a year. This might be extended unilaterally into a second year as a proconsular command, but after that it was going to dawn on even the most loyal of Sulla's followers that their general had no actual legal basis for commanding his army. And questions about exactly what gave Sulla the right to lead an army of Rome would become more pointed more quickly if Sulla could not notch up some solid achievements whilst he was (at least in the eyes of his army, if not of the government in Rome) officially consul.

Therefore, Sulla decided to spend the autumn of 87 BC conquering Athens. Militarily, this was not strictly essential. Certainly Sulla would not want a hostile base behind him when he moved north, but his main motivation was political. He wanted to be seen as the man who had driven Mithridates out of Greece, and whilst Athens was fallen from its former glory, it still had enough lootable wealth to sustain his army until the main Pontic force arrived. Both Sulla and his men would have been encouraged by a report which reached them at about this time.

Mithridates, a connoisseur of both theatre and music, was in Pergamum at a performance in the theatre. The city fathers had staged an event where Mithridates was to stand on the stage and receive a crown from Nike, the goddess of victory. The goddess was literally a *dea ex machina*, a goddess from the machine – a statue which, crown in hand, was winched down from the overhead awnings. Just as the goddess was about to place the crown on Mithridates' head, she broke apart. The crown dropped from her hand, hit the ground and shattered.[1] The symbolism did not need an expert in omens to translate, especially as Sulla was embarking for Greece at about the same time.

Athens and the Piraeus

The siege of Athens later that year was a premier league affair. The Pontic army had known nothing but victory, and was both tough and well generalled. It had strong walls and high morale to sustain it. The Romans had Sulla, now on his fourth campaign, and, like their commander, were themselves veterans of the war of 90 BC, which, having been fought between equals of the highest military ability, had brought the Roman army to a pitch of excellence not seen since the Hannibalic war of a century before.

Sulla's first move was to rip through the lines of communication between Athens and Piraeus. The 'long walls' which Pericles had built half a millennium before to connect Athens to its harbour were no longer up to the job, and consequently, though Archelaus in Piraeus could still count on being supplied from the sea, the Athenians under Ariston could not. This did not stop Ariston himself from mounting the walls and mocking Sulla to the full extent of his Greek eloquence. The Athenians took to referring to Sulla's complexion as 'oatmeal sprinkled with mulberries', and any Roman soldier who looked at his commanding officer could confirm for himself that the blonde Sulla had not exactly bronzed under the Greek sun.[2]

Athens could be left to starve, but the Piraeus needed to be stormed. Without hesitation the Romans set about doing just that. If the Pontics were surprised by the promptness and ferocity of the assault, the Romans were equally startled by the bravery and vehemence of the defence. There were substantial casualties on both sides, but in the end, the deciding factor was the walls of Piraeus. These were made of massive stone blocks and were up to fifty feet high in places. Baffled, the Romans fell back to Megara to lick their wounds, and came to the conclusion that more than mere siege ladders were going to be required to surmount this particular obstacle.

Now aware of the extent of the problem, Sulla set about preparing Plan B with skill, determination and the ruthless lack of scruples which was his trademark when crossed. This was not his first siege operation. During the Social War he had captured Praenestae by decorating his siege engines with the heads of slain enemy captains mounted on spears, so in this case he hardly hesitated before hacking down the legendary groves of Academe in the suburbs of Athens. The trees which had once shaded philosophers such as Plato and Parmenides were converted to siege engines so numerous that Plutarch says 10,000 yoke of mules were needed to haul them into position.

Thebes was pressed into service as a factory, churning out and repairing catapults and their ammunition. At the same time, the soldiers were turned into navvies and given the task of building a siege mound to nullify the advantage the Pontics gained from the height of the walls. Sulla had a secondary motive for this. According to Frontinus, a later writer, Sulla's men had been deeply discouraged by their first attempt and had decided that Piraeus was unassailable. Their general's response was to give them so many tedious tasks that, by the time he was ready for the next assault, not only was everything ready to the last detail but the men were positively clamouring for the attack to begin.

Sulla believed that the gods would provide funding for this massive, and correspondingly expensive, operation. Not that Sulla was particularly devout – quite the contrary. He sent messengers to the great sanctuaries of Greece, blandly informing them that in these troubled times it was not safe for so much treasure to be left about lightly guarded, and that the treasure should be handed over to him forthwith for safe keeping. Amongst the booty from Delphi, Sulla found a small statuette of a goddess that took his particular fancy and it became his habit before battle to pray publicly to the statuette for victory.

Within Piraeus Sulla found unexpected allies. Two slaves decided that their fortunes might be better served by taking the Roman side. Consequently they mounted the ramparts and enthusiastically hurled lead slingshots at the Romans. The legionaries only discovered the friendly intent behind this when they found the messages engraved on the missiles. One such message read: 'Tomorrow expect a sally against your siege works whilst the cavalry hit your army on both flanks'. So matters did indeed come to pass and Sulla, always happy to exploit betrayal among his enemies, made sure that things went badly for both sets of attackers.

This sally was one of many mounted by the spirited Pontic defence. Archelaus had no intention of sitting passively behind his walls. Mithridates was sending him a steady trickle of reinforcements and Archelaus' confidence grew with their numbers. The siege mound received particular attention, but, after the success of the first strikes, Archelaus observed that the mound was extremely well-guarded and any damage he inflicted was speedily repaired. He therefore took the (literally) more constructive approach of building a tower of his own opposite the mound, and as Sulla's earthworks grew, so did the walls it was meant to surmount.

Finally, following the arrival of a particularly large contingent which Mithridates had dispatched under the command of one Dromichaetes, almost an entire army was pent up behind the walls of Piraeus. This led Archelaus to test the Roman strength. He waited until Sulla had found fault with a particular legion and sent it off on wood-gathering duties, then led his army out of the gates. He did not go too far, having reinforcements positioned at sally ports within the walls and ensuring that his entire force benefited from covering fire from the archers and slingers on the ramparts. Archelaus himself led the sally and, by force of personality, pulled his troops together when they started to buckle. A ferocious fight ensued with the advantage going first to one side and then the other, with Sulla's lieutenant, Murena, forced at one point to plunge into the fray to steady a legion as it began to break.

Finally the wood-cutting detail returned and, perceiving the situation, exchanged firewood for swords to make a concerted charge. By now the Pontics were tiring and the arrival of fresh enemies forced them back within the walls, having suffered some 2,000 casualties. Archelaus himself stood his ground for so long that the gates had to be closed in his face to stop the Romans following him into the fort, and the furious general had to be hauled over the ramparts on a rope.

Winter set in but there was no slackening the pace of the siege. As fast as the Romans constructed entrenchments and earthworks, Pontic sallies knocked them down and filled them in. Winter storms came laced with additional showers of arrows, javelins and lead shot, ferried in by regular supply convoys from Euboea. Unfortunately for the Athenians, the plenty in Piraeus was mirrored by desperate want in Athens. Cut off by Sulla's armies, the Athenians were starting to boil leather boots and belts, and to gather edible weeds from about the temples. Negotiators sent to Sulla got a few paragraphs into their prepared speeches when the Roman general curtly informed them that he was there to teach the rebels obedience, not to learn rhetoric from them.

The contrast between the situation in Athens and Piraeus finally convinced Sulla, who was, like many Romans, a landlubber to the core, of the importance of sea power. He sent to Rhodes, Rome's traditional naval ally, demanding ships with which to choke off the Pontic naval supply line. The Rhodians replied that they had too few ships to break the Mithridatic blockade on their island, let alone give Sulla naval superiority in Athens. Unstated but implicit in this reply was the observation that the Romans might like to think a little more deeply next time before they decided their allies were too unreliable to be trusted with a navy.*

It was a sign of the importance that he now attributed to sea-power that Sulla chose his second-in-command, Lucullus, for a mission to gather ships. Basically, Lucullus' task was to assemble a scratch navy from whatever he could find floating in the eastern Mediterranean, and to extort, bribe or demand ships from allied and neutral states, starting with Egypt. Sulla hoped that the Ptolemies were suitably nettled by the loss of their treasure to Mithridates at Cos, and were in any case sufficiently worried about the extent of Mithridates' new empire and further ambitions to help the Romans. Accordingly, Lucullus was ordered to make for Alexandria, notwithstanding that the sea between him and his destination was swarming with pro-Pontic pirates and Mithridates' own ships.

There was no slackening of the pace of the siege. Both sides showed considerable energy and initiative, as was shown by the incident in which a

* As explained in Chapter 1, the Romans had severely limited the size of the Rhodian fleet after they suspected the city of leaning towards the cause of Philip VI of Macedon.

Roman patrol observed that the guards on a particular section of wall had dozed off. They promptly alerted the rest of their cohort, who furtively returned with siege ladders. The sleep of the sentries was converted to a more permanent repose, but, before the promising opportunity could be exploited, the Romans were spotted and thrown off the walls in a fierce and chaotic fight. Some of the Pontics, observing that the Romans were distracted, charged out and took the opportunity to ignite a few siege engines. With honours even after this spirited exchange, everyone settled down for the rest of the night.

Soon afterwards came the long-awaited battle of the two towers, as Sulla moved his machine to take on the Pontic tower within the Piraeus fortifications. An epic battle of men and siege engines followed, which was eventually won by the Romans, who used a sort of spring-powered blunderbuss to fire huge lead balls at the enemy in volleys of twenty at a time. With the Pontic tower becoming distinctly wobbly, Archelaus was forced to pull it out of the fight.

Then it was the turn of the siege mound. This had been going up faster than the wall opposite, and now had reached the point where Sulla could mount a formidable array of catapults on his new firing point. Infuriatingly, just as all was ready, the mound subsided into the earth. The Pontics had been digging under the mound as fast as the Romans had been piling the earth on top, so it all had to be done again. First, however, there came the grim business of counter-mining, in which groups of soldiers fought vicious battles underground, swapping shovels for swords as they dug into the enemy's tunnels. Finally, when the mounds were able to support battering rams securely, the Romans launched another major assault and managed to break part of the wall and set a tower on fire. Another hellish fight followed for possession of the building whilst it was still ablaze.

Meanwhile, Sulla had been doing some undermining of his own. A number of tunnels had reached the foundations of Piraeus' walls, and these walls were now supported by solid Roman props of timber. The props were soaked in oil and ignited at random intervals, so that the defenders could never be sure whether the section of wall they were fighting on might not suddenly cave in and take them down in the collapse. Archelaus rallied his men magnificently, even as Sulla threw wave after wave of attackers at the breaches. Between the irresistible Roman army and the immovable Pontic defence, something had to give. In the end it was the exhausted Romans who called it a day.

As soon as the Romans pulled back, Pontic stone workers swarmed over the breaches, knowing that the Romans would be back to try again before the damp masonry could properly set. Sure enough, the next day the Romans threw themselves at the walls once again and smashed their way through the Pontic repairs – just as Archelaus had expected. Behind the breaches were new fortifications, curved like dam walls to hold back the Roman flood. But these curves were concave, so the attacking Romans faced a hail of missiles not only from the front, but from the sides as well. Realizing that these defences (known in the siegemaster's trade as 'lunettes') were literal death traps, Sulla pulled his army back, and turned his malevolent attention on Athens.

The situation in Athens was desperate. Three times Archelaus had tried to get supplies to the city's starving people, and each time his plans had been betrayed from within. After his second attempt failed, Archelaus suspected what was happening. To confirm his suspicions, he ordered, in the strictest secrecy, an attack on the Roman lines at the same time as a further push was to be made to get supplies to the Athenians. Sure enough, the Romans were away attacking the Pontic supply train when Archelaus' attack took place. The Romans returned to find that the defenders of the Piraeus had made a bonfire of their siege weapons for them to cook their captured food on.

To make sure the famine within Athens was effective, Sulla had built forts and surrounded the city with a ditch to make sure that no-one got out. Consequently, hunger had weakened the defenders to the point where rumours of cannibalism abounded, and the walls were no longer adequately defended.[3] Hearing that there were no longer any guards on a particularly vulnerable section of the walls, Sulla first reconnoitred the spot personally to ensure this was not another diabolical Pontic trap, and then, on 1 March 86 BC, he sent a storming party over the walls. Plutarch describes what followed:

> At around midnight, Sulla entered the breach, accompanied by the triumphant howl of an army turned loose to rape and slaughter. They swept through the streets with naked swords ... even without mentioning what happened in the rest of the city, the blood from the Agora spread across the area of the Ceramicus, poured under the Double Gate and ran through the gutters of the suburbs.[4]

Eventually, the extent of the slaughter turned even Sulla's stomach and he ordered an end to the killing. In a reference to the city's glorious past, he magnanimously announced 'I shall spare the living for the sake of the dead', though one Greek historian bitterly remarked 'by then there were few enough living to spare'. Ariston and his cronies took refuge in the Acropolis, the ancient citadel of Athens. The Romans saw no point in losing lives in storming the place, and waited until thirst did their work for them. Ironically, an hour after Ariston surrendered, a squall descended on the hill and deluged it with water whilst the Romans were busily helping themselves to the Athenian gold and silver reserves stored within.

With Roman morale boosted, the attack on the Piraeus resumed with renewed fury. Catapults, siege towers and rams hit the walls in a coordinated wave, while a rain of arrows and javelins sought to clear the walls of defenders. The Romans smashed through the lunette, only to discover that Archelaus had built another lunette behind that, and others in sequence almost the entire way back to the dockyards. There was, however, a maniacal determination behind the Roman attack which forced the slightly-stunned Pontics to give ground despite themselves. Finally, Archelaus pulled back right to the Munychia, the central harbour of Piraeus, which, for the time being, was out of the Romans' reach.

In fact, by this time Archelaus was only in the Piraeus at all because the Romans were so determined to take casualties by smashing themselves against its walls. The Pontic general was well aware that the entire bloody episode at Athens was something of a diversion from the main contest. Mithridates' main army had now arrived. Under the command of Arcathias, a son of Mithridates, this huge force (estimated in the Roman sources at 100,000 men, 10,000 horse and 90 scythed chariots) had effortlessly swept the Roman legions of Macedonia aside, conquered the province, and hurried down to Greece. Even given the enthusiasm with which Roman historians over-estimated the size of Asiatic armies, there is no doubt that this was a formidable force. Archelaus had been a distraction to keep the Romans from interfering whilst the army of conquest arrived. Now it was here, Archelaus embarked his troops and sailed to join the main army, probably as he had always intended.

The Roman army took possession of the Piraeus and Sulla, in a fit of evil temper, ordered the burning of the famed Athenian dockyards. Then, like the Pontic army, he abandoned Athens and the Piraeus, and took his men to Boeotia where the decisive battles for Greece would be fought.

There was good reason why Sulla, having fought so hard for possession of Attica, was in a hurry to leave the place. The environs of Athens had been host to a Roman army for the better part of a year, and a Roman army which was not getting supplies from home at that. Consequently almost anything edible that grew or walked had ended up in the bellies of Sulla's soldiers. Athens was certainly not going to supply any more food, so, unless Lucullus was able to eventually return with sufficient ships to beak the Pontic stranglehold on the sea, Sulla had to move. Boeotia was flatter and much better suited to cavalry in which the Mithridatic army had overwhelming superiority. Even so, facing the enemy there was better than remaining in Attica and waiting for the Pontics to take up a strong position and wait until hunger forced the Romans to attack it. Besides, Sulla had achieved his objective and knocked Athens out of the war – so thoroughly that it would be a generation before the place achieved even a shadow of its former glory.

There was a final reason for moving out, and that was the significant Roman force in Thessaly under the legate Hortensius – quite probably the remnant of the Roman force in Macedonia which had fought its way southward.* Hortensius had some six thousand men under his command and Sulla was desperate enough for the extra manpower to run considerable risks, especially given the other pressing reasons for leaving Athens already mentioned. Hortensius had his own problems, as the Pontic vanguard was pressing him hard. Using native guides, he made his trip laboriously through the mountains, taking care never to cover ground wide or flat enough for the Pontic superiority in numbers to be brought to bear. Fighting by day and retreating by night, the small Roman force eventually joined with Sulla's on a defensible hill on the Plain of Elatea, near the opening to the Boeotian plain.

Even united, the Roman forces were hardly sufficient to strike terror into Pontic hearts, numbering some 15,000 foot and well under 2,000 cavalry. On the other hand, every one of these men was a hard-bitten veteran, and in ancient warfare quality counted for much more than quantity. It was only possible to bring a certain number of men face-to-face in a battle line and, because the Romans fought more or less shoulder-to-shoulder, it was not uncommon for them to have local superiority over more numerous enemies who fought in more dispersed formations.

Mithridates' son, Arcathias, had died at some point in the march into Greece, and the army fell under the command of one Taxiles until Archelaus took over once the Pontics joined forces at Thermopylae. Archelaus was unable to bring the Romans to battle. His men, deployed in battle order, almost covered the plain – a splendidly-armoured, multi-national force, with the chariots and cavalry dashing about in front of the main army. This so intimidated the Romans that they refused Sulla's

---

* Sadly, because none of the characters in whom the ancient sources were interested fought in the Macedonian campaign, the story of Rome's unsuccessful defence of the province is unknown, especially as the Romans were not particularly keen on discussing their failures.

demands that they go out and fight. Sulla responded with his usual tactic of giving the men hard labour that made fighting seem the easier option. While the Romans were making up their minds what to do, Archelaus employed his army in devastating the towns and cities about him. He had no inhibitions about this, as they had changed sides to Rome when Sulla had arrived in the country.

The first sign that the Romans were girding for battle came when Archelaus sent a unit called the Brazen Shields to take a hilltop fortress, and the Romans, urged on by Sulla, managed to beat the Pontic unit to take possession of the position. Thereafter, when the Pontic force descended on Chaeronea, a Roman detachment managed to get in ahead of it and garrison the town against attack.

The move on Chaeronea gave an indication of Archelaus' thinking. Sulla was secure on his hill and had plenty of fresh water (indeed, one of the tasks he had given his legionaries as a cure for timidity had been to divert a nearby river to a more favourable course). However, 18,000 men and horses needed a lot of feeding but Sulla, without enough cavalry to protect his men, could not let them forage for supplies. The Roman supply lines ran through Chaeronea – block these and the Romans could be starved into battle.

Sulla in his turn was more than ready to transfer operations south to Chaeronea. This fortress town was on a massif, the highest point of which was Mount Thurium. With Mount Hedylium opposite to the north and the river valley of the Cephisus between, Chaeronea controlled access to the northern plain of Boeotia. Because of its strategic position it had seen a major battle once already in its chequered history, in 338 BC when Philip II of Macedon had conquered the Thebans. Its position meant that Chaeronea needed to be defended for its own sake, but, as Sulla's advance party would have made clear, the rocky plain between the mountains was much less suitable for the manoeuvring of large bodies of men and cavalry – a situation which favoured the Romans.

Nevertheless, having got himself into the northern part of the plain, Archelaus had either to get through the Roman army which now blocked his passage to the south or abandon the current position altogether and make his way into Boeotia by a completely different route, an option which involved a long and tortuous journey. A third alternative was to stay put and await developments. Given that Sulla was a thoroughly proactive commander who had realized that he had his enemy in as advantageous a position as he was likely to get, developments were not long in coming.

The Battle of Chaeronea[5]

The troops whom Archelaus had sent to seize Chaeronea in the first place had retreated to a fortified position on Mount Thurium, above the town, while the main Pontic army had established itself in a pocket where the River Cephisus bent northward past Mount Hedylium and Mount Acontium blocked the end of the valley. This meant that Archelaus' forces were in a highly secure position, having Mount Thurium to their right, Acontium behind and the River Cephisus to the left with Hedylium beyond that.[6] However, as the modern military maxim explains, 'make it too hard for them to get in, and you can't get out'. The only escape for the Pontic forces lay to the left, where the River Cephisus flowed between the mountains. This was certainly too small for a large army to leave in a hurry, but then, given the numbers involved, a Pontic defeat was unthinkable.

Sulla was a general with a lot of practice at thinking the unthinkable, and fighting the cavalry armies of Numidia had given him considerable experience about the options available to an infantry army faced with a mobile enemy. Regarding the Pontic infantry, he, like other contemporary commanders, knew what any traveller on the London Underground can confirm: push a large body of men closely enough together and they cannot even scratch their noses, let alone defend themselves. The Pontic cavalry could be countered given the right terrain (as Archelaus had just done for Sulla) and the large number of enemy infantry could work against itself.

Whilst Sulla was girding himself for battle, Archelaus was not yet certain that Sulla was serious about fighting. The opening engagement of the battle appeared more like the sort of skirmish which had been part of the background noise over the previous fortnight. What Archelaus probably had not yet realized was to be the Second Battle of Chaeronea (Spring, 86 BC), kicked off with fighting around Mount Thurium. A group of native Chaeroneans had approached Sulla, offering to use their local knowledge of the terrain around the mountain to outmanoeuvre the Pontic force ensconced there. The idea was to get above the Pontics and throw and roll rocks down on them until they abandoned their position.

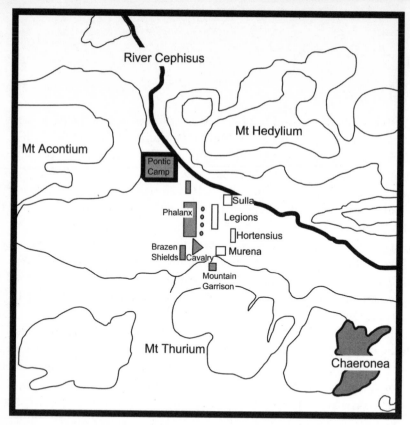

Reconstruction of the opening phase of the Battle of Chaeronea based largely on the description by Plutarch

Sulla agreed to the proposal and drew up his forces for battle in such a way that the Pontics, as they left the mountain, would receive a warm welcome from his lieutenant, Murena, who commanded the Roman left flank on the plain below. Murena had the support of whatever cavalry Sulla could give him, whilst Sulla took the rest to guard the right (river) flank. As the plain sloped slightly downhill towards the main Pontic army, Hortensius and his Macedonian veterans, in reserve to the rear, had a view of where they should prepare to deploy themselves.

The Chaeronean ambush was a disaster for the Pontic troops on the hill. They were driven off in confusion and lost some 3,000 men without striking a blow. Archelaus, hastily drawing up his men to meet the Roman challenge, was in time to see his force from the mountain run into Murena's welcoming party, and from there break in confusion to run pell-mell for the shelter of their own ranks. This was frustrating because the Pontic scythed chariots were ready to go and the clear field they needed for their run-up was cluttered with fleeing friendlies. To make matters worse, the Romans were following-up fast; by the time Archelaus was able to unleash his chariots

1. Bust of Mithridates, now in the Louvre, Paris. This is a unique survival as the Romans generally disapproved of images of those who opposed them with any measure of success. The 'lionskin' helmet may be to identify Mithridates with Hercules (photograph courtesy of Sandra A Whiteway).

coin of Mithridates showing him as a llenistic monarch. The hole in the top of the coin suggests it was worn as a ıllion by a tribesman in the Black Sea region where it was found ɛrre R Monney, with kind permission).

3. Cornelius Sulla – a highly capable general. His uncompromising ruthlessness made him a suitable foil for the equally-merciless Mithridates, though it made life extremely difficult for those civilians caug[ht] between the competing armies (bust in the Staatliche Antiksammlungen und Glyptot[ek] Munich; photograph ©P Matyszak).

4. Coin of Tigranes of Great of Armenia, son-in-law of Mithrida[tes]. Whilst he was happy to collabor[ate] with Pontus in invading Cappadocia, Tigranes was unhap[py] when his family connection caus[ed] him to be dragged into war with [the] Romans, and he eventually mad[e] separate peace with Pompey.

5. Bust of Gnaeus Pompeius, kno[wn] today as Pompey. Behind this ra[ther] smug and vapid expression was [an] astute politician with a formidab[le] military talent. (bust now in Ny Carlsberg Glyptotech, Copenhag[en]; photograph ©P Matyszak)

picture of Modern Sinope showing why the natural advantages of the landscape made it the
antile centre of the Pontic kingdom.

e Black Sea forests of modern Turkey are well watered and far from the popular concept of
olia as a uniformly arid environment. Much of the timber of the Pontic fleet came from here.

8. Rock tombs of the Pontic kings at the ancient Pontic capital of Amaseia. Note also the steep terrain which ma[kes] Amaseia a highly-defensible positio[n] (©Luc Wouters, with kind permissio[n])

9. Cappadocian landscape. This view of the parched interior of Anatolia shows the difficulties of maintaining a large army in the field. Such terrain was very suitable for the delaying tactics of Mithridates in later years.

Asclepion (temple of Asclepius) at Pergamum. During the Pontic massacre thousands of Romans [fled] to shelter in temples such as these, but were cut down anyway, a sacrilege for which the cities of [Asia] Minor paid dearly (©Tom Brosnahan, with kind permission of www.TurkeyTravelPlanner.com)

11. A reconstruction of how the major features of ancient Rhodes might have looked at the time of the siege of Mithridates (montage constructed by the author from aerial photographs of modern Rhodes and architectural sites throughout Greece).

12. Merchant ship and lighthouse from a mos... floor at Ostia Antica. ... successful were the pirates sponsored by Mithridates that they managed to bring maritime traffic to a n... standstill, not only in eastern Mediterranea... but also on parts of th... Italian coast (photogr... ©P Matyszak).

13. A warship, possibly a trireme, travelling under sail with oars shipped, from a mosaic at Ostia Antica. Note the prow shaped for ramming (photograph ©P Matyszak).

14. Drawing of a bireme by author. These light and spee... vessels were used by all sid... during the wars. They were slightly larger and heavier t... the 'Liburnian' vessels whic... made up the staple of the pirate fleet, but were sometimes adopted as the pirates gained greater resources (©P Matyszak).

…oman auxiliary soldiers from a relief in the …an Museum. These soldiers sometimes …red radically from their legionary …terparts in their armour and weaponry. … the scale armour, and apparent protection …e lower arm which seems to have been …acteristic of soldiers of the western Black …oast (photograph ©P Matyszak).

16. A Roman (left) battles with warriors identified as Bastarnae, from the Adamklissi monument. The Bastarnae, known as 'the bravest warriors of all' played a key part in the capture of the harbour at Chalcedon. (photograph ©Adrian Goldsworthy, with kind permission).

…omans fight Sarmatian horsemen. This relief from Trajan's Column shows the Sarmatians and … horses clad in tight-fitting scale armour. It is probable that their ancestors who fought for …ridates were similarly dressed (photograph ©Adrian Goldsworthy, with kind permission).

18. Thracian horseman. Thracians served on both sides as mercenaries during Mithridates' wars. This cloaked figure holds a spear, but his lack of armour suggests that on this occasion his equestrian skills were deployed in hunting (photograph ©P Matyszak).

19. Scythian Cavalrymen. The range of the Pontic kingdom gave Mithridates a wide variety of cav which greatly contributed to the flexibility and striking power of his army. Scythian horse archers were lightly armed, but almost impossible for the more heavily-armed Romans to catch (photogra ©Giovanni Lattanzi, with kind permission of the Archaeological image resource at www.archart.it

they were unable to get up the momentum they needed. When they saw the chariots coming, the well-drilled Romans opened their ranks in the manner their forefathers had once practised with Hannibal's elephants; rather than creating carnage in the Roman ranks, the chariots rushed madly through the Roman lines without actually hitting anyone. Once through, Mithridates' men screeched to as much of a halt as the maddened horses could manage and attempted to wheel round and take the Romans in the rear. Sulla, however, had anticipated this and had laid on javelinmen to take down the chariots at their most vulnerable moment. Archelaus saw a bad day getting worse as his vaunted chariots vanished into the Roman ranks, their disappearance followed by howls of derision and the traditional chant of spectators at the Circus Maximus in Rome, demanding that the next set of riders come out to race.

Having hardly paused for the chariots, the Romans came on and launched their trademark shower of *pila* (heavy javelins) at the Pontic phalanx. Archelaus had put freed slaves in the front line, and these, knowing that victory or crucifixion were the only alternatives, fought like men possessed. Sulla's men in turn were incensed that they had been matched against slaves, and tried frantically to break through the hedgehog spears of the Pontic phalanx. Meanwhile, the Romans put to use some of the lighter engines left over from the siege of Athens. Making good use of their position on slightly higher ground, they lobbed assorted ordnance, including 'fiery bolts', over the heads of their own men into the Pontic phalanx, which, given the confined space at the end of the valley, was necessarily drawn up in depth.[7] Whilst making life uncomfortable, the engines were less effective than they might have been because the soldiers in the back ranks left their 16ft spears pointing upward at an angle, creating a sort of wall which deflected arrows and broke the force of heavier objects on their way down.

Despite his early setback, Archelaus had achieved the classic Hellenistic battle plan. His phalanx had pinned the main block of enemy infantry and it was now time for him to sweep, Alexander-like, around the flanks with his superior cavalry, take out the enemy reserves and bring the battle to a climax as his massed cavalry crashed into the backs of the main Roman force and crushed them against the phalanx.

Of course, Sulla had read of Alexander as well, which is why he had made sure his flanks, being the side of a mountain and a river respectively, were not ideal for sweeping around. In any case, a Roman cohort was not a phalanx and on running into mounted opposition its members were able to group into tight hedgehog formations about which cavalry could only swirl ineffectively.

Archelaus' first target was Murena's corps, still overstretched and disordered from following up the routed troops from the mountain. Hortensius saw the danger and came rushing down the slope with five cohorts, intending to hit the Pontic horse in the flank. However, he had underestimated the superb control and discipline of the Pontic cavalry, which swerved violently and hit Hortensius men in mid-charge, though not before they could stop and brace for it. This, in turn presented Archelaus' flank to Murena, but Murena's men were busy reforming, and once they had done that they had urgent business approaching in the form of Taxiles, who was following up with his Brazen Shields. For the moment, Hortensius was on his own.

Sulla, on the river flank (the Roman right), had not yet engaged. Realizing how desperate things were getting on the left, he pulled what forces he could spare from the battle line and hurried to retrieve the situation. Meanwhile, Hortensius' infantry formations had evidently kept their shape in the face of Archelaus' charge and were beginning to contemplate a counterattack. As infantry will generally beat cavalry in a static situation, Archelaus decided to pull back in the face of Sulla's reinforcement and try his luck on the weakened Roman right wing. There followed a race to the river flank. Sulla ordered Hortensius to join Murena in throwing back the Brazen Shields and took his reserves back across the rear of the main battle line (still fruitlessly trying to get to grips with the Pontic phalanx) to meet Archelaus again on the Roman right. For the first time in the battle, Pontic numbers told against Archelaus. He had to get his cavalry around the mass of his army, reform and hit Sulla's right wing. Before he could manage it, Sulla's right wing hit him. Archelaus found himself trying to steady troops reeling from the Roman assault. Despite his efforts, these eventually fell back in disorder toward the gap between the river and Mount Acontium, where Archelaus had fortified his camp in order, as he had expected, to stop the Romans escaping from the valley.

Now under the ramparts of his camp, he ordered his men to stand and fight and it is a tribute to his personality and the discipline of the Pontic forces that they gamely attempted to do so. However, the Romans followed up too fast for the Pontic forces to pull themselves together and the tightly-packed, confused soldiers stood little chance against the wall of Romans hemming them ever closer. Satisfied that the river flank was under control, Sulla made a third commute across the rear of his battle line to see how Murena was getting on. On arrival, the Roman commander was greeted by the gratifying sight of the backs of Taxiles' Brazen Shields in open rout.

With the left and right flanks gone, the phalanx stood little chance. Whilst its multiple ranks of spears made it almost invincible from the front, the Romans, hardened by years of fighting the similarly-armed Macedonians, had long known that there was nothing that phalangites hated more than hostile troops at the sides and rear. Those same massed ranks of spears made turning sideways to fight extremely difficult, while dropping the spears to achieve this pitted lightly-armed men with tiny shields against well-armed legionaries. The phalanx crumbled into a mass of panicked men scrambling for the safety of the camp; a safety which the guards at the gates were reluctant to give without orders, and Archelaus was still rabidly insisting that his men fight to the last.

When, finally it became apparent, even to Archelaus, that the day was lost, the gates of the camp were opened. But the Pontic commander had left it too late. The Romans burst in on the heels of their fleeing enemies, and once they were in the camp the rout was complete.

The slaughter did not end when the final remnants of the Pontic army managed to squeeze out of the bottleneck at the end of the valley. Though a phalangite who had dropped all the tools of his trade could outrun the most enthusiastic legionary, Sulla's cavalry had come through the battle intact and made the most of a relatively open plain and a defenceless, fleeing enemy. Safety for the Pontic troops was only found far to the northeast at Chalcis in Euboea, to which point the Pontic navy brought those they were able to evacuate from the Greek mainland, some 10,000 men in all from an army that was originally estimated at 120,000 strong.

Sulla's estimate that he lost fourteen men in the battle (two of whom were not dead and returned later) sounds wildly optimistic under any circumstances. However, it was a truism in ancient warfare that the serious casualties came when a unit broke. In fact, apart from the serious fighting against the Brazen Shields on the left, much of Sulla's army had spent the battle being held off by the spears of the phalanx; a process which - if the Romans did not press too hard - would have done little harm to the front ranks of either side. If, as is assumed here, Hortensius' men did manage to brace for Archelaus' cavalry charge, then again, casualties would have been minimal, for the cavalry would have been no more able to penetrate the Roman formations than the Romans were able to get through the front of the phalanx. In short, Sulla's propaganda claim is more plausible than it first seems.

Archelaus had lost a huge number of men and materials to the Romans (Sulla burned what captured supplies he could not make use of), but thanks to the tireless logistic work of Mithridates, plenty more of both were forthcoming. Pontic command of the sea made transporting these from Asia Minor relatively straightforward, whilst lack of sea power meant that the Roman attempt to finish off the remains of Archelaus' army ended at the mainland shore, despite Chalcis being clearly visible across the strait.* Though defeated, Archelaus could try again. If Sulla was defeated, he was finished. As Archelaus probably reassured his men, one victory would be enough; the Greek campaign was far from over.

* It is reached by bridge today.

Chapter 6

The Road to Dardanus

It was to the credit of Mithridates that his immediate response to the catastrophe in Greece was not to look for scapegoats but to attempt to limit the political damage. Whether he succeeded in this aim cannot now be determined, as it is impossible at this distance in time to determine what the consequences would have been had he not acted as he did. Nevertheless, it can be said with certainty that the political situation in Asia Minor deteriorated disastrously after Mithridates acted – either despite his measures, or because of them.

Chaeronea went beyond a mere military setback. Mithridates had dispatched a huge, well-organized and experienced army of veteran soldiers. Morale had been boosted by an almost unbroken string of victories in Asia Minor and the Crimea. Yet this army had not only been beaten, it had been crushed by an enemy force less than a quarter of its size which had taken minimal casualties in the process.

This enemy force had been dispatched by Rome while that city was still wrapping up a major war with its own allies, and despite being on the brink of civil war between different factions within the city. Unsurprisingly, the people of Asia Minor began to ask themselves what Rome would be capable of once it got its act together and launched a coordinated assault on the region which had murdered 80,000 Romans and Italians. It was noted that those cities in mainland Greece which had switched their allegiance to Rome at the earliest opportunity had generally got off with swingeing financial penalties, whilst the loyalty of the Athenians to Mithridates had earned them starvation and massacre. Finally, Mithridates' conquests were too recent for Pontic rule to be the accepted status quo, and after Chaeronea it dawned on many that Mithridates had just lost the army he had done his conquering with.

Under the circumstances it would be surprising if Sulla had not received a series of unofficial delegations delicately enquiring what treatment an early surrender would gain them. Mithridates, a man who liked to be well-informed, was quick to scent betrayal. An early example came from the island of Chios; possibly whilst Athens was still under siege. Word reached

Mithridates that a delegation had gone to Sulla, apparently with the blessing of the city government. It did not help the Chian case in Mithridates' court that there had always been a strong pro-Roman faction on the island, or that it had been a Chian vessel which had collided with Mithridates' ship during action off Rhodes.

Therefore the commander of the troops sent by sea to reinforce Archelaus stopped off at Chios en route. The citizens of the island woke up to find their walls occupied by Pontic troops, the leader of which ordered the islanders to disarm and hand over hostages for their good behaviour. Rather than accuse the islanders of treachery (which might lead others with treasonable intentions to suspect that their sentiments were widespread), the charge laid by Mithridates was simple embezzlement, in that the Chians had allegedly failed to hand over the proper share of loot from the Romans whom they had murdered – a charge which contained a reminder of the collective guilt which the cities of Asia Minor shared.

Appian quotes a letter which he claims came from Mithridates himself. In it the king complained

> You benefit from the yields of the lands taken from the Romans, yet want to give nothing to us. When your trireme collided with mine at Rhodes, I wanted to believe this was an error of the ships pilot alone ... now you send your leading men to consult with Sulla, and you have made no attempt at all to deny that they acted with public authorization.[1]

Mithridates announced that the Chians deserved death for their betrayal, but the sentence would be waived if they stumped up a 2,000 talent fine. This was no easy matter at a time when trade was depressed and Pontic taxes were rising to pay for the expense of the war. Nevertheless, the citizens managed to raise the sum by stripping their temples and donating items of personal jewellery. Having accepted the sum into Pontic coffers, the leader of the occupying forces cheerfully announced that the Chians had given short weight. The punishment for this further act of peculation was to be the effective destruction of the islanders as a people. Men and women were put into separate groups and shipped off as colonists to different parts of Colchis. This would both provide a welcome Greek influence in the area, and, in this hostile environment, make the former Chians practically dependent on Mithridates for their continued survival.

However, it appears that this scheme was never put into effect. The historian Memnon reports that the transports were intercepted by the ships of the city of Heraclea, and the Chians restored to their homeland. By the time Mithridates was aware of these developments he had much larger problems on his plate and could not do much about Chios in any case. Certainly the archaeological record shows no break in human occupation of the island, indicating that if deportation took place, it was almost immediately reversed.[2]

Another group whose loyalty was not so much suspect as non-existent was the Galatians. This people had never forgiven Mithridates for annexing a chunk of northwestern Galatia, but they had been kept quiescent by good wages for mercenary service and the threat that, if sufficiently provoked, the Pontic army would go on to annex the rest of the country as well. Nevertheless, Mithridates felt it expedient to take hostages, sixty in all, from the leading Galatian families. These were treated as prisoners, further increasing hostility toward Mithridates. Nevertheless, the presence of a large Galatian contingent at the Pontic court raised the possibility that one of them might be able to achieve the assassination of Mithridates, thus freeing Galatia and earning the undying gratitude of the Romans.

Of course, achieving this desirable goal necessitated beating Mithridates, the master of the double-cross, at his own game. The devious king of Pontus invited the tetrarchs, rulers of Galatia, to join their hostage families at a banquet. The invitation implied that a weakened Mithridates had chosen to attempt the conciliation of his restless subjects. In fact Mithridates had a more radical solution in mind. His men massacred everyone who attended. Regrettably (from the Pontic viewpoint), killing off most of the Galatian leadership simply removed the rivals of those who were left. This allowed the Galatians to respond with a degree of coherence and coordination which political infighting had previously rendered impossible. The satrap whom Mithridates sent to rule Galatia did not have enough troops to withstand the wave of rebellion raised against him. Within months he and the Pontic garrisons had been expelled and Galatia was on its way to becoming a unified kingdom.

The citizens of Ephesus, another city of dubious loyalties, carefully noted these events, and when a Pontic force appeared at the city gates, the soldiers found those gates firmly closed against them. The fact that the commander of the Pontic soldiers was Zenobius, the same man who had masterminded the stealthy takeover of the defences of Chios, probably added to Ephesian paranoia. Zenobius tried to ease the suspicions of the Ephesians by asking for a conference with the leading pro-Pontic citizen in the city, the father of one of Mithridates favourite wives, Monima. Zenobius was allowed into the city with a few attendants, and he promptly called a meeting of the Ephesian assembly. The Ephesians equally promptly adjourned the meeting until the following day, and in the meantime threw Zenobius into prison. At the meeting the citizens decided on revolt, killed Zenobius, and sent envoys to Sulla, explaining that they had cooperated with Mithridates whilst they must, but were now throwing off his shackles at the first opportunity.

A slew of cities followed the example of Ephesus, leaving Mithridates with a dilemma. He had assembled another large army in haste immediately after receiving the news from Chaeronea. Now he could either send that army to deal with the rebellion in Asia Minor, or he could stick with his original intention and send it to Greece to give Archelaus another go at beating Sulla. Eventually Mithridates decided that, while Pontus itself remained steadfastly loyal, there would be more rebellions among the Greeks unless Sulla was beaten; if Sulla was defeated, the Greeks would fall back into line on their own. He sent the army to Greece, but kept back a detachment to harass the rebels in the countryside and make a gruesome example of anyone they caught outside their city walls.

Whilst so far Mithridates had attempted to govern the Greek cities well, he now set about making them ungovernable. Probably this was a deliberate tactic which assumed that if the Greek cities were worthless as allies, they should be rendered equally ineffective as enemies. He declared the cancellation of debts, the freeing of slaves, and citizenship for the resident aliens of each city. Predictably, the winners and losers from these declarations became respectively and fervently pro- and anti-Mithridates, and their cities were paralyzed by the resulting civic strife (appropriately known in Greek as 'stasis'.)

Nor was undivided loyalty to be found in Pergamum, which Mithridates had made the seat of his rule. Several high-ranking courtiers formed a cabal to plot the overthrow of the king. They were betrayed by one of their number, a man called Asclepiodotus. Mithridates was not prepared to have these men killed on the word of an accuser alone, so he personally eavesdropped on a meeting of the conspirators, who cheerfully discussed their plans unaware that their intended victim lay seething quietly under one of the couches.

Arrest and torture of the cabal led to the discovery that another eighty leading Pergamenes were engaged in a similar enterprise. After this Mithridates abandoned his former restraint and sent out inquisitors to all the major cities. Evidence was collected from informers in return for rewards, and some 1,600 people died messily in the purge which followed. Not unexpectedly, this did not greatly increase the loyalty or affection of the king's Greek subjects.

Mithridates could at least console himself that Sulla too was feeling the political heat. Even before Chaeronea, Sulla was joined by his wife and family in Greece. Things had become too dangerous in Rome, where Sulla had been declared a public enemy. His rival, Marius, had returned from exile and was energetically exterminating Sulla's supporters in Rome even as Mithridates was doing in the same in Asia Minor.

A further item of news which would have pleased neither Sulla nor Mithridates was that the government in Rome had prepared a rival army under the consul Flaccus and were preparing to send this across the Adriatic to join the fray. Given that Sulla was officially an outlaw, this raised the spectre of a three-sided war in which Roman army would fight Roman army whilst Mithridates fought the pair of them.

In fact the Pontic army had already engaged the advance guard of Flaccus. Archelaus was not taking his defeat lying down. In the absence of an army he had turned pirate and passed his time harassing enemy naval traffic and sending commando-style raids against the Romans. Using the island of Euboea as a base, he attacked and besieged the island town of Zacynthus and sent his ships into the Adriatic where they harassed the transports of Flaccus as he attempted to cross with his army.

The beleaguered Sulla could only await events. He made camp at Melitaea, a position which enabled him to keep a weather eye for any appearance of hostile Romans on the approaches from Thessaly, yet which was still close enough to Boeotia for him to be able to return in a hurry if word came that Archelaus was on the move. In fact, Archelaus was already embarking from Euboea, his 10,000 men reinforced by 80,000 troops brought over from Asia Minor by Dorylaus, another of Mithridates' generals. The return of a large Pontic army automatically meant the revolt of Boeotia from the Romans, so Sulla immediately returned to give his old enemy a rematch.

However, Archelaus had learned his lesson from Chaeronea. He had no intention of going through another head-on encounter with the Roman legionary meat grinder. Instead Sulla was frustrated to find his enemy was using the strategy that the legendary Roman general, Fabius the Delayer, had used against Hannibal, and refusing to engage in battle. This move demonstrates that Pontic intelligence was well aware of Sulla's predicament. Sulla needed both victories and money for his position to be tenable. By refusing to fight, Archelaus denied Sulla the victory he needed, whilst Sulla's army still needed to be paid.

The Battle of Orchomenos

Sulla's response was to offer Archelaus an all-or-nothing shot at the battle he desired. Instead of fighting within the confines of a rocky valley such as that of the Cephisus at Chaeronea, Sulla took up station near Orchomenos, some fifteen miles away. Here the valley opened out into the Boeotian plain, offering Archelaus' cavalry a treeless playground which stretched from the small city of Orchomenos across to the marshy banks of the River Melas some thirty miles to the east. Archelaus took the bait and moved his army on to the plain, though taking care to leave a well-fortified camp to his rear in case anything went wrong.

The battle which followed was a more confused affair than the set-piece of Chaeronea and this is reflected by the descriptions in the ancient sources. Though these are not so much contradictory as giving emphasis to different aspects of the battle, they are nevertheless hard to follow. All accounts agree that having got Archelaus on the plain where he could use his cavalry, Sulla immediately set about cancelling the cavalry's advantage by setting his men to digging long ditches ten feet wide, thus making parts of the plain impassable to horsemen.

Archelaus was not going to yield his treasured edge over the enemy lightly, and his cavalry came boiling out of the Pontic camp so quickly that the Romans did not have time to properly form up. Seeing the Pontic cavalry coming down upon them in their thousands, Sulla's men began to panic and break for the safety of their camp – which most had no hope of reaching before the cavalry took them to pieces. At this point the battle was almost lost before it had properly begun.

Sulla saved the day single-handedly by taking his stand at the earthworks and bellowing at his wavering troops. 'Orchomenos! Remember the name. I'm ready to fight and die here. When people ask you where you ran away and left your general, tell them: at Orchomenos!'[3]

Abashed, Sulla's officers came to join him, and with their encouragement the legionaries made a stand. These held out long enough for two unengaged cohorts to hurry to their rescue. The Pontics fought fiercely and it is probably at this point that Diogenes, the son of Archelaus, died in combat. However, the Pontic cavalry stood little chance in a stationary battle against infantry, especially with more Sullan troops joining the fight all the time, and they were eventually forced to retire. The Romans followed up into the Pontic archers who were attempting to support the cavalry, and these fought back with fistfuls of arrows which they wielded as impromptu swords.

Back in the safety of his camp, Archelaus saw that Sulla had again returned to constructing earthworks at a furious pace. Consequently he led out his troops once more, this time in more formal battle array, and it is quite likely that we have this array from the memoirs of Sulla himself, via Frontinus who recorded it in his Stratagems.[4] The first line consisted of the scythed chariots, which finally had a perfect run-up against the Roman lines. Then, ready to follow up the confusion the chariots should create, came the Macedonian-style phalanx, and behind the phalangites came the escaped Italian slaves who had proven their ability for dogged resistance at Chaeronea, though now these renegades were armed in the manner of Roman auxiliaries. The cavalry were massed on each flank, though their effectiveness was crippled by those earthworks which Sulla had succeeded in constructing, each terminating on the farthest point of the flank with an earthen redoubt.

Sulla's own army was arranged in three lines, though there were spaces between the files through which light infantry, and even cavalry, could rush if need be. Sulla had also arranged his *postsignati* (those drawn up behind the eagle standards) differently to his *antesignati*, with the latter forming a denser frontage, but with more space behind. The reason for this peculiar formation became apparent to the scythed chariots once they were hurtling irrevocably toward the Roman lines. The front-rank legionaries stepped smartly sideways and backward to reveal serried rows of stakes driven into the ground at angles carefully contrived to achieve maximum impalement. As the first chariots raced to their doom, Roman javelinmen rushed through the back ranks to take pot shots at those chariots which managed to skid around and head for safety. 'Safety' proved a relative term, as the phalanx was hurrying forward to exploit the confusion created by the scythed chariots. Chariots met phalanx head-on to their mutual detriment, though the collision did at least prove that scythed chariots could indeed create chaos when they hit poorly-prepared infantry.

With Sulla urging his men forward, Archelaus had little choice but to throw his cavalry into the fray in the hope that his phalanx could pull itself together whilst the Romans braced to receive the horsemen. Here Sulla's considerable military experience came into play. He had foreseen this move and countered it by hurling his own cavalry through the paths in the Roman ranks that had now been cleared of javelinmen. Sulla's cavalry were vastly outnumbered, and could only hope to check the hordes of Pontic horsemen for a moment, but a moment was all that was needed. The infantry had not faltered in their advance, and they hit the Pontic cavalry standing as it engaged in a mêlée with Sulla's horsemen.

Cutting through the cavalry, the legionaries closed with the phalanx, which had not, as Archelaus had hoped, been given time to reorganize. However, the Pontic general was a quick learner, and this time he had made sure that the phalangites had a clear line of retreat into the camp. Consequently, his infantry losses were relatively light – some 5,000 men, but each phase in the battle so far had led to butchery among the cavalry which was down by some 10, 000 horsemen.

This ended the proceedings for the day. Sulla was well aware that even after the mauling he had given Archelaus' army, that army outnumbered his own forces. If he allowed Archelaus to get away, the Pontic general would return to imitating Fabius the Delayer, and Sulla's victory would have been pointless. Consequently he kept a substantial portion of his men on stand-to overnight, and as soon as day broke, he set about constructing a further set of earthworks less than 600 feet from the camp.

Archelaus, meanwhile, harangued his men, pointing out that they still outnumbered an enemy who had the audacity to put them under siege. The Pontic force responded with the indomitable spirit which characterized that army in battle and surged over the ramparts just as the Romans, urged on by Sulla, attempted a sortie of their own. The result was another titanic and highly-confused struggle in which the discipline and flexibility of Sulla's legionaries was balanced against the numbers and spirit of their adversaries.

Finally the Romans succeeded in tearing down a corner of the Pontic ramparts. They were faced by another wall within, this one consisting of grimly-determined Pontic soldiers standing shoulder to shoulder. The Romans hung back until a junior officer called Basillus hurled himself at the Pontic soldier opposite and killed him. The Romans surged into the gap and a massacre began.

Trapped against the marsh, the remnants of Archelaus' army which abandoned the camp had nowhere to run, and the waters turned slowly red with blood. Plutarch reports that even in his day, two hundred years later, bows, breastplates and barbarian swords were still regularly unearthed from the mud. Sulla's men were in no mood to take prisoners (there was no boasting of the lightness of Roman casualties after this battle) and in any case, being a renegade army, the Sullans could not have done much with any captives that they did take. Consequently a Pontic army was yet again chopped to pieces by Roman swords. Archelaus survived the defeat, managing to slip away from the battlefield and get back to Euboea in a small boat, doubtless pondering how Mithridates would take the news of this latest catastrophe.

The Fimbrians

The dysfunctional state of Roman politics had produced the odd result that Mithridates' best hope was now the army which the Roman government had sent against him. If this could be encouraged to fall on the Sullans, perhaps the rival Roman armies might cancel each other out. Therefore, in order to encourage Sulla to turn his attention to the new arrivals, Archelaus deliberately adopted as unthreatening a posture as possible. Garrisons were unilaterally withdrawn from anywhere that Sulla might be tempted to attack. After Chaeronea, Archelaus had stepped up naval activity as the only means of hurting the Romans then available, but he now ceased operations altogether. These measures were confirmed by Mithridates, who went further and suggested that now might be a good time to sound Sulla out about a more formal cessation of hostilities.

Sulla responded to the calm after the storm by moving back to Thessaly where he could better keep an eye on Flaccus whilst setting up his winter camp. Three coastal towns facing Euboea had their harbour facilities destroyed in case they tempted the Pontic navy to make use of them. At the same time, having heard nothing from Lucullus, Sulla finally began to start work on a navy of his own. The cost of this, along with the wages of his troops, doubtless came from the pockets of the Boeotians, who were thus punished for their readiness to change sides every time a Pontic army came calling.

Mithridates would have found both interest and consolation in the reports reaching him on the new Roman force. Flaccus was making heavy weather of his trip across Greece. The Roman government in Italy had chosen the army commander for political reasons, as they wanted a general who, above all, would not simply hand his army over to Sulla once he got to Greece. Consequently, because his skills as a general were somewhat lacking, Flaccus also had with him a legate to advise on military matters, in this case a senator called Fimbria. Fimbria was becoming increasingly frustrated. Flaccus did not just insist on commanding the army himself, he was also doing an exceptionally bad job of it. Unlike Sulla, who had an immediate empathy with those under his command, Flaccus had no idea how to handle his men and seems to have veered erratically between excessive leniency and injudicious punishments. At the same time, Flaccus evidently regarded his command as a means to wealth and blatantly took every opportunity for enrichment that came his way.

His men were none too enthusiastic about taking on the man and the veteran army busily expelling Mithridates from Greece. After a steady flow of deserters from his army to Sulla's, Flaccus apparently decided on some morale-raising victories against the Pontics before challenging his fellow Roman. A brutal winter march to Thrace followed. If the newcomers wanted to fight the Pontics rather than Sulla, Mithridates was ready to oblige, and his garrisons along the route resisted bitterly.

By the time the Romans reached the Hellespont, relations between Fimbria and Flaccus had deteriorated to bitter enmity. Fimbria threatened to leave Flaccus and return to Rome, whereupon Flaccus appointed a man called Thermus in Fimbria's place. When Flaccus had left the army on business, Fimbria returned, knowing that the soldiers vastly preferred him as a commander. Faced with a mutiny, the furious Flaccus had to flee and it soon occurred to him that he was running for his life. Fimbria pursued him from city to city, finally capturing Rome's consul and army commander as he hid in a well. Flaccus' inglorious part in the expedition ended with his murder, with some reporting that Fimbria cut off Flaccus' head and hurled it into the sea.

Peace talks

Whilst Sulla delicately fenced with the envoys of Archelaus on talks about talks, Fimbria took his army into Asia Minor and, by damaging Mithridates there, improved Sulla's negotiating position. Sulla had a single overriding concern. He had to get back to Italy and sort out the situation there before his enemies became too entrenched. Yet if he gave too much to Mithridates he would lose the support of his own legions as well as his political credibility back home.[5] For his part, Mithridates knew that if he surrendered too much he would lose the respect of his subjects and mutiny and rebellion would cost him what little he managed to retain in negotiations. And Mithridates still had his fleet and possession of all of Asia

Minor to bargain with. Militarily he was weak, but by no means finished. Politically, his strength, and possibly his survival, depended on getting a good settlement from Sulla.

It helped that, from the siege of Piraeus onward, Sulla and Archelaus had come to respect each other as adversaries. In the first face-to-face meeting of the pair, at a place on the coast called Aulis, the serious bargaining began. Archelaus made the opening proposal: Mithridates and Sulla should each keep what they now held and become allies in memory of the family friendship the Mithridatids had enjoyed with Sulla's father.[6] Mithridates would supply everything that Sulla was not getting from Rome – ships, supplies and money. All Sulla had to do was wipe out Fimbria's army and return to take command of Rome.

Sulla dryly remarked that it was unfortunate that it had taken the death of 160,000 of Mithridates' soldiers to remind the king that he and Sulla were friends. As for being allies, there was the matter of 80,000 dead Romans and Italians still unavenged. Abandoning their cause would be tantamount to treason. Talking of which, Sulla could certainly assure the senate that guilt for the Asian massacre lay with Mithridates alone. If a more suitable candidate for the rule of Pontus could come forward, say Archelaus himself, Sulla would certainly back him to the best of his considerable ability. To sweeten his offer, Sulla made Archelaus a unilateral grant of ten thousand acres of land in Euboea, his to keep no matter how the negotiations turned out.

Archelaus diplomatically refrained from pointing out that he held Euobea for Pontus at present in any case, and if hostilities resumed Sulla would certainly try to conquer his 'gift'. Instead, he and Sulla agreed that neither man was going to betray his side, so they had better settle on terms. After considerable debate, it was agreed that Archelaus would take the following proposal to his king. Mithridates would return Cappadocia to Ariobarzanes, and Bithynia to Nicomedes. He would withdraw from Paphlagonia, Greece and the Cyclades immediately, and he would abandon at once his attempts to deport the Chians. Mithridates would pay the entire cost of the war – some 2,000 talents – and turn over all prisoners, deserters and escaped slaves in his dominions.* As a final condition, Sulla had noticed during the war the grave inconvenience caused by lack of a fleet, so perhaps Mithridates should give Sulla his? At least seventy first-class warships would do, provided these were fully kitted out and ready to sail.

That Archelaus was prepared to take such terms to Mithridates showed

---

* Sulla had already released many of his prisoners as a goodwill gesture. However, as Mithridates had no further use for Ariston, and Sulla had a personal grudge against the man, the former tyrant of Athens came back as a corpse.

the general's faith in his king. He had lost two armies in their entirety and was now carrying terms that amounted to the surrender of all his gains since 88 BC. And someone with Mithridates well-developed political antennae was bound to at least consider that Archelaus had colluded with Sulla. The pair were now so friendly that when Archelaus fell dangerously sick at Larissa on his return journey, Sulla halted his entire army so that he could stay and nurse him.

Sulla's army was on the move because the tribes invading northern Macedonia had become increasingly aggressive since the collapse of organized government in the region. Sulla intended to pass the summer of 85 BC hammering them (and incidentally cutting Fimbria's supply lines) whilst he awaited Mithridates' reply.

The sticking point in the negotiations was Paphlagonia. Mithridates had given up and retaken Cappadocia almost more times than he could recall, and was quite prepared to go through the process again. Bithynia, it might reasonably be expected, was about to go through a severe economic recession. Since Mithridates had to give the kingdom back anyway, he might as well first wring out of the place the 2,000 talents he had to pay in reparations. If there must be a hostile kingdom on Pontus' western border, it should at least be one which was too financially strapped to act on that hostility. But Mithridates had convinced himself that Paphlagonia was a part of his patrimony, almost a part of Pontus itself, and something he was prepared to stand up to Sulla to defend. Mithridates also denied that Archelaus had any authority to negotiate away his fleet.

Sulla himself was harbouring second thoughts about his own generosity, not least because his troops were carping that the liberation of Greece was all very well, but they had not signed up for a campaign which left their principal enemy undefeated and themselves low on booty. Consequently, when the news came that Mithridates was cavilling about giving up Paphlagonia, the Roman general erupted into a fit of temper.

He informed the cowering ambassadors that he was astounded that Mithridates was not prepared to throw himself at his feet in gratitude for being allowed to keep even that hand which had signed the death warrant of so many Romans. If Mithridates thought that he had some experience of war, he should wait until Sulla crossed over to Asia and explained his error to him in person. Archelaus desperately undertook to explain to his king that Sulla's terms were non-negotiable, whilst Sulla set about pacifying Macedon by the simple and brutal expedient of wholly depopulating any troublesome areas.

Three things encouraged Mithridates to take the negotiations further. Firstly, due to his exceptional circumstances, Sulla was offering to overlook the Asian Vespers and the execution of Aquillius, deeds for which an enemy of Rome would usually expect to pay with his head. Secondly, even though he was required to give up his conquests in Asia Minor, this still left the lands around the Black Sea in his possession. It was, after all, a family trait for the Mithridatids to take on more than they could handle, and then temporarily retreat to a more realistic position until favourable circumstances for further expansion reappeared. And thirdly, Fimbria was proving to be painfully annoying.

Cut off from Rome by Sulla, Fimbria had been forced, like Sulla before him, to supply his army from the land during the summer. Fortunately, Asia Minor provided rich pickings, and the richest of these were to be found at Mithridates' court in Pergamum. When Mithridates discovered that Fimbria's Romans were making a bee-line for his capital, he scraped together an army of half-trained levies and mercenaries commanded by his son, accompanied by the generals Taxiles, Diophontes* and Menander. This force was both large enough and commanded competently enough to cause Fimbria some difficulty. Nevertheless, Fimbria disposed of 6,000 of the Pontic cavalry by digging two lines of earthworks fronted by a ditch. He kept his men under cover until the cavalry had completely wandered into his trap, which he sprang with complete success. Thereafter, when the opposing armies encamped near Miletopolis, on opposite sides of the River Rhyndacus, Fimbria unexpectedly crossed the river at dawn under cover of a storm. He fell on the Pontic army and killed most of Mithridates' men while they were still in their tents.

The loss of its defending army meant Pergamum itself was threatened with siege. The walls of Pergamum were solid, but the loyalty of its citizens less so. Mithridates decided to return to his native Pontus and conduct operations from there. He abandoned Pergamum to its own devices and retreated to the coast at Pitane, opposite the city-state of Mytilene on the island of Lesbos, and waited for his fleet to pick him up.

This simple operation was almost Mithridates' undoing. Ever since the reforms of Marius a generation before, Roman armies had lightened their baggage trains by the simple expedient of making each soldier carry his own kit. This caused the legionaries to ruefully refer to themselves as 'Marius' mules' and it allowed Roman armies to move disconcertingly fast. Within an alarmingly brief time, Fimbria's legionaries were at the gates of Pitane. Even

---

* This is probably not Diophantus of Sinpoe and Bosporan fame.

more alarmingly, the sails which appeared on the horizon were not those for the voyage Mithridates had ordered, but Lucullus, finally turning up with his makeshift fleet at the worst possible time.[7]

Lucullus had made it to Alexandria after a hair-raising voyage in which he had been hard-pressed to outrun pirates on several occasions. With the blessing of Ptolemy and a seed grant of cash, Lucullus had raised a respectable flotilla. Even this was no match for the pirate fleet and, on his return to Cyprus, Lucullus got word that the pirates were preparing a massive ambush. Accordingly he had acted as though he intended to winter on the island, sending off to various cities to organize supplies. Then, as soon as the wind was favourable, he took off unexpectedly for Rhodes. On the voyage he literally kept a low profile, taking his sails down by day and sailing at night.

With the help of the highly-capable Rhodian fleet, Lucullus was easily able to drive off Mithridates' guarding ships and break the blockade of the island. The combined fleet brought Cos and several other islands back under Roman control and was greeted with immense relief at Chios. Now, off Pitane, Lucullus received an impassioned plea from Fimbria to block the harbour. With Mithridates unable to flee, and the walls of Pitane little more than a minor obstacle, the Mithridatic wars could be wrapped up within a week.

It is quite possible that at this point the cunning of Mithridates came into play. His best bet would have been to inform Lucullus that he had opened negotiations with Fimbria and now had no choice but to reach a settlement with the 'official' Roman army rather than Lucullus' commander, the renegade Sulla. A settlement with Fimbria, reached on any terms at all, would give Sulla's enemies the glory of finishing the war, and deny Sulla's men any back pay they would have otherwise expected from Pontic reparations. Nor was Lucullus' fleet any match for the full power of the Pontic navy, which could ensure that Sulla stayed cut off in Greece whilst a settlement was reached without him. Under such circumstances, it was unlikely that Sulla would keep either his army or his domestic support. In short, Mithridates could make a valid point that he and Sulla needed each other very badly at this stage.

Consequently, Lucullus blandly informed Fimbria that, as Sulla's subordinate, he was bound by the same de facto armistice as his general, and therefore he could not interfere. Fimbria's reaction can be imagined as Mithridates sailed away whilst Lucullus and his ships stood by benevolently looking on. With their king safely out of danger, a part of the Pontic fleet under an admiral called Neoptolemus attempted to put paid to Lucullus by launching a surprise attack on his flagship, which was a solid Rhodian quinquereme. The Rhodian ship's master, an experienced fighter, promptly turned away from the Pontic ship bearing down on him, and consequently Neoptolemus' ship rammed the bulky flagship in the stern whilst it was going in the same direction only slightly more slowly. The resultant collision was less of a bump than Mithridates had received from a friendly ship off Rhodes, and certainly was not enough to prevent Lucullus and his ships from turning sharply on their attackers and sending the Pontic flotilla scurrying after their royal master. Thereafter, Lucullus proceeded to northern Greece and ferried Sulla and his army across for a meeting with Mithridates at Dardanus on the coast of Asia Minor.

Mithridates arrived at the meeting determined to make his case. To show that he was far from beaten, he brought with him 20,000 infantry and 6,000 cavalry. Sulla made his case by having with him just four cohorts of legionaries (maybe 2,000 men), which, he implied, made the two retinues of equal strength.

When the two leaders came face to face, Mithridates extended his hand. Sulla did not take it, but bluntly asked whether or not Mithridates was going to accept the terms agreed to by Archelaus. In reply, Mithridates eloquently went through the wrongs the Romans had done him and his state. He reminded Sulla of the greed and injustice he had suffered under Aquillius and argued that all he had done was defend himself and his kingdom. In reply, Sulla said that he had heard that Mithridates was a powerful speaker and he had indeed proved that this was so. He went through the points the king had raised and refuted them one by one. Then he asked again, was Mithridates going to accept the terms agreed to by Archelaus or not?

When the king expostulated further, Sulla remarked that he was surprised that Mithridates was trying to justify those acts for which, through Archelaus, he had only recently asked to be pardoned. The time for speeches had been before matters had been settled by arms. Or did Mithridates think Sulla had come all this way just to have a debate? Was Mithridates going to accept the terms agreed to by Archelaus or not?

Faced with Sulla's uncompromising negotiating stance, Mithridates had little choice but to ratify his general's concessions, whereupon Sulla came forward and embraced him. Worse was to come, for Sulla had Ariobarzanes and Nicomedes in his retinue and insisted that the kings of Cappadocia and Bithynia be formally reconciled with their erstwhile conqueror. There was little Mithridates could do but get through the proceedings with what grace he could muster, hand over the ships which Sulla had demanded and sail home to Pontus with the remainder. The first war between Mithridates and the Romans was at an end.

Chapter 7

The Failed Peace

The post-war settlement

The peace of Dardanus was *realpolitik* at its most brutal, a peace made by two ruthless politicians because it was in their mutual interest that the killing should, temporarily, stop. In so far as both Sulla and Mithridates identified themselves with their respective countries, the settlement was good for Pontus and Rome. It certainly was not good for the cities of Asia and it was a disaster for Fimbria, though few shed tears for Fimbria's predicament. If Mithridates' misgovernment of the past year had caused many of the cities of Asia Minor to regret rebelling from Rome, the violence, savagery and greed of Fimbria's army served as a reminder of why they had rebelled in the first place.

To this the people of Ilium could give eloquent testimony. The city felt it deserved a special place in Roman hearts; better known as Troy, it was the birthplace of Aeneas, founder of the Roman race. When Fimbria besieged the city, ambassadors came to inform him that Ilium had entrusted itself to Sulla. Fimbria responded that since Ilium's citizens were already friends of the Romans, there was no reason why he should not be permitted to enter the city. Once allowed within the walls, Fimbria proved an even greater disaster to the city than Odysseus' wooden horse had been a millennium before. The Roman allowed his army to indiscriminately rape, pillage and slaughter the inhabitants, and to burn what was not worth stealing. Those who had been in communication with Sulla were reserved for special torture, whilst those who took shelter in the temples were burned with the temples themselves. 'Not a house, not a temple, not a statue was left standing', reports a later Greek writer.

Now Nemesis, the goddess of divine justice, had taken up residence outside the Fimbrian camp, her vengeance taking the shape of Sulla's army. As Sulla's circumvallation closed about him, Fimbria tried with ever-increasing desperation to stem the steady flow of deserters openly leaving to join Sulla, fraternizing with the enemy and even pitching in to help with the construction of the earthworks surrounding their camp. Fimbria was unable to persuade even his closest aides to swear an oath of loyalty to him. Weeping, he threw himself at the feet of his men, begging them not to abandon him; and when that failed, he tried bribing a slave to assassinate Sulla. This effort also failed as the slave confessed his mission to Sulla. Thereafter, predictably enough, Sulla was not disposed to meet Fimbria face-to-face when he requested a meeting. Instead, he passed the message that he would not bother killing Fimbria if the latter sailed back to Rome immediately and alone. Fimbria's pride reasserted itself. Informing Sulla that he knew of a quicker way home, he went to a nearby temple and stabbed himself, though it required one of his slaves to finish the job.

Fimbria's death and the surrender of his army removed one affliction from Asia Minor, but the region's troubles were far from over. As well as declaring that Rome was owed the stupendous sum of 20,000 talents in reparations and back taxes, Sulla ordered his soldiers to be quartered with individual families in the various cities.[1] Each family had to provide meals, an allowance and clothing to the soldiers whom they unwillingly hosted, as well as having to put up with the conduct of 'guests' who were less than sympathetic to the people who had killed 80,000 of their countrymen. On the other hand, those cities, such as Rhodes, which had stood by Rome were richly rewarded, partly because Sulla believed in standing by his friends, and partly to encourage resistance to any future invaders of the region.

Sulla then formally reported his settlement of the war to the senate, blithely ignoring the fact that this same senate considered him a public enemy under sentence of death. He then set off for Rome himself, leaving the administration of his settlement to Lucullus, who could at least be relied on to spread the misery equally and impartially. The Fimbrians, organized into two legions, were placed under the command of Murena, the commander who had distinguished himself at Chaeronea.[2]

Whilst the Romans were tidying their dominions, Mithridates too had sorting out to do at home. However much he tried to pass off the result of the war as a draw which left Pontus pretty much as it had been in 88 BC, the fact was that the king had been forced to terms by the loss of two major battles and 160,000 lives. This made Mithridates vulnerable to dissent, and this was being expressed in Colchis and the Bosporus vigorously enough to almost count as a rebellion. In part, this was probably due to poor administration as Mithridates had understandably been distracted elsewhere. To prevent this happening again, the Bosporans asked that they be given the king's son (another Mithridates) to rule over them. This son had acquitted himself reasonably well in the fighting against Fimbria, and should therefore have had his father's affection and attention.

However, the promptness with which the area returned to its allegiance once they had their requested ruler aroused Mithridates' suspicions. He suspected that much of the unrest had been deliberately engineered so that his son could get himself put in charge. Consequently, the governorship of young Mithridates was revoked; he was brought back to Pontus in chains (albeit chains of gold, since he was after all, the king's son) and executed on his arrival.

The execution of their chosen ruler aroused some dismay and anger among the Bosporans, as the wily Mithridates had foreseen and positively welcomed. To 'suppress unrest' on the northern shores of the Black Sea, he began assembling an army and fleet out of all proportion to the forces required to resolve the problem. That he did so not only indicates that he did not trust the Romans to stick to their peace agreement, but that he himself intended to test its limits as soon as he was able.

As part of the peace of Dardanus, Sulla had recognized Mithridates as *rex socius et amicus:* an allied and friendly king.[3] Though this was regarded in Rome and by many later historians as mutual acknowledgement of the king's client status, the title was a prized appellation among the kings themselves, as it obliged Rome to come to their aid if they were attacked. In theory, Mithridates could call for help to Murena and his legions of Fimbrians. In practice, Mithridates needed to become strong quickly enough to withstand the predatory interest of his so-called protectors. Sulla had a civil war to fight in Italy. This meant that Rome would be distracted by internal conflict exactly as had occurred in 90 BC, with the dangers and opportunities which this presented. And of course, if Sulla lost, then his settlement was null and void, and the war would be back on again.

The fact that he was able to kit out an army so quickly is further proof that Mithridates, foreseeing the probable outcome of the peace negotiations, had used the period before Dardanus to comprehensively loot the rest of Asia Minor before the Romans did the same with his leftovers. Add the fact that trade had been at a standstill and the cities disrupted by successive changes of power, dispossessions and repossessions, and it becomes clear why it took almost a century to make good the economic devastation thus caused.

Unlike the other leaders in Asia Minor, Mithridates was neither cowed nor submissive. Even as he ordered his troops to cease operations against Sulla, he was diverting funds and resources to the Cilician pirates. These, already a plague on the coast of Anatolia, expanded their operations accordingly. Whilst Sulla was at Samothrace on his way back to Italy, the pirates gave him a send-off by devastating the lands around him. Sulla had no choice but to endure this, as the heavy fighting ships handed over by Mithridates were practically useless against their swarms of small fast boats.

Pirate operations extended across almost the whole the Mediterranean – the pirates who assisted Sertorius, the anti-Sullan rebel in Spain, were probably Cilicians. Inland, the unholy alliance of Mithridates and the pirates combined to make the states east of the Meander river almost ungovernable. Isauria and Pisidia openly sided with Mithridates, and in Lycia a robber baron allied with the pirates wielded greater power than the Roman-sponsored authorities. Mytilene on Lesbos more or less openly repudiated Sulla's settlement and the Romans found it easier to accept the city's surly defiance than risk a protracted siege in which supply ships would require close escort through pirate-infested waters.

Another sign that Mithridates intended business as usual was that he was back to his normal tricks in Cappadocia, where Ariobarzanes was having a hard time getting comfortable on his throne. Mithridates occupied large chunks of the country, whilst blandly denying that he was doing anything of the sort. He had also suborned many of the most powerful and influential aristocrats during his earlier occupation of the country. Many of these, looking askance at the Roman treatment of the lands to their west, openly preferred that the rule of Mithridates should continue.

It is probably at this point that Mithridates gave some thought to the reorganization of his army. The comprehensive defeat at Chaeronea had followed similar victories of legion over phalanx in the Macedonian and Syrian wars, and Mithridates seems to have come to the conclusion that this formation was fatally flawed, at least as far as fighting Romans was concerned. He now concentrated on building up his forces in the areas where the Romans were weakest: missile troops and cavalry. Militarily, this combination could work, as the Parthians were to prove by conclusively defeating the Romans at Carrhae in 53 BC, but it required lots of flat open terrain which was easier to find in Syria than Pontus. Plutarch reports on the reforms:

> Instead of an inefficient army which made a good show but was less than useful...he knocked his forces into a leaner, more serviceable shape...gone were the mixed multitudes and howling threats of

barbarian tribes with their jewelled ornaments of gold which the enemy found more tempting than threatening. Now the men were armed and formed up in Roman style, with horses better suited for service than show.[4]

This army was taken to the Bosporus and practiced its skills on the native tribes of the interior, who had been exploiting the confusion to launch pillaging raids. Since the Bosporans seemed happiest when ruled directly by the Mithridatids, another of the king's sons, Menchares, was made governor. Archelaus was pointedly left out of these arrangements. The general's closeness to Sulla had been noted, as had been the Roman offer to make him Archelaus I of Pontus. And whatever his loyalty, Mithridates may have felt that there was no reason to give Archelaus, who had lost him two armies, the chance to lose a third.

Archelaus evidently felt that loss of influence was the precursor to loss of life, and he pre-empted matters by defecting to Murena. Possibly he may have considered whether the offer of kingship was still open, for he immediately attempted to move Murena in the direction of war. He claimed that Mithridates was developing his army for use against the Romans, which he certainly was, and that he intended to deploy it at any moment, which Mithridates almost certainly was not.

Hostilities resume

Murena did not need convincing to go to war so much as an excuse to do so. He had gained his present command through extraordinary circumstances and it would be years before such an opportunity came again. Pontus, just over the River Halys, was stuffed with the booty of Asia Minor and Murena was itching to get his hands on some of it. The restive Fimbrians were easier to manage in war than in peacetime, and had already proved that they could handle the Pontic army. And of course, not only riches but political kudos would go to the man who finished Sulla's war and avenge the Roman and Italian victims of the Asian Vespers.

Murena had already moved against the pirates, and annexed the city of Cybria. It might be at this time that he founded, as a deliberate provocation, a settlement right against the Pontic border which he gave his family name of Licinia. Therefore Archelaus' arrival in his camp provided the match to a fire already set. There was no point in waiting for authorization from Rome, as Sulla was currently campaigning in Italy with the object of conquering the place, so in the late summer of 83 BC Murena and his army crossed into Pontus. This was less an attempt at conquest than a massive plundering raid on the temple complex of Ma at Comana, the booty from which would have gone some way to fulfilling Murena's ambition of becoming very rich.

Mithridates sent a detachment of cavalry to find out what was going on and discovered that the Romans were hostile when he lost a large proportion of that force. He indignantly sent ambassadors to Murena, pointing out that his conduct was directly contrary to the agreement at Dardanus. Murena was unimpressed, possibly because Mithridates, in haste, had chosen Greek ambassadors who spent as much time denigrating the king as they did putting forward his views. Murena mockingly sent back to Mithridates asking him to show the provisions of the treaty in question, knowing full well that the agreement with Sulla had never been committed to writing.

All that could be said for the diplomatic interlude was that it lasted until the end of the campaigning season and allowed Mithridates to gather his forces and send vehement representations to Sulla, as well as a stern warning to the independent city of Heraclea to stay out of the brewing confrontation.

Perhaps word that an ambassador had come from Rome caused Murena to kick off the next campaigning season early. He had to cross the flood-swollen waters of the River Halys before he could start a massive plundering raid which swept through an alleged 400 villages. Mithridates did nothing but noisily protest about the injustice done to him, not least as Murena's repeated harassment allowed him to reinforce his claim that he was the victim of Roman aggression. It is quite probable that Mithridates still retained control of part of Cappadocia and that Murena was combining personal enrichment with politics, using the raids on Pontic territory to loosen Mithridates' bulldog grip on lands he should have given up immediately after Dardanus.

Back in Phrygia, and considerably richer, Murena was met by the expected ambassador. This was Calidius, a member of Sulla's entourage. Mithridates' old foe was now dictator at Rome and the (violently pruned) senate was only too happy to convert Sulla's orders into senatorial decrees. It was odd, therefore, that their message to Murena to leave Mithridates alone was not, in fact, couched as an official decree. Contemporary conspiracy theorists – Mithridates foremost amongst them – made much of the fact that Calidius spent far longer cloistered with Murena in a private conference than he did at the official meeting. The upshot of the intervention from Rome was that Murena invaded Pontus again.

This time Mithridates was compelled to act. Firstly, he had established his victim status beyond all doubt and further failure to react to the repeated Roman incursions would erode the bedrock of support in his native land. Secondly, the government in Rome had finally intervened and its intervention was apparently worse than useless. Thirdly, and most importantly, Murena seems to have moved from mere punitive raids to an attempt at conquest. His troops were driving north, almost certainly up the valley of the River Halys, with the apparent intention of capturing Sinope; in short, as Mithridates explicitly said, the Romans had now started an out-and-out war.[5]

Murena may have believed that he was following in the footsteps of Sulla, but in taking on Mithridates with an army composed mainly of Bithynian, Galatian and Cappadocian levies he was closer to the unfortunate Manius Aquillius. Murena in his turn was to discover how dangerous the Pontic army was when campaigning on home ground. His army was shadowed from across the river by Mithridates' general Gordius, and it soon became apparent that Gordius was keeping in touch with the Romans until Mithridates could arrive with the main Pontic army. When Mithridates did arrive, his men promptly crossed the river and soundly thrashed the Roman force. A startled Murena retreated to a strong position on a nearby hill, but before he could dig in the Pontic army swept over this too. There was nothing for it but for the remnants of the Roman expeditionary force to fall back through the trackless mountains of Phrygia, harassed all the way by Pontic skirmishers.[6]

As usual when he fell out with Rome, Mithridates helped himself to Cappadocia, driving out the Roman garrisons there. Then the king celebrated his victory with a massive bonfire to Zeus Stratios. Following the tradition for such bonfires, the king himself helped to carry the firewood. Milk, honey, oil and incense went on the wood as a sumptuous meal for the god, whilst the king treated his followers – their numbers considerably augmented by his victory – to a substantial banquet of their own. When the fire was lighted, Appian claims that the flames were visible over 100 miles away.[7] In part, this celebratory ritual was significant because with this fire on a mountaintop Mithridates followed the Persian tradition, in marked contrast to the Hellenistic image he had heretofore cultivated. This was a sign that he now intended to base his support more on his own people, and less on the fickle Greek cities. Another remarkable change of policy was that Mithridates, for only the second time in his three decades as monarch of Pontus, had commanded the Pontic army in person. At the age of fifty, the king seems to have decided that the general on whom he could best rely was himself.

Further opportunities for Mithridates to practice his new profession were prevented by the arrival of Gabinius, a much more senior representative of Sulla, who wanted to make it unambiguously clear that Sulla genuinely wanted the fighting to stop – or else. Given the speed with which this second ambassador arrived, it is probable that Gabinius was dispatched as soon as word arrived that Murena was attacking Pontus again, rather than as a response to the Roman defeat. Murena knew his master well enough to stop fighting as soon as he got the message, and whilst Mithridates truculently kept the extra slice of Cappadocia he had occupied so far, his experience of Sulla was enough to prevent him trying to do more.

Murena was put on the next boat home. Possibly Sulla felt his lieutenant had done enough damage to the Roman cause in Asia Minor, or perhaps Murena had simply completed his allotted time of duty. Or both, as the two reasons are not mutually exclusive. Sulla, who was as loyal to his friends as he was merciless to his enemies, allowed the man who had stuck with him through the Greek campaign the privilege of celebrating a totally undeserved triumph.

Gabinius stayed to effect yet another reconciliation between Ariobarzanes and Mithridates. This time Ariobarzanes was welcomed into the Pontic royal family by marrying himself or his son to a young daughter of Mithridates. The so-called Second Mithridatic War thus came to an end in a huge party thrown by the two kings. Significantly, the festivities were again in the Persian, rather than the Greek style, with prizes for eating, drinking, singing and telling jokes. Gabinius did not join in the jollity and Ariobarzanes' enthusiasm for his in-laws dimmed yet further when he discovered that Mithridates had unilaterally awarded himself a further slice of Cappadocia as a wedding present from his daughter. Nevertheless, after three years of intermittent hostility and a single significant battle, Mithridates was again at peace with Rome. On the whole, Mithridates could claim to have come out best from the war. The Romans were re-established as the prime villains in the region, and militarily, Mithridates had won the fighting on points. His star seemed to be in the ascendant once more.

The Cold war

As before, when blocked from expansion in Anatolia, Mithridates turned his attention to his empire around the Black Sea. His intention was to link Colchis in the east with the lands he held around the Bosporus by conquering the backward and recalcitrant Achaeans. The expedition against them was not a success and two thirds of the army of conquest never returned. They were victims of attrition, hostile conditions and, says Appian, 'an Achaean stratagem', though it is nowhere explained what this stratagem was.

Whilst Mithridates was attempting to tidy up the lands around the Black Sea, the Romans were doing the same with their lands in Asia Minor. Mytilene was finally brought to heel by a force which included the young Julius Caesar.[8] Antonius, the genial but incompetent father of the triumvir Mark Antony, made a floundering effort to stamp out the pirates, in the course of which he managed to start and lose a war in Crete. Antonius then died whilst the pirates, still flushed with Pontic money, continued to flourish. The Romans had more luck in southern Anatolia, where they went some way to sorting out Isauria, though the pirate heartland of Cilicia remained unaffected.

Meanwhile, the Pontic king had embarked on a series of foreign policy initiatives. He secured the neutrality of the Ptolemies by marrying off Nyssa and Mithridatis (two of the offspring which he produced with startling regularity from a string of concubines) to Ptolemy Auletes and his brother the king of Cyprus. As a further goad to the Romans, Mithridates subsidised the efforts of tribes in the eastern Danube region to harass Roman territories there and in northern Macedonia.

Meanwhile, after numerous plaintive embassies from Ariobarzanes, Sulla finally sent a peremptory message to Mithridates, telling him to give back the parts of Cappadocia he had seized. Mithridates did so, but having been reminded that the Peace of Dardanus had still not been put into writing, he sent ambassadors to Rome. These returned in 77 BC with the disturbing news that Sulla was dead and the senate was 'too busy' to see them. No-one, including Mithridates, had dared to go against Sulla even when he had 'retired' from the dictatorship and was living as a private citizen. But now that Sulla was dead, it would have occurred to many that the Peace of Dardanus had been made whilst Sulla was an outlaw disowned by Rome and that it had never been formally ratified afterward. Legalistically, it could be argued that Mithridates and Rome were still at war, which made the refusal of the senate to talk to the Pontic ambassadors all the more alarming. It was also a snub, and Mithridates was not the man to take insults meekly.

Urged on by deserters to his cause from the disaffected Fimbrians, he sent ambassadors across the Mediterranean to where the anti-Sullan rebel, Sertorius, was still holding out, and secured from him recognition of

Mithridatic suzerainty over Bithynia, Cappadocia and Galatia. Mithridates had wanted the Roman province of Asia as well and had offered forty ships and three thousand talents in exchange, but Sertorius replied bluntly that he was a Roman and was not going to give up Roman territory, in Asia Minor or anywhere else. Nevertheless, Mithridates could feel content that with his Fimbrian deserters and representatives from Sertorius among his entourage, he was slowly driving wedges into the ever-widening gaps in the Roman body politic. By providing support and encouragement to the losers in Rome's ferocious political battles he could foment and sustain confusion and unrest in the enemy camp.

Mithridates also decided to have a word with his son-in-law. During the years that the fortunes of Mithridates had waxed and waned, Tigranes had prospered.[9] He had given strong but indirect support to Mithridates during his war with Rome, but had concentrated his efforts on keeping Parthia out of Armenia, almost as Mithridates was intent on keeping Rome out of Pontus. In a sense the two kings were fighting back-to-back against pressure from east and west, and it is no coincidence that once their power was broken Rome and Parthia came directly into conflict. However, unlike Pontus, Armenia had the failing remnants of the Seleucid empire to batten upon. Tigranes had also made forceful and intelligent use of Parthian weakness after the death of the Parthian king Mithridates II and had advanced his borders well toward Ecbatana, the Parthian capital. By annexing parts of the Seleucid empire, Tigranes had extended his power far into Syria and, in about 83 BC, he took over part of Cilicia as well. As holder of the largest kingdom in the east, Tigranes now called himself by the ancient title of 'king of kings' and made a point of never appearing in public with less than four lesser kings in attendance.

This was the instrument with which Mithridates decided to test the Roman senate's assertion that they were impossibly busy. He invited Tigranes to help himself to Cappadocia. It was a typical Mithridates move, in that no-one would have doubted who was behind the initiative, yet it continued to give lip service to the treaty to which the king had agreed. Tigranes was happy to help because he was in a Hellenistic phase. He had begun to mint his own coinage (a first for an Armenian monarch) and had decided to build for himself a capital city worthy of Armenia's new power. This new city needed a population and the inhabitants of Cappadocia were elected to supply it. Some 300,000 Cappadocians found themselves rounded up and compelled to start a new urban existence on the border between Armenia and Mesopotamia (probably near present-day Silvan in Turkey).[10]

In Asia Minor itself, even Mithridates was looking like a benevolent ruler compared to the terrible exactions of the Romans, whom even later Roman historians likened to a flock of ravening harpies. The massive initial indemnity had been paid twice over, yet, thanks to the wonders of compound interest at exorbitant rates, the peoples of the region were even more indebted than before. Municipal properties were mortgaged to the hilt and private citizens first prostituted their offspring and then sold them into slavery in an attempt to pay their debts. It was not uncommon for Roman creditors to torture defaulting debtors to ensure that they had extracted the last of their assets before selling them on as slaves. A series of Roman governors, each more corrupt and venal than the next, paid scant attention to the suffering of the provinces they were maladministering. Some administrators, such as Verres (later prosecuted by Cicero for doing the same in Sicily), added to the woes of the region with flagrant injustice in the courts. Amid the misery moved the agents of Mithridates, whispering that the king had learned his lesson and was preparing to give the cities of Asia their freedom once he had thrown off the Roman yoke for them.

By the winter of 74 BC, Mithridates had an army of 140,000 infantry and 16,000 cavalry, as well as a fleet of 400 ships.[11] Mithridates had consulted his Roman advisors and this time his forces were designed less with the aim of overawing the enemy and more toward killing them. Drill and efficient practice became part of the Pontic military experience. This was all paid for because, in contrast to the misery in the west, Pontus had an efficient and well-organized economy. Ironically, this economy prospered all the more because the wealth flowing to Rome from Asia had stimulated the market for luxury goods from the east and the trade routes for this passed through the eastern ports of Mithridates' kingdom.

Mithridates was probably rather startled that the Romans had reacted tamely to Tigranes occupation of Cappadocia. The Romans were preoccupied with Sertorius and had been deeply embroiled in a succession question in Cyrene in Lybia, which finally ended up with them annexing the place, so their excuse that they were very busy had some validity. Furthermore, after virtually emptying Cappadocia of its population, Tigranes had withdrawn again, so the senatorial nominee, Ariobarzanes, was once more ostensibly in charge. Mithridates also knew that the Romans were desperately attempting to shore up their weakened presence in Anatolia as far as their stretched resources would permit, and they would never be so vulnerable as they now were. In short, Mithridates was ready to go another round with Rome. The time was right and he needed only a pretext. Then, at the end of the year, Nicomedes IV of Bithynia died. Claiming that he had left it to them in his will, the Romans annexed his kingdom.

Chapter 8

Mithridates Attacks

Prelude to war

Bithynia had been a buffer state between Rome and Pontus. Its removal put the two states into jarring collision, and in a way that Mithridates must have considered unfavourable to his interests. He had until now possessed a virtual naval monopoly in the Black Sea and his western flank had been secured against Rome by the mountain ranges which included Paphlagonia and Phrygia. But Roman Bithynia would have ports such as Cyzicus and Lampsacus on the Black Sea. Even assuming that Heraclea was allowed to retain its precarious independence, Roman control of Chalcedon would, at best, block Mithridates fleet from the wider Mediterranean.

Even worse, a future Murena would not have to march up the valley of the River Halys to reach Sinope, as the city was immediately accessible by the coastal plain from Bithynia. This may have mattered less, were it not that Rome fully understood and reciprocated the hostility and warlike intentions of Mithridates. Despite a legal challenge to the will from a putative heir, they accepted the legacy of Bithynia and dispatched both consuls east to perform the act of financial rape that passed for Roman governance in Asia Minor. Aurelius Cotta was to take Bithynia, but, even more alarmingly, Licinius Lucullus, Sulla's former henchman, had, after desperate intrigue, been given Cilicia as his consular province. According to Lucullus' biographer, Plutarch, this was explicitly because he wanted to be well situated for the coming war with Pontus and the glory and spoils that a victorious campaign would bring. Few doubted that conflict was inevitable. The instructions which the consuls took with them from the senate amounted, if not to orders to start the war, then at least to mobilize for when Mithridates started it. In short, the dispatch of both consuls to Asia Minor, and the eagerness with which the consuls contrived to get themselves dispatched there, shows that few in Rome expected Mithridates to take the Roman annexation of Bithynia calmly.

Mithridates was now fifty-seven years old. He could, perhaps, by a policy of careful diplomacy and judicious bribes and surrenders have eked out another decade of independence for his kingdom. However, it was only a matter of time before some Roman demagogue reminded the Roman people of the 80,000 Romans and Italians still unavenged, and of the fact that the treaty of Dardanus remained unratified. Better, then, to take the bull by the horns and challenge Rome now while Pontus was strong, rich and confident and Rome was still weak from its recent wars. Consequently Mithridates went to war. He did it properly, performing another mountaintop fire sacrifice to Zeus and driving a chariot pulled by splendid white horses into the sea as an offering to Poseidon. Then he mustered his army and delivered a speech which the historian Justin has immortalized, though how accurately none can now tell.[1]

Even if the case is hopeless, Justin has Mithridates declaiming, a true man will draw his sword against robbers, if only to achieve some measure of revenge. Yet Pontus could not only revenge itself against Rome, but follow the examples of the Gauls and Hannibal and bring the city to its knees. Nor was it a question of whether to go to war with Rome – merely a question of whether the time was currently right; Rome being Rome, war was inevitable at some point, as past Roman conduct had proven. 'Their founders, as they themselves claimed, were suckled by the teats of a wolf, so the whole race has the disposition of wolves, insatiable in their lust for blood and tyranny, desperately hungry for wealth'.

Rome had enslaved even its native land of Italy and was even now making war on its own peoples. As proof, the king pointed to his entourage, which included Romans of noble descent who had taken refuge with him from the violence of their own city. (These were the men sent by Sertorius, one of whom bore the renowned name of Marius. This Marius was Sertorius' candidate for governor of Asia if Mithridates succeeded in 'liberating' the province. It has also been suggested that enough disaffected Fimbrians and other deserters had joined the Pontic side to produce an Italian-style legion.) Mithridates pointed to the strength of Pontus, its conquests on the Black Sea, and his own lineage as a descendant of Xerxes and Cyrus, and promised his men that he would lead them personally to victory.[2]

The chronology of what happened next is uncertain.[3] The most probable scenario has Mithridates retaking control of Paphlagonia at the end of 74 BC, before the Roman consuls arrived in Asia Minor in the following year. This aggressive move by Mithridates would have given the consuls a clear idea of what they were in for; in fact, the young and energetic Julius Caesar had already interrupted his studies at Rhodes and taken over organizing the defence of Bithynia on his own authority. The manner in which the consuls went on to a full war footing from the moment of their arrival certainly suggests that Mithridates had already made his intentions clear. Furthermore, the Pontic invasion force that descended on Bithynia in the spring of 73 BC spring took only nine days to arrive, which suggests that it either moved by forced marches, or from nearby Paphlagonia.

Mithridates seemed to be following the same path as he had taken when he swept down from the mountains in 87 BC in the wake of the defeated Nicomedes and Aquillius, but the situation in 73 BC was significantly different. Lucullus, to the south, would probably be able to pull together a fully-fledged Roman army of four legions. Admittedly, the core of that army would be the Fimbrians. Surly, disaffected, and openly longing for their discharge papers, they were, nevertheless, veteran Roman legionaries, tough and deadly once they could be persuaded to fight. Cotta, in Bithynia, was the easier target, as he had few Roman troops under his command and was a somewhat inept commander himself, as Mithridates' spies in the Roman camp had undoubtedly informed their king. Furthermore, Mithridates was uncertain exactly how the Romans to his south were deployed, but he knew exactly how to get at Cotta. Therefore he sent his general Diophantes south with orders to hold the passes along the Halys, whilst he aimed to crush Cotta before Lucullus could swing into action.[4] With Cotta gone, perhaps Asia would rise again, allowing a vastly strengthened Mithridates to swing south with his full force, defeat Lucullus, and claim suzerainty once more over the full area of Asia Minor.

Chalcedon

The Roman operation was in many ways the mirror image of what Mithridates had in mind. Like Diophantes, Cotta was to try to stop the main enemy push, whilst the stronger part of their forces under Lucullus pushed into the enemy heartland, and then swung back to defeat the by-now hopefully demoralized and weakened main army. Lucullus, however, had first to whip the Fimbrians into shape, train up his raw levies and gather together the legions which had previously been deployed against the pirates in Cilicia. It is not surprising then that Mithridates' version of the plan, carried out by well-trained and prepared troops, came into operation first and forced Lucullus to change course.

Most of Bithynia welcomed Mithridates back with open arms. This was unsurprising since the province was still outraged by its first experience of Roman rule. Even in the cities of the province of Asia there was unrest, even though these cities had also experienced the weight of Roman vengeance. Heraclea tried hard to maintain neutrality, but Mithridates arranged the killing of Roman tax collectors and his popularity soared. The city government was forced to hand over ships and money to help with the Pontic war effort and to admit a Pontic garrison within its walls.

Cotta retreated to Chalcedon, where he had the Roman fleet at his back, and sent urgent messages to Lucullus to the effect that the invasion of southern Pontus could wait until the Pontic invasion of Bithynia had been dealt with. These messages became even more strident when Cotta unwisely allowed Nudus, his naval prefect, to take the field against Mithridates. Nudus located his men in fortified positions outside the city, but, like Murena before him, was utterly taken aback by the speed and professionalism with which the Pontic army swept over his defences.

The Roman force fell back to the city, but it was an untidy retreat with the rearguard already overwhelmed. After the Pontic archers had made the most of the tight-packed targets struggling to get into the city gates, the Pontic infantry charged. The city's defenders had no choice but to drop the portcullis to prevent Mithridates' men from getting inside. This left a large portion of the Roman force trapped outside the walls. Nudus and some of his officers were pulled over the ramparts by rope, but from there they could only watch as the rest of their force, some 3,000 men, was cut down.

Mithridates energetically followed up his success with a combined land and sea assault on the harbour. An advance guard of Bastarnae (this Danubian tribe, was called by Appian 'the bravest people of all'), managed to break the long chain of bronze that guarded the harbour entrance, and the Pontic fleet sailed in. The Romans lost four warships before their resistance collapsed. Then the defenders on the walls of Chalcedon could only watch in horror as their enemies calmly took control of sixty warships, the entire Roman naval strength east of Athens, and towed the ships away for later recommissioning as part of the Pontic navy. In the entire battle, Mithridates lost twenty men, those being from the Bastarnae assault force.

With Cotta bereft of his army and his fleet, his local support melted away. Nicaea, Lampsacus, Nicomedia and Apameia, all major cities in the region, either fell to Mithridates or opened their gates to him. Only the nearby city of Cyzicus held to the Roman cause, perhaps embittered towards Mithridates because some 3,000 of their citizens had died fighting at Chalcedon. Cotta's only hope was Lucullus, but the question was whether Lucullus would come. Mithridates former general, Archelaus, was now firmly and literally in the

Roman camp, either because the suspicions of Mithridates had driven him there, or because those suspicions were justified in the first place. Archelaus argued that Diophantes and his army guarding the southern passes could easily be defeated, and thereafter, Pontus would be defenceless. This was a tempting option, not least because a Roman army in the heretofore unplundered Pontic heartland could get very rich before Mithridates returned from Bithynia to defend his kingdom. Nevertheless Lucullus put saving Cotta first.

Finding the enemy

For once, Mithridates' excellent intelligence network seems to have failed him. He ordered Diophantes to send out probing raids to try to find Lucullus, and sent another general, Eumachus, plundering across Phrygia and Psidia to see what reaction this would draw. After initial success, Eumachus did indeed encounter serious opposition – but not from the Romans. Mithridates' vindictive purge of the Galatian leadership during the first Mithridatic war had sufficiently thinned the field for a single Galatian, Deiotarus, to become king of the hitherto disunited country. Deiotarus knew that one of the best ways to unite his people under his rule was to lead them against a foreign enemy, and no other foreigner was as well-hated by the Galatians as Mithridates. Accordingly, he attacked Eumachus and duly sent the somewhat battered general back to Bithynia to report that, despite the absence of Lucullus, Phrygia was emphatically in enemy hands.

Eventually Lucullus was located and scouts reported him to be moving north up the valley of the River Sangarius to confront Mithridates. Consequently, Diophantes was released from garrison duty to take his men raiding the new Roman conquests in Cilicia and Isauria, and a large force was sent under Marius, the Sertorian 'governor' of the province of Asia, to confront the Romans. The two sides met in the Bithynian lowlands between Nicaea and Prusias, at a place called Otryae, for the most puzzling confrontation of the war.

It appears that Lucullus had been expecting to meet a small detachment guarding the Pontic rear and probing for his whereabouts. He was nonplussed when he found that the enemy force was almost as large as his own contingent of 30,000 men, and confident enough to offer battle. This challenge, unless he was to lose all credibility with his unruly legions, Lucullus had to accept. The battle lines were drawn up and there followed an odd delay. Perhaps Lucullus was reluctant to engage in case his army received a severe mauling even before it had encountered the main Mithridatic force. And it has been credibly suggested that the Sertorians were confidently waiting for the Fimbrians to come over to their side. They had, after all, been sent out whilst leaders of the faction of Sertorius had been ruling Rome, and should still be sympathetic to that cause. However, for the moment, it appeared that the Fimbrians were giving Lucullus the benefit of the doubt and they stayed firm in their loyalty to their general.

Thereafter, proceedings were interrupted by a strange event. In the words of Plutarch 'without warning the skies opened, and a large glowing object fell to the ground between the two armies. It was the size of a substantial barrel and glowed like molten silver'.[5] Uncertain what to make of this strange and undoubtedly-supernatural prodigy, the two armies withdrew from contact and did not re-engage thereafter.

This reticence was partly due to the fact that Lucullus, astonished by the size of the detachment that Mithridates had sent against him, decided to make serious enquiries about the size of the Pontic force. When he established that it numbered just less than 300,000, the Roman general determined on a new strategy. Even the resources of Pontus would be stretched to keep that many fed and Mithridates had to transport the food to them. The way to defeat so large an army was memorably described by Lucullus as 'stamping on its stomach'. In fact the Pontic army numbered about 140,000 infantry and about another 20,000 cavalry. But a cavalryman is effectively a man and a horse, giving the combined pair a tremendous appetite, and though the rest of the 300,000 were camp followers, these had to eat too.[6]

Apart from supplies and whatever nefarious plans the Romans were cooking up against him, Mithridates had other worries. It was becoming clear that, despite the Pontic success at Chalcedon, the occupation of Asia Minor was not going to be the triumphal procession of 87 BC. Young Julius Caesar was keeping much of the western coast loyal to Rome, and the Asian cities, with their brutal experience of Roman resilience and vindictiveness, would not commit to the Pontic side again unless victory seemed certain.

The siege of Cyzicus

To encourage the others, Mithridates looked for a recalcitrant city to make an example of, and chose nearby Cyzicus. There were strategic as well as political reasons for this. It was becoming probable that the fate of Asia Minor would largely be determined by a single confrontation, rather as the Romans had broken the power of the Seleucids in 190 BC at the Battle of

Magnesia. The Pontic king would undoubtedly have paid careful attention to what was required to prevent the Romans enjoying a similar victory on the forthcoming occasion. Pontus had a good army that hugely outnumbered Lucullus, and their cavalry was vastly superior. In the Bithynian lowlands, there would be none of the cramped conditions experienced at Chaeronea, and if Lucullus did as Sulla had done and dug in, Mithridates would simply leave the battlefield and go elsewhere. In short, Mithridates was prepared to play a waiting game if need be. It had probably also occurred to him that Lucullus, too, would stand off from a crucial battle until lack of supplies had

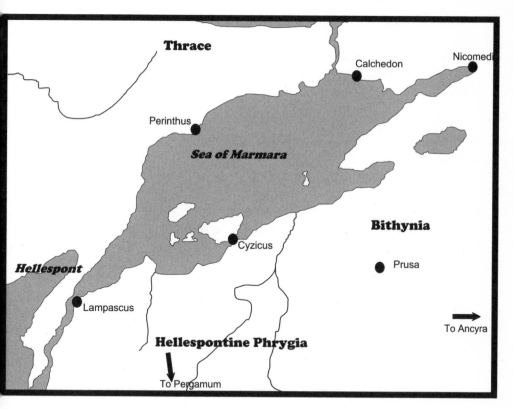

Area of the Cyzicus campaign, showing the position of Cyzicus in relation to access to the Black Sea and Pontic coastline to the north and east

worn down the Pontic army, and he was determined that this lack of supplies would not happen. Mithridates' current supply base was at Lampsacus, where the harbour was good enough to shelter his fleet, but was totally unequipped to handle the tons of war materiel required by his huge army. In fact, by detailed questioning of prisoners, Lucullus had satisfied himself that the entire Pontic army was virtually living from hand-to-mouth, with just four days of reserves.

Cyzicus had an eminently-suitable harbour for the grain ships which would supply the Pontic army, and the city's capture and salutary punishment would signal to the rest of the region that Mithridates meant business. Furthermore Cyzicus was already weakened by the loss of thousands of its soldiers outside Chalcedon. In short, it was ideally suited to become Mithridates' next conquest.

If Cyzicus was politically and strategically the correct choice, the drawback was geographical.[7] Cyzicus was difficult for the Pontic army to reach, let alone besiege. For all practical purposes, the city was on an island. This island was called Arctonnesus; shaped roughly like a broad spearpoint about to plunge into the mainland of Bithynia. Cyzicus occupied the triangle right at the tip of the spearpoint. From this tip the only contact with the mainland was a narrow causeway.[8]

On the approach of Lucullus, Mithridates withdrew his army by night and set off for Cyzicus. On arriving at the city the following morning, Mithridates opened hostilities with psychological warfare. The Cyzicans were treated to the sight of boatload after boatload of ships transporting the soldiers of Mithridates from the mainland in their tens of thousands. These immediately set about taking control of the harbour and walling the city off from the outside. In clear view of the besieged, Pontic engineers under the direction of Niconides of Thessaly, Mithridates' chief engineer, began assembling a 150-foot wooden tower, battering rams, catapults and other siege weaponry, including giant crossbows. The intention was to make the Cyzicans feel that Mithridates was concentrating all his strength on their small, friendless city.

The psychological pressure was stepped up even further when another large force moved onto the slopes of Adrastia, a mountain overlooking the city. Pontic heralds gleefully informed the Cyzicans that Tigranes of Armenia had sent tens of thousands of extra troops to join the siege. The Cyzicans readily believed this, for they knew that access to the heights was by way of a narrow valley which Mithridates would certainly have guarded.

Mithridates had indeed done so, but was betrayed by the Romans in his camp. Some of these, despairing of the cause of Sertorius in Spain, were preparing to turn their coats once more and defect back to the Roman side. After secret negotiations with Lucullus, they advised Mithridates that the Fimbrian legions were preparing to desert, and needed only a secure position from which to do so. Trustingly, Mithridates withdrew his guard from the pass, and allowed Lucullus to establish his troops on the mountain – a position from where they had clear access to the Bithynian hinterland, from which Mithridates was now blocked. The besieger was now himself besieged, and the Cyzicans, regarding what seemed a hopeless situation, were unaware that their rescuers were now camped in plain view on the hillside before them.

For Mithridates, the situation was grave, but not critical. True, he was effectively blocked from the mainland, but he still had his fleet and, at a pinch, he could evacuate much of his army by this means. And if he could get into Cyzicus and use the docks there, he could evacuate his forces in their entirety, leaving Lucullus to watch over a gutted and empty city. Thus the capture of Cyzicus, which had earlier seemed advisable, was now imperative. Furthermore, because the weather was deteriorating with the onset of the first storms of winter, sustaining a long siege would have been tricky, even if the Pontic army had somehow contrived to find itself supplies with which to do so.

The psychological pressure was then stepped up by the launch of Mithridates' naval siege weapon, an improvement of the model which had been deployed unsuccessfully at Rhodes. This device was intended to start the hostilities. Before it was deployed, a convoy of ships sailed slowly under the city walls. Aboard were 3,000 Cyzican prisoners, either captured at Chalcedon or those who had failed to take shelter in time within the city. The prisoners had been told that their only chance of survival lay in persuading their fellow-citizens to surrender. In a piteous scene the hostages raised their hands in supplication to friends and relatives within the city and pleaded to be saved. They were given the resolute reply from the city's general that they were in the hands of the enemy and should bear with courage whatever fate awaited them. That fate is unknown, but was probably grim. The unsentimental Mithridates was hardly going to waste scarce supplies on hostages whose purpose had failed.

The reason for this literally unyielding Cyzican response is probably that the citizens had finally made contact with Lucullus. Because the causeway to the city was held by Mithridates, Lucullus sewed his letters inside two inflated animal skins. Choosing one of his best swimmers, he got the man to straddle the skins so that his weight pulled them partly underwater. In the dimness of the night the resultant shape gliding through the water looked more like some marine animal than a man, and the swimmer had brought Lucullus' message across the seven-mile strait.

The Cyzicans had by then received word from Archelaus that a relief force was coming and hastily interrogated a shepherd boy, who had escaped from the Pontic hostage-takers, as to whether he had heard anything of Lucullus' whereabouts. The boy looked from his questioners to the Roman camp plainly visible outside the walls, and assumed this was some kind of joke. Even when the confusion had been cleared up, the Cyzicans had hardly dared to believe the boy, so Lucullus' confirmation of the situation was extremely welcome.

The Pontic assault began badly. The naval assault ship ran itself up to the walls, dropped its bridge, and a group of soldiers ran straight onto the ramparts of Cyzicus. The speed of the attack took everyone by surprise, including the rest of the Pontic assault force. The Pontic soldiers – all four of them - frantically urged their comrades onto the walls, but the Cyzicans got their act together first. The unfortunate Pontic vanguard was unceremoniously tipped into the sea, and the naval assault craft was forced to back away beneath a waterfall of burning oil. After this somewhat farcical start, the attack began in earnest. Mithridates repeatedly switched the pressure from the landward to the seaward side so that the defenders were constantly rushing from one section of walls to the other.

The defenders had not been caught by surprise when Mithridates turned up, and now their preparations paid off. Burning oil splashed over the ships and stones were dropped with pinpoint precision on the heads of battering rams. Other rams were caught in nooses and the heads were yanked out of the machines operating them, while the impact of the remaining rams was blunted by wool-packed baskets lowered in front of their area of operation. Fire-fighting teams stood by within the walls with buckets of water mixed with vinegar, ready to pounce upon any flaming missiles which Mithridates launched over the walls. As further protection against incendiary attack, large screens of loose, damp cloth projected above the walls to literally dampen the impact of burning projectiles. After an afternoon of intense but unproductive activity, Mithridates called off the assault as the weather was worsening.[9]

It continued to worsen through the night, and developed into a full-blown storm. This was bad news for the infernal engines constructed for Mithridates by Niconides, as the wind pushed them from directions they were never intended to be pushed, and many were flipped over or blown down and totally destroyed. The people of Ilium later reported that Athena appeared to many of them that night in a dream. Breathless, and with her garments torn, the goddess reported that she was just back from helping the people of Cyzicus in their struggle. Either the gods or skilled propaganda continued to help the Cyzican cause thereafter. It was customary for the citizens of the city to sacrifice a black heifer to Prosperina, and as the siege had rendered heifers unobtainable, the Cyzicans were preparing to sacrifice a substitute made of dough. But lo! A black heifer of perfect dimensions bolted from the meadow where the sacred cows were grazing and swam across the strait. Untired by its exertions, it showed aquatic abilities hitherto unseen in the bovine species by diving under the chain blocking the harbour and heading for the docks. Returning to terrestrial mode, this prodigy navigated perfectly through the city and found its own way to the temple, where it trotted up to the altar and took its place under the knife.

Mithridates' advisors pointed out that this 'divine' phenomenon gave him a perfect excuse for abandoning what increasingly seemed a profitless undertaking. Mithridates was unimpressed by the wonder cow and obstinately continued to press the siege. Nevertheless, whilst the bulk of the Roman forces were engaged in storming an outlying Pontic fort, Mithridates took advantage of their distraction to send away his cavalry. The horses were short of food and useless in siege warfare, and were in any case the core of the Pontic army about which a new force could be built if disaster befell the present one. After this, Mithridates occupied Mount Dindymus, which rose near the city walls. He had a mound constructed which connected this elevation with Cyzicus, and used it as a missile platform for his remaining towers. At the same time, Pontic engineers set about the long job of undermining the city walls. The Romans under Lucullus were not idle, and the historian Eutropius remarks that they fought 'many battles' with Mithridates' men in the course of the siege, so the Pontic army was probably in action on two fronts at once.[10]

Winter set in, and with it the plague – probably dysentery, which often laid low ancient armies that stayed in one place for too long. With Lucullus blocking the supply lines from the mainland, and winter storms making deliveries by sea few and infrequent, hunger was a serious problem. There were rumours of cannibalism in the army and men became sick from eating almost any vegetable matter they could put in their stomachs.

Then came the news that the cavalry force had suffered a disaster during its withdrawal, ambushed by the Romans in falling snow and bitter cold as it crossed the River Rhyndacus. Some 15,000 men were reported lost, along with a substantial amount of baggage. The Cyzicans took advantage of the weakened and demoralized state of the Pontic army and sallied out, burning many of the beseigers' engines before their assault was contained. Nothing was going right for Mithridates. It was time to take the hint offered so plainly by Prosperina all those weeks before. With grim reluctance he set about preparing his withdrawal.

In military terms, the endeavour Mithridates was contemplating was at the masterclass level. He had to disengage a large, demoralized force from two fronts simultaneously in the face of active and spirited opposition and brutal winter weather. However, it was probably that same vile weather that allowed the army, even lacking its cavalry, to break Lucullus' stranglehold and struggle toward Lampsacus, with the Roman army gleefully in pursuit. Starved, half-frozen and demoralized, the Pontic army suffered huge casualties as it limped toward safety. River crossings were a particular problem. There were two of them, at the Granicus and the Aesepus, and both rivers were swollen with icy rain. At the bottleneck of the narrow fords the Romans massacred thousands of the Pontic army as the remainder struggled to cross. At Granicus alone, 20,000 were slain and tens of thousands more perished of cold and hunger during the march. With the Romans closing fast, the sick and wounded had to be abandoned to their fate. They were found by an advance guard of Cyzican soldiery, and these, probably remembering the killing of their own hostage citizens, had no compunction in killing every one of the helpless men.

Mithridates himself had departed by ship and he now sent his entire fleet to evacuate the army from Lampsacus. So few were the survivors of the once mighty force that had besieged Cyzicus that there was room for the people of Lampsacus to embark as well, and so escape Roman vengeance. Ten thousand men and fifty ships stayed with Marius with orders to garrison Lampsacus, guard the Hellespont and cause as many problems for the Romans in the region as possible. This garrison might have counted itself fortunate, as the vengeful gods were not yet done with the hapless Pontic army. The fleet was hit by a storm en route to Nicomedia and many of those who thought they had found safety after being evacuated were drowned. Of the 300,000 who had set out for

Bithynia that spring, only about 20,000 effective troops remained. The siege of Cyzicus could be considered an unmitigated disaster.

Mithridates after Cyzicus

Perhaps the most formidable aspect of Mithridates' character was his indomitable energy and resolution in the face of defeat. Far from giving in to despair, the king gathered his forces and took stock. Above all, he needed time. Mithridates still held all of Pontus and most of Bithynia, both of which were rich in resources. Another well-equipped army could be raised if the Romans could be kept out of Pontus long enough. The obvious course was to plunder as much as possible of Bithynia before the Romans got hold of it and to use the mineral and human wealth of Pontus and the Black Sea kingdoms to build another army.

Meanwhile, the Pontic forces remained supreme at sea and Mithridates intended to use this advantage to harass and slow the Romans. As another obstacle to the Roman advance, forts and cities around the kingdom were strengthened to withstand the coming storm, starting with those to the west. If Lucullus wanted Pontus, Mithridates intended to make him fight every step of the way.

The measures Mithridates was taking were not intended to simply delay the inevitable. The Pontic king knew his enemy, and he knew that Roman soldiers were also Roman voters. Perhaps he could make the war sufficiently unpopular at home to force a Roman withdrawal, or perhaps the progressive collapse of the Roman political system would see the Roman army needed elsewhere, ideally for a nice internecine civil war. Either way, Mithridates had nothing to lose. There was no question of surrender being either offered or accepted. Both sides knew this was a fight to the death.

Whilst Mithridates re-armed, Lucullus entered Cyzicus to a hysterical welcome from its citizens, who instituted the Lucullan games in honour of the occasion (these were held regularly for centuries afterwards). After Cyzicus, the Roman turned his attention to the war at sea. Every bit as much as did Mithridates, Lucullus appreciated the importance of sea power. He was, after all, the man who had risked his hide getting a fleet together for his general when Sulla belatedly realized the impossibility of finishing off the Pontic force in Greece without a navy. It would appear that even before the Romans settled down before Cyzicus, Lucullus had dispatched his agents across the islands of the Ionian Sea to commission warships. Consequently, Mithridates found that his fleet had to contend not just with the lethal vagaries of the eastern Mediterranean in winter, but also with a nascent Roman fleet.

Mithridates had forty ships which he had sent to support Sertorius in Spain. After the Roman victory there, these ships were on their way home. Marius had another fifty ships, and the remainder, probably just under 100 ships, were with the king.[11] Mithridates kept these at hand for the planned evacuation of himself and the remainder of his army from Nicomedia to Pontus itself. Such an evacuation was foreseen as the Pontic position in Bithynia was expected to become increasingly untenable.

The war which had looked as though it would climax with one decisive battle had instead degenerated into a messy series of disjointed conflicts, yet these nevertheless had a single underlying strategic theme. Lucullus wanted to drive into the Pontic heartland before Mithridates could organize a defence, and Mithridates was intent on making conditions for such a drive as difficult as possible.

Marius and his admirals on the Hellespont, Alexander and Dionysius, were not only protecting Pontus from naval attack but were also starting to cooperate with the pirates in interfering with Lucullus' supply lines across the Aegean. This was the first and greatest roadblock placed by Mithridates in the way of the Roman advance, and this Lucullus and his new fleet set about removing.

The Romans caught Marius and his ships off a small barren island in the Ionian Sea near Lemnos. Despite a Roman effort to lure Marius into a deep-water battle by sending their ships against him in ones and twos, the Pontics beached their ships and prepared to resist on land. The Romans kept the Pontic troops engaged without fully committing themselves, while sailing a large proportion of their force to the other side of the island. When these made their appearance, the Pontics were forced aboard their ships, but were now trapped between the ships of Lucullus offshore and the army onshore. They took heavy casualties before they broke, and thereafter there was nowhere for them to run. Marius and his admirals hid themselves in a cave, where Dionysius anticipated his capture by drinking poison. Lucullus had the other Pontic admiral shipped to Rome to await his eventual triumph. Since a Roman senator, even one of an opposing faction, was no proper ornament to a triumphal parade, Marius was killed on the spot. Lucullus returned to the mainland to prepare the next stage of the Roman invasion.

This was the signal for Mithridates to evacuate Bithynia. Though he had twice marched an army into the country, the king chose to leave by ship. The fleet was standing by anyway, in case the Romans cut off land communications, and it is possible that Mithridates decided that since the ships were there, he might as well use them. The earlier casualties inflicted on his army had evidently not convinced Mithridates that the winter sea was unsafe, so now he was to learn the lesson from personal experience.

The storm that hit his ships on the way to Pontus not only sank several Pontic transports, it threatened Mithridates' flagship itself. With the storm-lashed vessel waterlogged and foundering, it became essential to get the king to safety. Yet 'safety' was a relative term – the rescue ship was not Pontic, but owned by a pirate called Seleucus. In vain, Mithridates' advisors pointed out that pirates were, by definition, motivated by profit. Once the pirate ship had Mithridates on board there was nothing to stop Seleucus from proceeding straight to Lucullus and a huge reward. Mithridates was no coward, and he had great – usually justified – confidence in himself as a leader of men. Consequently, he felt more confidence in his ability to handle the pirates than in his flagship's ability to handle the storm. In the prevailing weather, transferring the royal person to the pirate ship (probably a sleek little galley of the type called a 'liburnian', after the part of the Dalmatian coast where these ships originated) was itself no-risk free manoeuvre; but for once one of Mithridates' gambles paid off. The pirates were true to their word and took the king to the safety of Sinope. When Mithridates' battered fleet showed up, the pirates cooperatively took the flagship in tow and brought it safe home to Pontus. There any relief at a safe landfall and homecoming was wiped out by the news that the part of the Pontic fleet returning from Spain had been brought to battle and wiped out at Tenedos, near Rhodes.

Now Mithridates was to find who his friends were. He sent an ambassador with a huge war chest of gold to recruit the Scythians. Instead of undertaking this risky mission, the ambassador, a man called Diocles, defected to Lucullus. In return he probably received a generous cut of that same gold. Diocles was not alone in his treachery. For another example of how the Pontic elite began to consider an accommodation with Rome, the later geographer of the region, Strabo, admits that his own maternal grandfather defected at this time, handing over to Lucullus the fifteen forts of which he had command. If courtiers could not be trusted, family were just as unfaithful. Tigranes, the son-in-law of Mithridates, sheepishly admitted that it was not in Armenia's interests to go to war with the Romans. Even more wounding, Mithridates' own son, Menchares, remained deaf to his father's messengers. Menchares had apparently decided that though Pontus was a lost cause, he could still set himself up very nicely as a small independent kingdom in the Bosporus. Indeed, it later became apparent that he was already negotiating with Lucullus to achieve this objective.

Bereft of fleet, army and allies, Mithridates and his kingdom stood alone against the vengeance of Rome.

Chapter 9

Defeat and Exile

In 72 BC Mithridates was in his sixtieth year, and the seventeenth of his struggle with Rome. Among the levies now facing him might be found the children of the Roman legionaries he had fought in 88 BC. Certainly, one of his opponents – the Murena now cruising the Propontis with the Roman fleet – was the vengeful son of the Murena who had so spectacularly failed to defeat Mithridates in the war of a decade previously.

Mithridates grimly continued to keep faith in the eventual political collapse of the Roman polity. As well as the continued exertions of Sertorius and the depredations of the pirates, Italy itself was now racked by the rampaging Spartacus. It is probable that Mithridates, like almost everyone else, underestimated Spartacus' military genius. Otherwise he would undoubtedly have attempted to give a fellow enemy of Rome substantial support. However, even if the phenomenon of Spartacus was considered a slave revolt of the type that the Romans quashed with monotonous regularity in Sicily, the sheer scale of this insurrection meant that no reinforcements would be coming to Lucullus in 72 BC. In fact, with Spartacus in Italy, Mithridates in the east, Sertorius in the west, and the pirates right across the ocean in between, the Roman colossus was beleaguered on all sides. Hope was by no means lost.

Out of consideration of the stringency facing Rome, Lucullus had declined an offer from the senate to help his war effort with 3,000 talents of silver. The Roman had decided to use the resources of Pontus to finance the war against that country's king, but first he had the challenge of getting there. He had by now established that Mithridates had evacuated Bithynia, and had no doubt that the king was preparing to resist his advance through Paphlagonia or Phrygia. This left the choice of routes as either through Galatia or along the Black Sea coastal plain.[1]

The coastal route was straightforward as far as Heraclea, but going further involved taking that city out of the war, and this probably meant another protracted siege – something that Lucullus could ill afford. His Fimbrians had already endured the gruelling siege of Cyzicus, and were unimpressed by the thanks of the grateful citizenry. After almost a decade in Asia Minor, they wanted plunder and to go home. In the event, the siege of Heraclea was left to

Cotta. Through a mixture of Pontic determination and Cotta's woeful military ineptitude, the siege dragged on for two years. It was only brought to a halt when Menchares, on the other side of the Black Sea, was persuaded to become an official 'friend' of the Romans and to stop smuggling supplies to the besieged citizens.

This left Galatia, and across Galatia went the Fimbrians, complaining bitterly about the lack of supplies as they went. Deiotarus had foreseen this problem. As many as 30,000 Galatians followed the Romans, not as reinforcements but as a supply chain. Every one of these men carried a bushel (a measure equivalent to about eight gallons) of wheat on his back, and in this way the Roman army crossed the barren highlands of Galatia, and descended into the unprotected heartlands of Pontus.[2] This fertile and well-populated area had been Pontic for generations, and had thrived under the aegis of the Mithridatic dynasty. With Mithridates still attempting to gather an army at Cabira to the east across the river Lycus, the Fimbrians were finally free to plunder the abundance of the countryside to their heart's content. In the Roman camp the price of an ox dropped to under a day's wages, and a slave could be had for four drachmas. When the Romans could plunder no more they simply pillaged and despoiled what was left. The degree of human and economic damage that this entailed partly explains why Mithridates had opted to fight Sulla in Greece rather than in his Anatolian conquests, which he had been more confident of holding. Warfare was more damaging than any typhoon for the lands a hostile army passed over.

With plunder aplenty, the Fimbrians became more particular about their choice of loot. Agricultural produce was all very well, but retirement pensions needed gold, and gold was to be had from the cities and towns. These, annoyingly, Lucullus refused to take by storm. Instead he camped before them and negotiated their surrender, giving easy terms to encourage the next fortification down the line to give itself up as well. This far-sighted strategy was both intended to expedite the surrender of Pontus and to allow the province, once yielded, to become as much a cash cow for Rome as it was for Mithridates. The problem lay in explaining all this to an army fixated on pillage and plunder. It did not help that by and large the Roman leadership shared the Fimbrian outlook. Lucullus later attempted to prevent further uprisings in Asia Minor by fixing the payment of the Sullan indemnity with a twenty-five per cent tax (on virtually everything) and freezing interest rates at twelve per cent. As Lucullus also ruled that interest should not accrue beyond the amount of the original debt, the ravages of galloping compound interest were cut at a stroke. It also meant that if Mithridates were to arise, vampire-like once more from defeat, Asia would be less likely to succumb to his promises of financial relief. By these measures the foundations were laid for the economic recovery of Asia Minor, and by way of thanks Lucullus incurred the bitter enmity of those at Rome who had been making their fortunes from the suffering of the region – a group which included many senators and their equestrian partners in extortion.

The Cabira campaign

Mithridates could not prevent the despoiling of his lands, because he lacked an army with which to do so. However, he had the cavalry which had survived Cyzicus, and the largely-intact forces which had been defending the southern approaches to Pontus during the Bithynian campaign. This probably totalled some 40,000 men – not enough to defeat Lucullus, but certainly enough to trouble him.[3] Certainly, there was no way that Pontus could be considered conquered whilst this force remained in the field. By way of reminding the Romans that he was far from a spent force, Mithridates began raiding with a goodly proportion of his cavalry over the Lycus. He engaged a Roman force on the other side and soundly defeated it. Plutarch relates that one of the leading Romans captured was a man called Pomponius (possibly a relative of Pomponius Atticus, the friend of Cicero). Mithridates offered to spare the man's life in return for his friendship. Pomponius defiantly replied that he would remain Mithridates' enemy as long as Mithridates was an enemy of the Romans. 'The king was amazed by the man, and did him no harm', reports Plutarch.[4]

In the hope of bringing Mithridates to battle, Lucullus settled down to a leisurely siege of Amisus. There was not much else he could do. The ever-strengthening cavalry of Mithridates meant that the Romans could no longer plunder the plains with impunity, and Pontic irregulars would make life difficult in the hills. If pushed, Mithridates would retreat to the fastnesses of Armenia Minor, and Lucullus certainly did not relish persuading the Fimbrians to undertake the unrewarding task of chasing a highly-mobile Mithridates around the mountains. Mithridates knew that Lucullus was already facing criticism for dragging out the war, and believed that Amisus – fortified as it had been – was capable of outlasting Lucullus.*

Therefore Mithridates remained at Cabira and waited for the Romans to come to him. He placed a small garrison, commanded by a relative called Phoenix, on the mountain passes and gave orders for a signal fire to be lit if the

---

* One of the precautions the defenders of the city had taken was to lay in a stock of wasp nests and wild bears. When the Romans began the traditional attempt to undermine the walls of the city, the Pontic defenders countermined the tunnels and unleashed bears and wasps, singly and in combination, upon the Roman miners.

Romans moved, as he felt Lucullus would be forced to do. Eventually, in the spring of 72 BC, Lucullus left the siege of Amisus to Murena and two legions, and reluctantly made his way to Cabira with the rest of the army.

Details of the campaign which followed are hopelessly confused, with different sources giving different and incompatible chronologies. However, a number of events are commonly agreed on, though not the order in which they occurred. Militarily, it would appear that Lucullus had first to storm the fortress of Eupatoria, which Mithridates had constructed specifically to guard the approaches to Cabira. It may be that this was where Phoenix was stationed, for we are told that after informing Mithridates that the Romans were coming, he promptly defected to them. However, as the historian Memnon is clear that this fortress was captured at the end of the Cabira campaign, this suggests that Lucullus left the fortress in native hands and at some point it returned its allegiance to Mithridates.[5]

It is also clear that Mithridates gave Lucullus a warm welcome to Cabira and inflicted a sharp setback on some of his troops in a highly-confused skirmish which seems to have developed from an attack on Roman foragers. Confronting Mithridates in Cabira had been a bold move by Lucullus and, despite this setback, the Roman proceeded to push his luck even harder. Some local Greeks offered to lead the Roman force to an advantageous position and Lucullus accepted. Since this involved passing through a dangerously narrow valley, he took advantage of the fact that he had veteran troops under his command and performed the manoeuvre at night. To slow the enemy reaction, the Romans first lit camp fires and generally gave the impression that they were settled until dawn.

In fact, dawn saw the Romans occupying an old fort on the heights overlooking Cabira. This was a secure position defensively and one from which the Romans could easily move to the plain.

But that narrow defile meant that Lucullus was cut off from his recent conquests in Pontus and was now dependent on supplies from Cappadocia in the south to keep his army fed. The vulnerability of that supply line was soon demonstrated by a violent skirmish with the Pontic cavalry. At first the Pontics got the worse of this confrontation but Mithridates himself led a countercharge, and gave the Romans such a fright that they continued to retreat long after the Pontic forces had pulled back.

Now fighting on his home turf, it was Mithridates who offered battle on the favourable ground of the plain, and Lucullus who declined. While this stalemate dragged on, Mithridates appears to have attempted to decapitate the

Roman force with the assassination of Lucullus. He fell out very publicly with a barbarian chieftain called Olthacus, and this man promptly followed the prevailing trend and defected to the Romans. Olthacus gave Lucullus intelligence which was checked and proven trustworthy, with the result that Olthacus himself became a trusted member of Lucullus' entourage. One midday, the barbarian presented himself at the commander's tent with urgent news, and as was his custom, a dagger on his belt. An officious attendant told Olthacus that Lucullus was asleep and had ordered that he should not be disturbed no matter how urgent the tidings. Olthacus must wait until the general had awakened. This was far from convenient, because the would-be assassin had parked his horse just outside the camp for a quick getaway, and it was only a matter of time before this suspicious positioning was noted. After being physically prevented from forcing his way into the Lucullan bedchamber, Olthacus gave up the attempt. Since he was hopelessly compromised anyway, he mounted his horse and rode back to Mithridates. As Plutarch commented, many a general has come to grief from being asleep at the wrong moment, but only Lucullus was saved by being asleep at the right time.[6]

The war of attrition continued. At Cyzicus, Mithridates had been taught that a strong position with poor supply lines was at least as bad as a poor position with good supply lines, and he was determined to give Lucullus the benefit of this lesson. The Pontic cavalry made a violent attack on a supply convoy which was bringing corn from Cappadocia. The convoy had an escort of ten cohorts of infantry, commanded by one Sornatius, and these succeeded in holding off the attack, so Mithridates decided that the next attempt by the Pontics would constitute a mixed force of infantry and cavalry.

Some 4,000 infantry and the Pontic cavalry fell upon the next Roman supply convoy but, possibly due to poor coordination between foot and horse, the battle took place in the narrow valley where the horsemen were almost unable to deploy. The infantry and half the Pontic cavalry were wiped out. The infantry were not a serious loss but, with his cavalry crippled, Mithridates was unable to dominate the plain. Almost certainly, as soon as Lucullus comprehended this he would descend from his hill and either force the Pontic infantry to battle on the plain or, if battle was declined, lay siege to the Pontic camp. Mithridates, harbouring no illusions as to what would happen to his foot soldiers if the Fimbrians got to grips with them, made ready to withdraw.

In order to minimize panic in his camp, the king gave out that in the recent fight his men had merely got the worst of a minor skirmish. He instructed his guards to stop anyone from leaving the camp and discreetly ordered the royal treasure to be evacuated on muleback. Rumours of a major Pontic defeat were exaggerated by the survivors of the battle in the valley as they trickled back into camp. It also became clear from the loaded waggons approaching the Roman camp that the Pontic attack had failed miserably. Those who knew of Mithridates' plan to evacuate his treasure took the chance to send away their own baggage as well. It did not take long for the soldiers to connect the crush around the camp gates with the reports of a major defeat, and the dissimulation of their commanders led the normally-obedient infantry to conclude that their betters intended to leave them in the lurch.

Mithridates in his tent became aware of general tumult outside. It was too late to rally his troops, who had decided that it was now every man for himself. No one listened to the king; he was knocked from his horse and one of his priests, Hermaeus, was trampled to death by the crowd trying to get out of the gates. With commendable promptness, Lucullus divined what was happening and sent his army to harry the retreating force, giving explicit instructions as to which members of Mithridates' entourage he wanted captured alive. The Romans reached the camp and slew the few who had remained as they were attempting to pack tidily.

Lucullus knew his men and had specifically told them to ignore the camp and concentrate on killing as much of the Pontic army as possible whilst it was disorganized and vulnerable. However, the Fimbrians finally had the chance to get what they had signed up for – loot in portable, easily-converted form. They stopped to plunder the camp. Even then they might have caught Mithridates, for the king was reduced to just another body in the flow pushing its heedless way out of the gates. Fortunately, one of the king's entourage observed the plight of his sovereign. He forced his horse through the throng and, at considerable personal risk, gave his mount to the king. Being on horseback once more allowed Mithridates to put some distance between himself and the Romans and to become reunited with his treasure train.

The Roman cavalry were still closing and Mithridates again became in danger of capture. The enemy had him in sight when the king tried a last desperate stratagem. He – with his own hand, by some reports – slashed open the bottom of some treasure sacks and drove off the mules. A fortune in gold and jewellery was scattered across Mithridates' line of retreat, and no pack of hounds ever swerved so readily after a red herring as the Roman pursuit which took off on the treasure trail.

A frustrated Lucullus learned that Mithridates had slipped through his fingers and that Callistratus, the king's chief attendant and one of the men whom Lucullus was most eager to question, had been killed by soldiers who suspected him of concealing gold. Of course, that is exactly what Callistratus had been doing – not in his girdle as the soldiers suspected, but by the waggon load in fortresses and strong points out of Roman reach. This fortune had now to be ferreted out item by item. However, with the Pontic army all but destroyed and Mithridates in headlong flight, Lucullus was prepared to dedicate plenty of time to the job.

The exile

Not all fortresses surrendered readily to Lucullus but, as well as treasure, many Roman sympathizers captured by Mithridates over the years fell into Roman hands and were freed from their imprisonment. Also, Nysia, the sister of Mithridates, became a Roman prisoner, which caused Mithridates to determine that the same would not happen to his wives and concubines. These were kept at a place called Phernacia along with Roxane and Statira, two unmarried sisters who, though in their forties, the king was keeping in secluded reserve for a diplomatic marriage if required, and to prevent them from producing any rival heirs for the Pontic throne in any other case. Since it was impossible to evacuate this harem to safety, Mithridates decided that their death should come before the dishonour of falling into Roman hands.

A eunuch was sent with the king's order that the harem commit suicide. It is reported that reactions varied, with some praising the king for taking the time to consider their honour even in his hour of need, whilst others, as they died, wished their own fate upon their royal husband. Each chose death as she felt most appropriate. Some took poison but one Monime of Miletus* chose to hang herself by her royal diadem. This was because she had held out against the courtship of Mithridates until she received the status of wife and queen. She got her wish, only to discover that the honour meant that she was secluded in a harem and ignored for long periods by 'more of a keeper than a husband'. The stifling boredom of the royal seraglio had replaced the usual social interactions of a Greek noblewoman and now Monime decided that the the diadem which had brought her so much misery could release her from it as well. Even in this, her crown failed to meet her expectations. It refused to bear Monime's weight once she put herself into the noose she had attached to it. After spitting on the broken crown, the unhappy girl finally presented her throat to the eunuch's dagger.

Mithridates, with 2,000 horsemen, headed for the last sanctuary available to him, the kingdom of his son-in-law, Tigranes. Given that family solidarity

* This may or may not be the same person as Monima of Stratonice (p.41)

was not a strong point among the royal families of the region, it is unlikely that Mithridates was counting on Tigranes welcoming a relative fallen on hard times. Rather, once he had publicly made himself a supplicant to the Armenian power, Tigranes had either to accept his inconvenient guest or openly show his subservience to Rome by meekly handing him over. This was something that the man who titled himself the King of Kings would not do readily, and it was this pride rather than family sentiment on which Mithridates gambled for his salvation. Yet family ties were indeed to save him, albeit in an unexpected way.

Unsurprisingly, Tigranes was less than thrilled with the arrival of Mithridates on his metaphorical doorstep, but, as the Pontic king had calculated, Tigranes was not prepared for the damage which his public image would suffer were he to simply abandon his son-in-law and erstwhile ally to his fate. Mithridates was kept in in the manner to which his royal person was accustomed, but in a castle well away from the Armenian court and guarded so closely as to almost be a prisoner. Tigranes hurried himself off to Syria to further distance himself from whatever happened in Anatolia, and to gain time to prepare for the inevitable envoy from the Romans.

This is where family ties came to the help of Mithridates. Lucullus was hosting in his camp the noble, pig-headed and dissolute Clodius, scion of Rome's ancient and patrician Claudian house, and his brother-in-law. The antipathy which Lucullus rapidly developed for his brash and arrogant relative probably inspired the idea of sending him as envoy to Tigranes the demand the person of Mithridates. Clodius duly set off for Armenia, leaving Lucullus to settle down to conquering Armenia Minor and returning to the sieges of Amisus and Sinope without the distraction of his demanding relative.[7]

Arrogant and ignorant he may have been, but Clodius was no fool. He soon determined that Tigranes was trying to run him in circles, from the guides who literally attempted to do so with a highly-circuitous route to the capital, to the messengers who regularly informed him that the king would welcome him personally in the very near future. Clodius ditched his guides and made his own way to the capital, and, by way of encouraging the king to speed up his audience, he began intriguing with various members of the Armenian court, promising some aid from Lucullus if they moved against Tigranes.* Clodius also showed admirable dedication to his duty. Regularly offered an abundance of treasure by Tigranes as 'presents', Clodius reluctantly accepted but a single cup – not enough even to avoid insulting the king, let alone enough to count as accepting a bribe.

---

* One who listened to the Roman promises too attentively was King Zarbienus of the Gordyenians, who paid with his life for being a suspected conspirator.

This stubbornness on Clodius' part boded ill for the meeting with Tigranes. What Tigranes hoped to gain from the meeting will never be known. Perhaps he hoped that Rome would leave him alone in exchange for a promise that Mithridates would never leave his gilded captivity. It is fair to guess that a suitable incentive, such as offering Tigranes suzerainty of Cappadocia, would have seen Mithridates promptly handed over in chains. However, as his refusal of bribes had shown, the Roman had come with a different purpose in mind.

Clodius, who like all Roman aristocrats was essentially a politician, deliberately chose to imitate Gaius Popillius Laenas, who in 168 BC had drawn a line in the sand around King Antiochus IV and bluntly told him to decide on peace or war with Rome before he stepped out of the circle. This Republican plain speaking and scorn of kings played well at home and Clodius had a political career to build. So, he bluntly told Tigranes to hand over Mithridates or face the consequences. No bribes or concessions were offered apart from this naked threat.

Almost all that could be said for Clodius' style of is that it produced prompt results. The Roman demand was flatly rejected and Clodius was sent packing. After almost twenty months in a marshy backwater, Mithridates was brought to the Armenian court, honoured by Tigranes as his father-in-law and given a place on the royal council. Whether intending to or not, Clodius had immensely helped the cause of Mithridates by making Tigranes an offer he had to refuse and almost certainly bringing Armenia into the war on the side of Pontus against the Romans.

Mithridates celebrated his return to a position of power in typical fashion, by throwing himself into palace politics and ensuring that those who had shown insufficient passion for promoting his cause came to a sticky end. Mithridates would have been dismayed by the news that the last of his strongholds in Pontus had finally fallen, but would have certainly been encouraged by the dogged loyalty shown to his cause by the defenders of cities such as Sinope and Amisus. Nevertheless, by 69 BC, Pontus was effectively in Roman hands, although the Bosporan kingdom remained under the rule of Menchares, Mithridates' traitorous son, who was now officially a 'friend of the Roman people'.

The Armenian campaign

It is possible that Mithridates did his best to convince Tigranes that the Romans would never dare to come against him in Armenia – after all, he wanted his son-in-law to assemble his army for a campaign in Asia Minor.

Tigranes himself might or might not have been considering a foreign adventure against the Romans, but he literally refused to consider the idea that the Romans might have the temerity to march on him. The first messenger who came with news that Lucullus was indeed on his way was beheaded for being alarmist.

Nevertheless, the news was correct. Whether Lucullus jumped at the opportunity which the undiplomatic Clodius had presented, or whether Clodius had been requested to produce exactly the outcome which transpired will never be known. In either case, it was Lucullus who went onto the offensive. He did this against a major foreign power which had so far stayed scrupulously neutral, and absolutely on his own authority. The senate in Rome was more than somewhat astonished to hear that they were now at war with Armenia, and that Lucullus had taken the army on what many regarded as virtually a massive private plundering raid. Lucullus, already unpopular in Rome for his sensible settlement of Asia, could expect very little sympathy if anything went wrong with his unauthorized invasion, and could confidently expect to have to defend himself in court even if everything went right.[8]

Clodius did not accompany his brother-in-law. He had fallen out with Lucullus and took his revenge by stirring up the Fimbrians to the point of mutiny. Being unceremoniously booted from Lucullus' presence, Clodius joined the army of Marcius Rex in western Anatolia. Marcius gave Clodius a minor command against the pirates. After being captured and ransomed by the pirates, Clodius rejoined the Roman land army and this time did successfully instigate a mutiny, in the course of which he almost lost his life. After this it was decided that Clodius and Asia Minor were not suited to each other and Clodius returned to Rome.*

Meanwhile, in the spring of 69 BC, Lucullus handed command of Pontus to Sornatius (who had acquitted himself well in the Cabira campaign) and headed for Tigranocerta, the Armenian capital. He was accompanied by Murena junior, who probably commanded auxiliary troops, and two picked legions under Lucullus' personal control. In the context of the Fimbrians, 'picked legions' meant the two legions least likely to mutiny, though they were far from delighted with the honour which their commander had done them. Overall, Lucullus probably had some 12,000–18,000 foot and 3,000 horse. Given the length of their service, the two legions were probably severely under-strength and the infantry numbers were made up with auxiliaries – Lucullus prided himself on using native resources whenever possible. The Roman general was marching his surly, unwilling little army

---

* One of the first things Lucullus did on returning to Rome was to break the family connection with Clodius by filing for divorce.

into the heartland of an enemy who could be confidently expected to raise ten times as many infantry, and at least twenty times the cavalry. No wonder Tigranes was incredulous.

Tigranocerta lay slightly north of due east from Comana in Cappadocia (which was probably the jumping-off point of Lucullus' invasion). Therefore, there was only one sensible route for the Roman army to follow – which is along the east-west valley of the anti-Taurus which has Edessa on the other side of the mountain range, and which finishes at the head of the River Tigris, where Mosul stands today. This is the route which Crassus later scorned in favour of taking his army along the more direct route to Parthia, 150 miles to the south, which in his case finished at Carrhae in 53 BC when the Parthian cavalry wiped him out.

The initial part of the route wound between snow-covered mountains and torrents still swollen with snowmelt. There was some apprehension at the prospect of crossing the headwaters of the Euphrates into the small, Armenian-controlled principality of Sophene, but it turned out that the Euphrates was at its lowest in living memory.[9] The army could simply wade across, something Lucullus did not hesitate to point out as a signal of divine favour. With Tigranes still wilfully ignorant of their coming, the Romans made their way eastward, the Fimbrians muttering darkly about not being allowed to plunder the countryside as they went along. However, Lucullus would not have wanted his army either slowed down by loot, or to have lost its appetite for plunder before it reached its destination. Besides, nothing encouraged a native population to help an army on its way more than if it was friendly but showing signs of changing its mind.

The Romans rounded the headwaters of the Tigris and were set to fall on Tigranocerta itself before one of the favourites of the King of Kings decided to literally risk his neck by bringing his royal master up to date with developments. For his reward, this man, Mithrobarzanes, was given a force of cavalry several thousand strong along with instructions to crush the impertinent Roman army and bring its commander to Tigranes alive.

Mithrobarzanes seems to have decided that his only chance of surviving his mission was to hit the Romans suddenly with all his strength and hope that they had been lulled into complacency by the total lack of opposition along their march so far. However, Lucullus was an old hand at fighting in Asia Minor and, unlike the average Roman general, he appreciated the importance of scouts. Warned of Mithrobarzanes' approach, Lucullus sent out a force of some 3,500, infantry and cavalry in equal proportion, and told them to stand the Armenians off until the Romans had fortified a camp. This Roman force met the Armenian cavalry, which attempted to disperse it with a headlong charge. Against experienced infantry who knew how to stand their ground such a cavalry charge was suicidal, and the Fimbrians were very experienced. Mithrobarzanes and most of his force duly perished on the spot.

The Battle of Tigranocerta

The brusque treatment of his advance force finally convinced Tigranes that the Romans were both a serious and imminent threat. As his levies had not yet completed their muster, he decided to withdraw from his capital to Taurus and gather his army about him there. En route, he discovered that he would have to do without his Arab levies, as one of Lucullus' commanders, Sextilius, came across the Arabian camp, attacked it and dispersed the entire force. Murena junior, meanwhile, was hot upon the trail of Tigranes. At one point he was so close on the king's heels that Tigranes had to abandon his baggage and make a dash for safety. While this was going on, Lucullus settled down to besiege Tigranocerta. This was the standard Roman campaign tactic – find something the enemy valued and march straight at it. The enemy would eventually muster an army to defend the target of the Roman advance and would be defeated. Indeed, the massive walls of Tigranocerta would not have been an easy nut to crack, had Lucullus intended a serious investment rather than a provocation to Tigranes.

At this early stage of the campaign Tigranes was still confident that he could handle the Roman threat, and paid little heed to Mithridates. In fact Mithridates was not even included in the retinue of the King of Kings and had to make do with frantic letters and pleas transmitted through an ambassador called Taxiles. After his experiences at Cyzicus, Mithridates had become a convert to the idea of victory by malnutrition. Now he pointed in vain to the long and exposed Roman supply lines and argued that Tigranes and his hordes of cavalry could starve the Romans into submission without a battle. His proposal fell on deaf ears. With his precious new capital under siege and a massive multi-national army gathering about him, Tigranes was determined to fight. The hard-won experience of Mithridates was construed as envy that someone else was going to crush the Romans, or alternatively as proof that the Romans had broken his spirit.

It is hard to determine the size of the Armenian force, as Roman chroniclers are prone to exaggeration, but Appian gives Tigranes credit for raising the suspiciously-round numbers of 250,000 foot and 50,000 horse.[10] Plutarch claims as his source the actual report of Lucullus to the senate, and this allowed him to give a more detailed breakdown. By this account, 35,000 of the Armenian army were a pioneer and engineering corps, supplying their comrades with wood, bridging small rivers and making roads. The backbone of the army was 150,000 heavy infantry arranged into cohorts or phalanxes according to the preferred disposition of the subject people who had supplied the troops. Of the 55,000 cavalry, Plutarch says 17,000 were completely armoured, probably in the style of Parthian cataphracts. At the fore of this massive force were 20,000 light missile troops, a mix of slingers, archers and javelineers, who by themselves easily outnumbered the entire Roman force.[11] By way of contrast, an independent account, admittedly late and fragmentary, comes from one Phlegon of Tralles. He puts the number of effectives in the Armenian infantry at 40,000 – perhaps a more realistically-sized, but still formidable, force. Phlegon's assessment of cavalry numbers is still high at 30,000.[12] Even by this lowest estimate, however, the Romans were still massively outnumbered.

The high morale of the Armenians could be seen in the heroics of a force of 6,000 cavalry who broke through the Roman siege lines into Tigranocerta, then broke out again with Tigranes' royal harem and a good portion of the royal treasury in tow.

The substantial Armenian garrison of Tirganocerta, strengthened by a large number of Greek mercenaries, was yet another problem for Lucullus. If he turned to face Tigranes, he risked having the garrison fall on his back, yet an army of up to a quarter of a million men was impossible to ignore. The only solution was for Lucullus to divide his already-tiny army, leave Tigranocerta to Murena and 6,000 foot, and take the rest against Tigranes. This gave Lucullus twenty-four cohorts, or about 10,000 men, with about another 1,000 mixed cavalry and skirmishers and an unknown number of auxiliary troops. These formed up on the plain beside 'the river'. Because we do not know the exact location of now-vanished Tigranocerta, it is not certain what this river was, though it was either the upstream Tigris or a tributary thereof. The river today called the Zgran is a very plausible candidate. We know the battle took place within sight of Tigranocerta (wherever it was), but given the paucity of detail about the battle and the incompatibility of the details we do have, only a rough outline of events can be reconstructed.[13]

It is reasonable to suppose that Lucullus first intended to take on the Armenians as they attempted to cross the river. Since Lucullus had to use a ford when going the other way, it seems certain the river was not something which could be crossed by an army in battle formation. Therefore it would appear that Lucullus intended to hit the relieving force as it came across the river with an eye to defeating its units in detail as they crossed. However, as the huge Armenian force hove into view, another possibility, based on the enemy's line of approach, presented itself to him. His scouts had shown him a ford perhaps slightly to the north, where the river curved westward, its course affected by a gently rising plateau on the other side.

At this point the Armenians were not fully deployed and, in any case, were working on the not-unreasonable belief that they were going to be the aggressors in the coming battle. Indeed, Tigranes was far from certain that there was going to be a battle at all. Eyeing the diminutive Roman force, he remarked jokingly 'if that's a diplomatic mission, it's too big. If it's an army, it's too small'. Consequently, he was unsurprised when the Romans wheeled left, and trotted away along the river bank. Taxiles pointed out that the Romans were not backing off. The men of a retreating Roman army would have put their shields back into their leather covers – not presented them freshly polished. The Romans were dressed for battle, with plumes affixed to their helmets, a sure sign that they were expecting an engagement.

There was considerable confusion as the large and unwieldy Armenian force was reconfigured to fight its battle on the east bank of the river, a confusion which was more acute because Lucullus had screened his infantry with his cavalry. Consequently, Tigranes was unaware that the Roman infantry had not stopped going once it had crossed the river but instead the legionaries were looping round to gain the higher ground of the plateau at the rear of the Armenian right flank. 'Are they on us?' asked the bewildered Tigranes. Still uncertain of where his enemy had got to, he closed the main body of his infantry about himself at the centre, and sent a large force of cataphracts to push the Roman cavalry aside.

Cataphracts were a reasonable choice, since these were very heavily-armoured cavalrymen, and thus more capable of standing against the infantry which Tigranes expected to find behind the Roman horsemen. However, rather than stand and fight, the Roman cavalry gave way. By this hypothesis, they gave way rapidly along their river flank, falling back more slowly toward the plateau, whilst the Armenian cavalry probed forward along the line of least resistance looking for the legionaries who should be there. The cavalry nearest Lucullus on the plateau (Lucullus had chosen to fight on foot with his legionaries) were now almost on the right flank of the cataphracts furthest from the river, and Lucullus saw his chance. His cavalrymen were sword-armed

Galatian and Thracian irregulars, and hitting the lance-armed cataphracts on the flank meant that the lighter-armed horsemen could use their swords to beat down the Armenians' lances before they could be swung around.

This was not going to do more than delay the cataphracts, but it would keep them busy long enough for the Roman infantry charge to hit them standing. The Romans did not bother with their usual preliminary shower of javelins, mainly because the Galatians and Thracians were already engaged, and would be far more affected by friendly fire than the well-protected Armenians. The infantry's intention was to use their swords to slash at the unprotected shins and thighs of the Armenians, but the cataphracts did not give them the chance. Still struggling with the Roman cavalry, they chose the only possible line of disengagement – a line that sent them crashing into the advancing Armenian infantry.

Either at this point or slightly earlier, Lucullus decided that it was time for the rest of his infantry to make their presence known. Raising his sword, he bellowed 'Soldiers, we are victorious', and led the downhill charge. The Armenian baggage train was as confused as the rest of the army, and was keeping close behind the right flank on the assumption that the Romans were still some way ahead. The unexpected sight of Lucullus and his legionaries thundering downhill toward them prompted those manning the baggage train to retreat precipitately, directly away from the Roman advance – and again into the right of the Armenian infantry, which was by now in a state of total chaos.

Lucullus had achieved his initial objective – given his enemy's overwhelming superiority in cavalry and missile troops, the last thing he had wanted was to be pinned by cavalry whilst his forces were picked off by bows and javelins. This was not an unreasonable fear, and exactly what the Parthians later did to Crassus. Instead, Lucullus had brought his men to close quarters with hardly a casualty, and his legions were now chewing through the right of the Armenian army whilst the rest of Tigranes' force was still working out what had hit them.

Unsurprisingly, the Armenian right broke, and their panic communicated itself to the troops next in line. The baggage handlers were already in full flight along with much of the cavalry and to the unsteady Armenian levies it seemed that the battle was already lost. The same thought was preoccupying Tigranes, who had been off-balance since before the battle commenced, and who was keenly aware that the tumult of the Roman advance was getting uncomfortably close to his own position. This was the moment to make a headlong charge at the Romans and hope that the remainder of his army would take inspiration from his valour. Of course, there was the embarrassing and all-too-likely prospect that this charge and Tigranes' subsequent death would be in vain, which left the second option – to follow the example of those even nearer to the Romans, and make a timely exit from the battlefield.

Tigranes opted to depart, and with him went the last chance of Armenian arms salvaging anything from the day. The battle became a rout.

The following series of diagrams offer a highly speculative look at how the battle of Tigranocerta might have happened. Though this sequence is consistent with the available evidence, other interpretations are certainly possible. Tigranes' army is in black, Lucullus in grey. Thin lines represent cavalry in skirmish order.

Battle of Tigranocerta

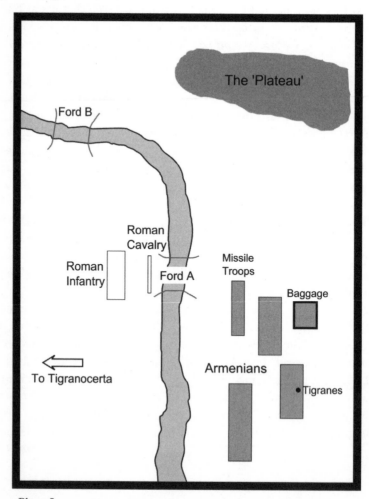

Phase I

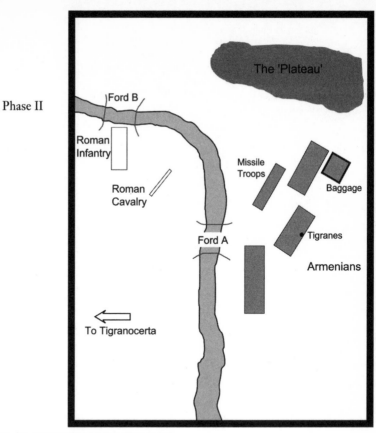

Phase II

The 'Plateau'

Ford B

Roman Infantry

Roman Cavalry

Missile Troops

Baggage

Ford A

Tigranes

Armenians

To Tigranocerta

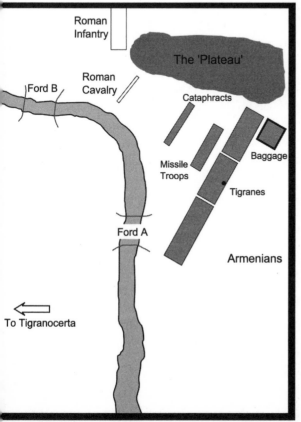

Roman Infantry

The 'Plateau'

Ford B

Roman Cavalry

Cataphracts

Phase III

Missile Troops

Baggage

Tigranes

Ford A

Armenians

To Tigranocerta

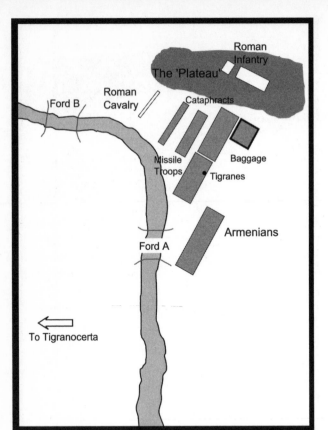

Phase IV

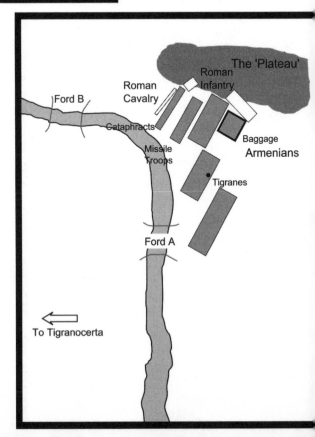

Phase V

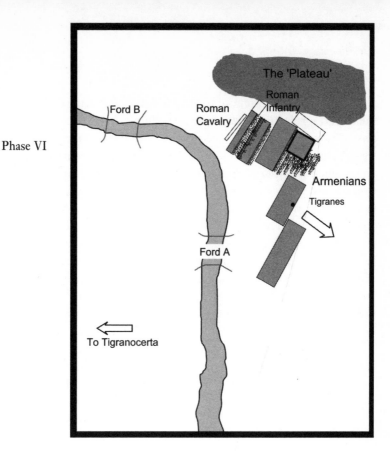

Phase VI

The 'Plateau'

Roman Infantry

Ford B

Roman Cavalry

Armenians

Tigranes

Ford A

To Tigranocerta

After Tigranocerta

Just as with the numbers of the army before the battle, the number of casualties afterwards are highly unreliable. For a start, it is improbable that anyone was counting, and secondly the Romans pursued the Armenian rout for a considerable distance. Therefore we get a body count as high as 100,000 (Plutarch) and as low as 5,000 (Phlegon). Nor are the two incompatible. If Plutarch drew his figures from claims that Tigranes lost 100,000 men and Phlegon says the Romans killed 5,000, it may be that 95% of the army lost their taste for soldiering and headed directly home without stopping to collect their back pay.

Lucullus was well aware that scattering an enemy army was not the same as destroying it, and he had given very strict orders that killing and not plunder was to be given priority. The Fimbrians, whatever their other faults, were a dependable force on the battlefield. But they would have been aware that tens of thousands of cavalry were still unaccounted for, and were not going to break into very small groups to hunt down their scattering foes.

Indeed, had they done so they would may well have come to grief, because there were probably 2,000 highly-disciplined cavalry close at hand. This was the personal guard of Mithridates who had been late arriving on the battlefield, quite possibly because he had a pretty good idea of what was going to happen there. If pessimism was indeed the cause of his tardiness, he would have been unsurprised to meet first a trickle and then a flood of panicked Armenian troops heading in the opposite direction. In any case, once he had ascertained that there would be no further fighting that day, he directed his energies to finding Tigranes. Given that Tigranes' negotiating position had just sharply deteriorated, Mithridates now needed the goodwill of his son-in-law more than ever. Therefore he carefully refrained from pointing out that he had told Tigranes so. Instead he concentrated on raising the chastised king's morale, handing over his personal guard with instructions that they should look after his crestfallen relative.

The Romans now received an unexpected bonus. The commander of the garrison of Tigranocerta, one Mancaeus, had witnessed the dispersal of the Armenian army from the walls. Given that the Romans were now in command of the land outside, he began to doubt the loyalty of his Greek mercenaries. Therefore he ordered them to hand in their weapons. This the Greeks took as a preliminary to their arrest and possible massacre, so they gathered together and started making themselves clubs from whatever heavy objects were at hand. When Mancaeus sent troops to disarm them once more, the mercenaries wound their cloaks about their shield arms and attacked with their makeshift weapons. Success gave them access to real weaponry from the defeated Armenian detachment. The Greeks fought their way to a section of the walls between the towers, and invited the delighted Romans to enter the city as their allies.

Finally the Fimbrians had all the plunder they could carry, though Lucullus reserved the state treasury for himself. For the next week or so he amused himself by having the Greeks in the city put on a series of plays and pageants before allowing any who so wished to return to the original homes from which Tigranes had forcibly transplanted them.

Chapter 10

The Return of the King

King Mithridates to King Arsaces [of Parthia], greetings. ...

If you were looking at eternal peace with no perfidious enemies just beyond your borders, and if crushing the power of Rome would not bring you glory and fame, I would not dare to ask that you unite your prosperity with my misfortunes and join in an alliance....Fortune has deprived me of much, but has given in return the experience which underlies my advice.[1]

So begins a letter to the king of Parthia from the new commander of the Armenian army, Mithridates of Pontus. Tigranes had belatedly seen the benefits of putting in charge someone with almost two decades of experience in fighting the Romans. While Lucullus was delayed in sorting out Tigranocerta, Mithridates was looking for allies and doing what he did best – raising another army. Whether the letter to Arsaces is genuine has been the heated topic of debate for centuries. It comes from the papers of Sallust, a contemporary historian. He might be quoting the letter verbatim from papers which later fell into Roman hands. Alternatively, he might have used a genuine letter as a topos, the basis for a literary exercise, or he might have invented the entire composition on the basis of what Mithridates *should* have said.

Either way, we get some spirited anti-Roman invective:

From the beginning of their existence, they have nothing, not homes, wives, nor empire, which they have not stolen. Parentless, homeless vagabonds, created to be the scourge of the world, no laws, human or divine are allowed to stand in the way of rapine and destruction ... The Romans are the enemies of mankind, most vicious where the loot is greatest. By audacity and deceit, leapfrogging from war to war, they have grown great. They will destroy humanity, or themselves perish in the process.[2]

The argument of Mithridates was simple. Rome was an out-of-control juggernaut. Ultimately foiled in the west by the Atlantic shore, the monster had turned east, successively destroying Philip of Macedon, Antiochus of Seleucia and Pontus itself. 'Do you think that when we have all been crushed, that the wars will end, or that you can withstand the Romans otherwise?'

Though this last comment was both prescient and correct, the Parthian king chose to send sympathetic responses, but no help. Arsaces had in fact also sent envoys to Lucullus assuring him of his complete goodwill, so it was as well that Mithridates was not basing his survival strategy on Parthian intervention.

The campaign of 68 BC

It was fortunate for Mithridates and Tigranes that the Battle of Tigranocerta had taken place late in the campaigning season, in October, as this allowed the pair to withdraw their remaining forces to the fastnesses of upper Armenia. This meant leaving lower Armenia to its fate, but the Romans would not venture to follow their enemies through the mountain passes so late in the year. The two kings had until the start of the campaigning season of 68 BC to brace for the storm.

Mithridates had the smithys of every town working overtime to produce weapons, and set about raising a sizeable infantry force. This was organized and trained legionary-style by his Pontic officers, who had learned their skills from the Romans. Indeed, there were still some genuine Romans in his entourage, simply because these men had nowhere else to go. Tigranes meanwhile mustered the cavalry. Since we can discount out of hand Appian's figure of 70,000 men, all that can be said with certainty is that the two kings had a handy army, albeit raw, partially trained and fragile, with which to withstand Lucullus when he arrived in the summer of 68 BC.[3]

As instructed by Mithridates, Tigranes avoided bringing his cavalry to battle, but harassed the Roman supply lines. The historian Cassius Dio tells us that the Armenian light cavalry, like their Parthian counterparts, were expert at shooting over the rumps of their horses even as they retreated. Not only were the legionaries unable to get to grips with their enemy, but those hit by bowfire suffered doubly, both because the Armenians allegedly poisoned their arrows, and because they deliberately made the heads loose, so that these came off in the wound when an attempt was made to remove them.[4]

Much of the summer was spent in marching and counter-marching about the mountains in a game of large-scale chess. Lucullus attempted to bring the Armenians to battle, while the Armenians attempted to isolate and cut off his columns, attack his forage parties and lead the Romans on fruitless pursuits. It would appear from the fragmentary evidence available that Lucullus attempted to advance to the west of Lake Van, though his exact route cannot be determined. Whichever of the two possible paths the Roman took, his army, and especially his foragers, would at some point have been exposed to the Armenian cavalry on the plain of Mutsch.[5]

However, when an increasingly confident Tigranes decided to challenge the Romans at a river crossing (probably the eastern Euphrates in the valley of Arsanias), he received a sharp setback. This eased the pressure on the Roman supply lines and allowed Lucullus to set his course for Artaxata, the capital of Armenia proper, where he hoped to repeat the success he had enjoyed before Tigranocerta, the former capital of Tigranes' Armenian empire. However, Mithridates' delaying tactics had achieved their purpose. Winter came early in northern Armenia and it was already too late in the year for a major initiative. A frustrated Lucullus was forced by his cold and hungry troops to swerve westward and try to draw Tigranes into battle by besieging Nisbis.

Both sides were disappointed, Tigranes because he wrongly calculated that the walls of Nisbis were equal to the highly-practised skills of the besieging Romans, not least because the city was well garrisoned and commanded by his brother and Callimachus, the man who had for so long withstood the Romans at Amisus. However, although Lucullus took the city and helped himself to another royal treasury, Mithridates and Tigranes ignored his provocation. Instead, working on the principle that Lucullus did not have the troops available to both fight and hold his conquests, Tigranes spent the time busily repossessing himself of Lucullus' conquests in southern Armenia, no doubt consoled by the thought that Nisbis too would fall back into his hands when Lucullus moved on.

Lucullus had in fact noted the same point, and sent to Sornatius for some of the remaining legions garrisoning Pontus. These, with true Fimbrian recalcitrance, simply refused to move. Nor could Lucullus press the point too hard. The truth was that he had overstayed his tenure in command, and that command had only been for Cilicia in the first place. It was not just the Fimbrians, but some very highly-placed senators in Rome who were asking exactly why the ex-commander in Cilicia was currently hundreds of miles away from there, charging around Armenia with several unwilling Roman legions in tow.

Partly because his legions followed orders with ever-increasing reluctance, the Armenian campaign of 68 BC was ultimately inconclusive. The military initiative lay with Lucullus, but the wile and experience of Mithridates ensured that he could not use it. It almost seems as though, despite the loss of his armies, his conquests and his kingdom, Mithridates was beginning to enjoy himself. The king who had once, like a true Asiatic monarch, sent generals and armies to war on his behalf had now matured into a hardened warrior king who led from the front. His early setbacks had given him a resilience and cunning which made him a formidable general, and though now in his sixties, Mithridates' sheer physical presence made him a terrifying opponent on the battlefield.

Certainly, Mithridates showed no traces of war weariness and threw himself into campaigning with gusto. Leaving Tigranes to tidy southern Armenia, Mithridates took a small expeditionary force of about 8,000 men to Armenia Minor. Half of this force was Pontic (perhaps including the cavalry detachment which had been with him since Cabira) and half loaned by Tigranes. With this force Mithridates began to harry the small Roman garrison in eastern Pontus, catching many small Roman detachments unaware and cutting them down before they were even aware that there was a serious enemy presence in the region.

Perhaps because of his inability to get Lucullus his desperately needed reinforcements, Sornatius was now gone, and command was with Hadrianus, another Roman commander with whom Mithridates had clashed in the past. Like many a Roman before him, Hadrianus found that Mithridates was not to be underestimated. For a start, Hadrianus lost the strong force of Thracian mercenaries which he had inherited from Mithridates after the latter's flight from Cabira. As soon as they heard of his return, these men defected in a body back to their old master. Shortly afterwards, an early clash lost the Roman legate 500 of his men. He withdrew to his camp and sent out desperate messengers seeking reinforcements. Even so, when the attack came, Hadrianus was in danger of being overwhelmed until Mithridates exposed too much of himself in his enthusiasm to take the walls. He received a dart under the eye and a stone, probably from a sling, damaged his knee. The attack faltered as the king was taken away, and for a while his men feared for his life.

The Romans remained quiet over this period, for they had wounds of their own to lick. Among the retinue of Mithridates were members of the Agari, Scythians who treated wounds with snakebite. This appealed to a king with an interest in pharmaceuticals, and the royal patient was entrusted to them. Evidently the Agari were up to the job. Valerius Triarius, another Roman general, had been bringing reinforcements to Lucullus. Hearing of the crisis at Cabira, Triarius promptly changed direction and headed to his comrade's relief. Mithridates, thanks to his exotic medical treatments (or despite them) was able to rise from his sickbed to resume command. A cowed Hadrianus handed his battered troops to the command of the newcomer, but it soon became evident that the only battle over the next few days would be against the elements. A terrific late autumn storm developed, which soldiers afterwards reported as lifting whole tents into the air, and blowing to their doom those who strayed too near cliff tops.

Mithridates pulled back before the combined Roman force, toward Comana. Even in retreat he was dangerous, for after crossing a river (probably the Iris) he prepared to attack Triarius as his men came over the same bridge. Meanwhile, a second force had been sent hurrying back post-haste with the intention of re-crossing the river by a second bridge, so that the Romans would be caught halfway over the river and attacked by Mithridates' men on both sides. However, the bridge collapsed, so Mithridates was forced once more to retreat after a brisk but inconclusive engagement. Thereafter he followed the Roman example and went into winter quarters.

Even after campaigning finished for 68 BC, the advantage lay with Mithridates, for - as was the case almost anywhere in Asia Minor that had experienced the benefits of Roman rule - the local population were desperately keen to assist anyone who might offer an alternative. This meant that hordes of volunteers flocked to the royal standards, and allowed Mithridates to extend his power to include several local fortresses.

This left Lucullus with the thankless task of persuading his surly troops out of their winter quarters and informing them that it was necessary to abandon the conquest of Armenia and return with all speed to prevent Mithridates taking back Pontus. In order to save fellow Romans, the troops eventually agreed, but the effort cost Lucullus the little credibility that he had left with his men.

Events of 67 BC

It was a sign of the renewed confidence of Mithridates that he took the initiative and opened campaigning. When Triarius declined his initial offer of battle, he followed this up with an attack on the Roman fortress of Dadasa. This showed two things. Firstly that the Mithridatic intelligence organization was back to its usual level of efficiency, and secondly, that having been informed by his scouts that Lucullus was on his way, Mithridates had determined to dispatch Triarius before his arch-enemy arrived. The attack on Dadasa was a neat choice, for it held the booty looted by the legionaries on their campaigns so far. Either Triarius would be compelled by his men to defend their hard-won gains, or Mithridates would help himself to a handy financial windfall.

In the event, it turned out that Triarius needed little persuading. He may have been regretting his earlier reluctance to engage. After all, the Pontic troops had fled the region once before when confronted by Lucullus at Cabira, and the Armenians could not be worth much as soldiers if the legionaries of Lucullus had defeated ten times their number at Tigranocerta. Now, with his troops motivated by the defence of their booty, he felt reasonably confident of being able to present Lucullus with a tidy victory by the time his commander and the rest of the army arrived, and in the process would have done his career no harm.

Mithridates chose to meet Triarius near Zela, a fortified town which guarded the approaches to Amaseia from the Anatolian highlands. Though the walls of Zela itself are buttressed by a hill, the surrounding plain gave the Pontic cavalry excellent room for manoeuvre. It is also possible that Triarius had not expected the local reinforcements Mithridates had picked up over the winter. Not all of these would have been raw recruits either, as it may be that many who defected after Mithridates' retreat from Cabira had, like the Thracian mercenaries, returned to their old commander.

Exactly what happened at Zela is unknown. The Romans are much happier giving details about their victories than they are fond of describing defeats, and nobody sufficiently prominent for a biographer to take an interest in fought on the Roman side. From the scanty details we have, we know that there were perhaps two legions on the Roman side, and that Mithridates had a considerable force of cavalry. It appears that Mithridates sized up the Roman approach, threw his entire force against one section of the advancing enemy and defeated it whilst holding off the other section. Thereafter his cavalry rode around to the rear of the remainder of the Roman force and broke that too. There are tight-lipped Roman references to 'a ditch' across the plain, which Mithridates may (with fond memories of Sulla) have constructed in preparation for the battle, and then flooded. Many Romans were trapped against this unexpected obstacle and cut down in great numbers. Appian ruefully lists 150 centurions among the Roman casualties, which other sources put at about 7,000 men.[6]

Things could have been much worse for the fleeing Romans, for the Pontic cavalry were ideally placed to cut down the survivors. However, in the confusion of flight and pursuit, a Roman centurion found himself alongside

Mithridates himself, who evidently took him for one of the Romans in his own entourage. This man ran up to the king as though bearing dispatches and stabbed him in the thigh, which was probably the only accessible point where Mithridates could be wounded, since he was armoured Armenian-style in a metal corselet.

The would-be killer was promptly cut down, but the damage had been done. The entire Pontic army came to a disconcerted halt. Fortunately the king's physician (a Greek called Timotheus on this occasion) was near at hand and he ordered the king to be lifted above the throng of worried followers, so that his men could see that their leader still lived. Not only was Mithridates alive, he was furious that the pursuit of the Romans had been halted. Despite his wound, he personally set the attack back in motion, directing it toward the Roman camp. However, Mithridates soon discovered that in the delay his birds had flown. The Romans made no attempt to defend their camp, but fled directly to Lucullus, who had to take pains to prevent his men from lynching Triarius.

This showed considerable restraint, for Lucullus probably felt like lynching Triarius himself. Zela was a very substantial defeat, and the fact that it had been incurred by a lieutenant of Lucullus totally undermined his only remaining grounds for continuing to wage war in the region – namely that he was doing so successfully. The sad thing is that Lucullus, had he been as uninhibitedly brutal as Sulla, could have become wildly popular by allowing his men far greater freedom to plunder and quartering them on the unfortunate cites of the region during the winter. He could also have taken the approach of many of his contemporaries, which was that the barbarism of the tax-collectors was dangerous to interfere with, and was in any case no harm to him personally. As it was, by restraining his troops and forcing them to winter in tents, Lucullus had alienated his army; and by protecting those he had conquered from the full avarice of the tax-collectors he had lost vital political support at home. In short, whilst his enemies claimed that he was prolonging the war in Asia minor for his own benefit, the real case against Lucullus was that he was not being greedy and brutal enough whilst doing so.

After Zela, there was a slight air of unreality about the campaigning. Troops were deployed, positions offensive and defensive were taken up, but everyone was waiting to hear what the reaction would be in Rome to one of the city's most substantial defeats for decades. Mithridates withdrew toward a fortress called Talaura in the direction of Armenia Minor, there to await reinforcements from Tigranes, who had finished mopping up after the

Roman invaders had left his territory. Indeed, an advance guard of cavalry under one of Tigranes' relatives was already operating in the area. The tide seemed to be turning in Mithridates' favour. Attidius, one of the Roman senators in Mithridates' entourage, had been planning to betray Mithridates when the time was right. However, the increasing strength of the Pontic position encouraged waverers to betray the plot. The senator was killed quickly through virtue of his rank and Mithridates excused the freedmen and servants, saying there was no fault in following one's master. All others involved met a horrible end by torture.

Meanwhile, Lucullus, desperate for the chance to pull his men's morale together by a successful battle, turned to meet the Armenian force. In the event, he turned alone. As soon as it reached a relatively secure position, his army downed tools and refused to advance a step further. The arguments of Clodius rang in their ears. The soldiers of Pompey, who had fought a brisk campaign in Spain before mopping up the remains of Spartacus' uprising, had been discharged and were now living on the grants of land which their commander had secured for them. In many cases called to the standards whilst Pompey's recruits had still been schoolchildren, the soldiers of Lucullus had chased Mithridates across the length of Anatolia, and all about Armenia. Now, after his victory at Zela, Mithridates looked set to take them around again and the exasperated soldiery were having none of it. When the distraught Lucullus came to them, sometimes taking individuals by the hand and pleading with them to continue the fight, his soldiers responded by throwing their empty purses at his feet. Since Lucullus was the only one making a personal profit from the war, they told him he could continue it on his own.[7]

This also seemed to be the attitude of Lucullus' official successors. Marcius Rex, proconsul of Cilicia and Lucullus' direct replacement, refused to do anything. He had a small fleet and three new legions, but his soldiers had heard of the merry dance Lucullus' men had been on and he claimed that they would refuse to march if he ordered them eastward. Acilius Glabrio, who had been appointed governor of the new province of Bithynia et Pontus, was making light work of taking control of the Bithynia part of his command. That was, however, the limit of his interest. Not even the Pontus part of his new province concerned him, let alone a nasty-looking war on the borders of Armenia.

It was all that Lucullus could do to keep his army together for the duration of the summer, with the newer legionaries extracting from the Fimbrians the promise that they would fight if attacked. Naturally, Mithridates (fully occupied with making himself at home once more in Pontus) and Tigranes (engaged in his customary occupation of kicking Ariobarzanes off the throne of Cappadocia) took care to offer no such provocation. Therefore, at the end of the summer, a good part of Lucullus' army packed its bags and unilaterally discharged itself. To complete the misery of Lucullus, a commission arrived from Rome. During the full flush of his victories he had earlier asked that this commission be sent to settle the affairs of Pontus and bring it into working order as a Roman province.

As 67 BC came to an end, it appeared that after twenty-one years of intermittent warfare costing hundreds of thousands of lives, with a front line that had moved over a thousand miles from west of Athens to east of the Euphrates, Mithridates of Pontus was right back where he had started.

Pompey and the pirates

This situation did not go unremarked in Rome. Standing before the assembly of the Roman people, the orator Cicero thundered:

> He [Mithridates], already conquered, has just been able to accomplish that thing, when he was in the full enjoyment of his powers, he never even dared even to wish for!' [ie victory over a Roman army in battle]).The kingdom of Ariobarzanes... is wholly in the power of the enemy ... and that man, who in one day marked down for slaughter all the Roman citizens in all Asia, ... has not only never yet suffered any punishment worthy of his wickedness, but, now, twenty-three years later, is still a king. Not only a king, but so much a king that he is not content to hide himself in Pontus, or in the recesses of Cappadocia, but seeks to expand once more from his hereditary borders.[8]

Cicero was speaking in support of a law proposed by the tribune Manlius, which suggested that powers greater than any heretofore awarded be given to a Roman general. The lucky recipient of these powers was to be Gnaeus Pompeius, better known to posterity as Pompey. Pompey was later to try to persuade his contemporaries to call him Pompeius Magnus – 'Pompey the Great' – though one senator on hearing the new title asked interestedly 'Really? How big is he then?'[9]

Pompey was an ambitious man who deeply scared many in the senate. As a teenager, he had thrown his support behind Sulla when the latter returned to take control of Italy after the peace of Dardanus. Pompey's enthusiastic and unscrupulous endorsement of Sulla's philosophy earned him the unofficial title of 'carnifex adulescens' – the 'teenage butcher'. But when young Pompey went to fight in Spain, he made a chilling discovery. He was a brilliant general. He was a master of logistics and manoeuvre. His strategic vision was unequalled. Tactically, however, he was weak and he could not win battles. When he tried in Spain, Sertorius came close to terminating his promising career on the spot and Pompey was only saved by the timely arrival of his colleague, Metellus Pius.

Consequently, Pompey appears to have decided that henceforth he would win his wars without major battles. Given that battles were in his day the customary way of deciding wars, this was no easy thing to do. But it was certainly possible and Pompey, as mentioned, was a brilliant general.

This brilliance had its full chance to shine in Pompey's next command, which was against Mithridates' old allies, the pirates. With Rome preoccupied with rebellion, Mithridates, civil war and then the uprising of Spartacus, the pirates had been left to grow from an irritant to a problem to a fully-fledged menace. Their dominance of the sea now seemed complete, to the extent that they were now extending their operations, storming minor cities and staying there for weeks at a time as they plundered far inland.

They no longer confined their operations to the Cilician coast, or even to the Aegean. The west coast of Italy now offered the most profitable plunder, and there the pirates had even kidnapped two praetors off the roads of Italy as they travelled in their full state and regalia. On another occasion a female relative of Mark Antony was captured and only freed after the payment of a substantial ransom. Clodius (as related already) and Julius Caesar were among others who had involuntarily experienced pirate hospitality. So profitable had their occupation become, says Plutarch, that their ships had sails coloured with expensive purple dye and oars plated with silver.

Now Pompey, who had successfully brought the war in Spain to a conclusion, was given a command which overrode that of all Roman magistrates, both along the coast and for a considerable distance inland. His orders were to wipe out the pirates and their stranglehold on maritime trade (which was in danger of ceasing altogether). Currently, Roman efforts against the pirates consisted of a campaign in Crete by a general called Metellus, and he was making heavy weather of it.

In very short order, Pompey assembled a fleet of 500 ships,and divided the Mediterranean into thirteen areas of operation. Starting around Rome, he swept the Mediterranean from end to end, rolling the pirate fleets back before him all the way to Cilicia. From start to finish, the entire operation was accomplished in three months, with the greater part in forty days; all with minimal loss of life and only a single minor battle. In part, Pompey was successful because he allowed the pirates to surrender on terms. All who came to him as suppliants were allowed to live and many were settled on lands in Greece and other areas still depopulated after the ravages of the war with Mithridates had passed across them. All this was accomplished, as Cicero effusively commented, with 'god-like' speed and efficiency.[10]

Now, with Lucullus undone, and Pompey sightseeing in the east of the Mediterranean where his campaign had concluded, it seemed a natural step to give Pompey a further extension of his command, and make him responsible for stamping out the resurgent Mithridates and Tigranes. In addition to his present powers, Pompey was to be made commander of Phrygia, Lycaonia, Galatia, Cappadocia, Cilicia, upper Colchis and Armenia – quite a swathe of territory, when one considers what Lucullus had got up to when he was merely in command of Cilicia. Exactly how much control Pompey had over Bithynia is disputed, and in any case moot, as he did not operate there.

The law was carried, mainly because Pompey was very popular with the people, for whom the cost of imported materials had dropped sharply since the defeat of the pirates, and because Lucullus was unpopular with those of the upper classes who considered that he had curtailed their right to plunder Asia. It should also be noted that the territory allocated to Pompey in Asia Minor was less substantial than it appeared. Apart from western Anatolia and the allied kingdom of Galatia, anywhere else that Pompey wanted to command would have to be wrenched from the grasp of Mithridates and his son-in-law.

It was hardly to be expected that Lucullus would take all this calmly, though he tried. When he met with Pompey, he started by complimenting the man on his achievements. Then he discovered that Pompey had rearranged his settlement of Asia; partly in such a manner as to show clearly that he, Pompey, was now in charge, and partly, one suspects, to reward those in Rome who had contrived to organise his present command for him. At this point cordiality broke down.

Pompey claimed that Lucullus had merely been playing at fighting Mithridates whilst he used the war to enrich himself (and Lucullus was by now fabulously wealthy). Only now that a proper general was in charge would the war be fought in earnest. Lucullus responded by calling Pompey a 'vulture' who gorged on the winnings of other men.[11] Metellus Pius had saved Pompey's bacon in Spain, Crassus had won the slave war in Italy that Pompey claimed to have torn up by the roots, and Metellus had been winning in Crete against the pirates. Now, despite Mithridates' temporary resurgence, Lucullus' war was all but won and Pompey had come to claim the spoils.

These pleasantries exchanged, the two men had to be physically kept from each other's throats by their friends. Thereafter Lucullus took himself homeward in a huff, leaving Pompey and Mithridates to square off for the latest round of the drawn-out war.

The Dasteria campaign

Whilst the Romans politicked, Mithridates was rearming for the inevitable confrontation. He had learned at Cyzicus and Tigranocerta that sheer numbers do not a conquering army make, and he was experimenting with a Roman-style force that emphasized quality and mobility. Despite his best efforts he was low in cavalry, partly because the Sarmatians of the Black Sea were now loyal to his undutiful son Menchares. He had some 30,000 infantry, the hard core of which was made up of Roman exiles prepared to fight to the death rather than fall into the hands of their mother city. However, the remainder consisted of raw recruits of fragile morale. He was also re-fortifying his cities for a further round of sieges.

The new round of conflict opened with diplomatic sparring. Tigranes, like Mithridates and any Hellenistic monarch, needed sons to prevent opportunistic aristocrats from fancying themselves as successors to the throne and forthwith expediting the death of the current monarch. Parenthood restricted the potential beneficiaries of regicide to royal sons, but made the lives of these sons correspondingly more dangerous. The necessarily-paranoid eye of Tigranes had lingered on one of his offspring long enough to cause that son to bolt to the court of the Parthian king, Phraates. With an Armenian heir in his keeping, Phraates began to consider championing the son against his father and gaining a compliant puppet king on his western border. When diplomats arrived from Pompey promising generous Roman support for the invasion he was already contemplating, Phraates decided to launch his attack.

The invasion of his heartlands immediately took Tigranes homeward and out of the war in Anatolia. This left an isolated Mithridates with the grim prospect of facing not only the Romans, but also the Galatians and the levies of Bithynia and Asia. Pompey may have felt that the prospect was bleak enough for him to get Mithridates to surrender without a fight, or he may have felt that he needed more time to assess the situation and assemble his levies. In either case, his next step was to send envoys to Mithridates to discuss the king's surrender.

It is likewise uncertain how serious Mithridates was about negotiations. He had managed to extract a very favourable deal from the Romans in the past; but that was when Sulla had been desperate to depart the theatre of operations in order to deal with pressing domestic problems. Pompey had come specifically to deal with Mithridates and Tigranes and it was unlikely that he would depart without a convincing victory to take to the Roman people. But still, Mithridates had men to train, the Bosporan kingdom to bring firmly back under his control, and perhaps his son-in-law's war in Armenia might prove short-lived, making him available once more for an Anatolian war. In short, Mithridates was quite happy to waste a bit of time talking.

Pompey made it plain that he merely wanted to skip the war part of the business and have Mithridates behave as though he were already conquered. He was to place himself entirely at Pompey's mercy and to hand over all his possessions and all the Roman deserters serving under his standards. Mithridates could not for a moment appear to contemplate such an offer. Had he done so, his worried Roman contingent might actually have done him physical injury. Indeed, by some reports he only managed to soothe his men by saying that he had sent envoys to the Roman camp only in order to gain from them some measure of the Roman strength.

This strength would appear to have been about 50,000 men, at a very shaky estimate. The magic of Pompey's name had caused many of the Lucullan legionaries to re-enlist, and even a few of the veteran Fimbrians had stayed on to have a last shot at a decent pension under a commander already well known for his care for his soldiers upon their discharge. The legions were supplemented by a large force of native levies, including cavalry, and from Mithridates' later conduct it seems likely he was outnumbered even in this, his favourite military arm. However, the key to the matter was that Mithridates 30,000 men seem to have been facing an equal number of Roman legionaries, which meant that he could never expect to win a direct confrontation.[12]

Given the imbalance in numbers and quality of the armies, Mithridates chose to make his stand in the eastern heartlands of his kingdom, near the northern borders of Armenia. He had decided to let Pompey come to him and to try his now-standard tactic of hitting the Roman supply lines, rather in the manner that had worked so well against Lucullus in Armenia. In fact, according to Cassius Dio, Mithridates used a scorched earth strategy, devastating his own lands along the line of the Roman advance in the hope of making them short of supplies.

Details of the actual campaign are vague and contradictory. It appears that Mithridates was happy to let the Romans approach and even camp alongside his army, but he refused to offer to fight except from highly-defensible positions, which the mountainous lands along the Armenian border offered in abundance. There were various clashes, including, for example, one in which Pompey ordered his cavalry to feign a confused retreat from a skirmish in the hope of drawing the Pontics into an ambush; but just as the trap was sprung, Mithridates led his infantry on a sally and forced the Romans to retire.

The strategy of Mithridates is reasonably clear. To win, he had simply not to lose. Every month that he kept Pompey fruitlessly traipsing about the mountains was another month in which the glamour would wear off the Roman's name, and the soldiers would once again tire of a war which offered all the privations of a campaign but no prospect of victory or loot. Eventually the wheel of Roman politics would turn again and Pompey would go the way of Sulla, Murena and Lucullus.

Had Mithridates known his man better, he would have realized that he was, in fact, fighting Pompey's preferred kind of war. Once again, Pompey's logistical genius ensured that his men remained adequately supplied, whilst it was Mithridates who had periodically to shift his camp due to lack of supplies. Pompey had his men working ceaselessly at a series of ditches and minor forts, which constantly harassed the Pontic foragers and which threatened to enclose Mithridates completely if he did not keep moving. On one occasion, Mithridates was caught and besieged by the Romans in his camp for over a month and, when he finally broke out, Mithridates had to sacrifice his sick and wounded, and all but fifty days of supplies.

His retreat had taken him up against the headwaters of the River Lycus, not far from the later city of Nicopolis. Again we have three historians who have recorded what happened here, and each gives a somewhat different version. However, it is evident that Mithridates had established his camp on a now-unknown hill called Dasteria. Approach to this camp was by way of a defile with a single road. At some point there was a sharp engagement between the Romans and the Pontic army in this defile – either because

Pompey had stolen a march on Mithridates and set up an ambush (according to Dio) or because Mithridates had set a strong rearguard to block the defile (Appian).

By Appian's report, some of the Pontic cavalrymen were dismounted and fighting as infantry and making a good show of it until the Romans showed up with a large contingent of cavalry. At this, the Pontic cavalrymen rushed back to the camp to get their horses, precipitating a general retreat by those who did not know why their companions were running off and decided not to wait and find out. According to Appian this marked the end of the battle, but it is more probable that, as Plutarch, our third source, says, the Pontics finished up back in their camp – a secure base with a steep drop on at least one side.

Plutarch reports that Mithridates, as his men made camp for the night, was disturbed by a dream in which he was sailing pleasantly along the Black Sea with the Bosporan coast coming into sight when suddenly conditions changed, and he found himself alone in a shipwreck and clinging desperately to a plank.[13] At that point his lieutenants came to him with the news that the Romans, fearing that he intended to cross the river and make for Armenia, were launching a midnight attack on his camp.

Here Plutarch and Dio agree that the moon was low on the horizon and the Romans attacked with the moon at their backs. This confused the raw Pontic troops, who launched their missiles early, mistaking the shadows thrown far ahead by the Romans for the soldiers themselves. It is in any case notoriously difficult to judge ranges up and down a slope, let alone in highly-confusing circumstances in semi-darkness. Once the experienced Roman legionaries got among the Pontic troops the battle was as good as won. The Romans fought shoulder-to-shoulder in close formation, using their stabbing swords to terrible effect on men who were more preoccupied with escape and flight than in holding the enemy off. Also, Mithridates' foresight told against him at the last. He had made his camp at a site which was hard to get to. As his desperate troops now discovered, it was equally difficult to get out of.

Mithridates did manage to escape, fighting his way clear with 800 hundred horsemen, but at least 10,000 of his men did not. They were cut down by the Romans or, in many cases, simply forced off the edge of the cliff by the panicking throng. The Romans were not inclined to take captives and Dio reports that prisoners were far fewer than the dead. Defeated once more, and with his army dead or dispersed, Mithridates was again on the run.[14]

Chapter 11

The Last Stand

When victorious, Mithridates was inclined to show the vindictiveness of many a Hellenistic monarch. When in difficulty he was vicious, and because of this he had alienated potential or existing allies when he was young. But when defeated, he was magnificent. In the past, the king's response to resounding defeats had been to pick up the pieces, retreat and attempt to gather his strength, all the while continuing to hurt his enemy with all the means still at his disposal. He did not fall into despair, or look for scapegoats. Still, after Dasteria he must have known that this defeat would be very hard to come back from.

Of the hundreds of thousands he had once had at his command, he now commanded a troop of mercenary horse and about 3,000 infantry who had escaped the disaster. Believing the Romans to be hot on his trail, Mithridates led this little force directly for the fortress of Sinora, which was situated right against the Armenian border. Plutarch romantically describes their flight thus:

> one by one his followers fell away until he was left with three companions, including his concubine. She was an excellent horsewoman, dressing and riding in the Persian style, which prompted the king to nickname her Hypiscrates ['horsemaster']. She, with a manly and daring spirit, accompanied the king on his flight, never tiring and never failing to attend to him even after the longest journey.

However, Plutarch contradicts himself and falls into line with other historians when he says that at Sinora he opened the treasury there and discharged his men, rewarding those who had stayed with him thus far with cash and rich clothing. Those who wanted to avoid falling into Roman hands at all costs were also given deadly poisons from the king's personal repertoire. Mithridates' original intention was apparently to return once again to the sanctuary of Armenia, but the beleaguered Tigranes was having none of it. Suspecting Mithridates of conspiring with his rebellious son, the Armenian king let it be known that there was a huge 100-talent bounty on Mithridates' head.[2] Tigranes suspicion may not have been unfounded, since the rebel son was, after all, Mithridates' grandson.

With Armenia ruled out, there remained a final, desperate option. The Bosporan kingdom under Menchares had early thrown in its lot with the Romans, but it had never formally renounced its allegiance to Mithridates. Mithridates therefore decided to stake his life that this formal allegiance continued because there remained a hard core of support for his rule there. Of course, before Mithridates could stake his life on this belief, he had still to reach the Bosporus alive. The Romans were now masters of the Black Sea, and the peoples of Colchis, on the land route through which Mithridates and his handful of followers had to pass, were not particularly welcoming. They had suffered under invading Pontic armies in the past, and were equally worried about Mithridates drawing the pursuing Romans after him into their lands.

This is precisely what happened, but not immediately. For a start, it may have been that the Dasteria campaign was harder than the Roman sources let on, for after beating Mithridates, Pompey went on to populate a city which he founded nearby with his sick, wounded and discharged veterans. The city was called Nicopolis in commemoration of the victory at Dasteria (Nike being the goddess of victory).[3] This victory had made Pompey master of most of the Middle East, and, with his genius for organization, he immediately set about tidying the place up. Under pressure from the Parthians, and with the threat of the Romans joining in against him, Tigranes realized that he had no alternative but to throw himself on Pompey's mercy. Once his ambassadors had conveyed the assurances of Pompey that such mercy would be forthcoming, he literally knelt at the conqueror's feet.

Apart from administrative issues, one of the problems with pursuing Mithridates was that no-one was yet sure where he had gone. The fugitive king seemed almost literally to have dropped off the face of the known world. All that Pompey could do was set a watch on the Black Sea ports, make diligent enquiries and wait for his enemy to resurface. He reportedly whiled away some of his time reading Mithridates' mail, as he had captured the royal correspondence along with those castles which were gradually accepting the inevitable and changing their allegiance.

Once such castle, Symphorium, was handed over by Stratonice, a wife of Mithridates who was irked that the king had left her without even the protection of a garrison. Stratonice had been the subject of a royal wooing whilst the king was at the height of his power. Her father, a musician, had sung with her at a banquet, and had afterwards been dismissed by the king without a word. But the next morning, he was awakened by servants stocking his tables with gold and silver plate and his cupboards with fine clothing, whilst a top-quality horse was brought up for him outside. Mithridates, it appeared, was taken with his daughter, and would like to wed her. The riches being bestowed on him were those of a local notable who had 'died suddenly'. Father and daughter took the hint and the fortune which Mithridates offered. The fortune of Stratonice – in terms of both luck and money – outlasted that of her royal husband, for whilst Mithridates fled into the wilds of Scythia, Stratonice was confirmed in her current possessions.

Pompey let on what he had been reading about Mithridates. No doubt for propaganda purposes, he let slip that Mithridates had poisoned a son he believed was getting too popular, and a famous horseman from Sardis who had been impertinent enough to beat the king in a race. He also released the saucy correspondence between Mithridates and one of his concubines, and it is probably from the same source that later Roman writers claim their knowledge of the king's pharmacological research into poisons and countermeasures.

Regaining a kingdom

While Pompey was settling the affairs of Pontus and combining it with Bithynia to form a single administrative unit, Mithridates was adding to his reputation. The land to the northeast of the Black Sea was as little known to the peoples of the Mediterranean as darkest Africa was to the Victorians, and it enjoyed much the same reputation. Yet even here Mithridates was something of a living legend. 'He pushed on through strange and warlike Scythian tribes', reports Appian, 'sometimes by permission, sometimes by force, so respected and feared was he, though a fugitive in his misfortune.' He wintered in Colchis during 66 BC and pushed on around the sea of Asov in the following year, apparently not only gaining secure passage from the local princes, but even securing the allegiance of some. We get further detail from Strabo, and though many of the peoples mentioned have passed from history, some of the epic flavour of the journey is conveyed by their names.

> The Heniochi had four kings at the time that Mithridates Eupator fled from the country of his ancestors to the Bosporus, and passed through their country, which was open to him, but he avoided that of the Zygi on account of its ruggedness, and the savage character of the people. He proceeded with difficulty along the sea-coast, frequently embarking in vessels, till he came to the country of the Achaei, by whom he was hospitably received. He had then completed a journey from the Phasis of not much less than 4,000 stadia (390 miles).

No doubt Mithridates promised them those lands and titles which were about to become vacant when he got his vindictive hands on his son's kingdom and began settling accounts. Not all his family had died or gone over to the Romans, for we hear of several daughters in Mithridates' entourage. Some of these were married to Scythian kings to secure their allegiance. The journey through the wilderness was not without cost. Mithridates was no longer a young man, and his constitution was irreparably damaged by the privations of the trip. He also developed a set of ulcers on his face which never fully healed.

In the spring of 65 BC Pompey set off in leisurely pursuit of Mithridates. It is uncertain whether he actually thought that this would amount to much, but it also gave him the excuse to do as Caesar was later to do in Britain and gain the kudos of having led his armies beyond the confines of the known world. Pompey rather liked the idea of being known as the Roman Alexander, and if earning this title meant taking his men far to the east as Alexander had done, then the pursuit of Mithridates provided a decent excuse.

He clashed with the Iberians, a people who lived in the area of modern Georgia, and after defeating them he proceeded up the Black Sea coast, keeping contact with the fleet which accompanied him. On discovering that circling the Black Sea on foot was not easy due to the mountainous country past the Phasis estuary, Pompey turned inland and fought several brisk battles with the peoples of the interior. According to the later writer, Pliny, Pompey had interested himself in the trade routes of the Silk Road which looped south of the Caspian Sea thereabouts, and which was, as mentioned, one of the possible sources of Pontic wealth.[5] Certainly Pompey was keen to bring his army to the shores of the Caspian Sea, though whether he succeeded in this is doubtful. Plutarch is probably right to assert that his men, suffering from dysentery, and apparently astounded by the number of venomous snakes in the region, began to complain. Pompey, mindful of the fate of Lucullus, heeded the early warning and took his army to the more salubrious climes of northern Armenia, where Mithridates had left several juicy castles stuffed with treasure.

This was as close as Pompey came in his pursuit of Mithridates, whom the Roman commander probably suspected was by now either a captive of the Scythians, who would hand him over in due course, or a set of bones mouldering in an unmarked grave somewhere on the steppes. The Caucasus wilderness could be safely exchanged for the wonders of Palestine, Syria and the Red Sea.

At almost the same time, news reached Menchares that his father was alive and, if not in full health, at least well enough to descend on the Bosporan kingdom like an avenging thunderbolt. The tidings caused considerable alarm and despondency in the royal court, not least because Mithridates had done his reputation no harm by arriving via the 'Scythian Gates', from wild country which no-one was known to have traversed before. At his back was a horde of Scythians, whilst at Menchares' back was a horde of courtiers who were hastily reconsidering their allegiance. Politically, Menchares was wrong-footed from the start. As soon as his father had reached the Taman Peninsula and his whereabouts were known with certainty, Menchares sent a stream of messengers to protest his unflinching loyalty and argue that the Romans had given him no choice but to act as he had done in the recent past.

It is significant that Menchares seems not for a moment to have contemplated military action, which suggests again that there was considerable support for Mithridates in the Bosporan kingdom. Mithridates crossed to Panticapaeum and there put to death another of his sons, Xiphares.[6] The fault of this lad was apparently no more than that he was also a child of Stratonice, and Mithridates was deeply annoyed that his wife had docilely handed his treasure over to Pompey. One of the conditions of that handover had been that Xiphares should be spared if Pompey caught him.

Menchares, meanwhile, had understood that his father was not in the mood for reasoned discussion and fled to the Pontic Chersonese, burning his ships to prevent pursuit. Mithridates followed inexorably in a makeshift fleet. Once he landed the game was up for his son, who either committed suicide or was pre-empted in his death by those with a pressing need to gain the old king's favour. Mithridates in victory surprised many by sparing the friends of his son, saying they had acted according to their position and loyalties. His grudge was with his own 'friends', whom he had sent to counsel his son on his behalf. He considered that these men had betrayed him, so he had them hunted down and imaginatively executed.

News of the re-emergence of the enemy he had been sent from Rome to fight failed to galvanize Pompey into action. By now he was set on establishing Roman rule firmly in the remnants of the Seleucid empire, ignoring a rather plaintive request from the last Seleucid emperor to be given back what Tigranes of Armenia had taken from him. Pompey's only reaction to Mithridates' re-establishing himself in the Bosporus was to send the fleet to blockade the Bosporan ports on the Black Sea, claiming that, like Lucullus, he would let famine do the fighting for him. This overlooked the fact that at Cyzicus Mithridates had the army of Lucullus across his food-supply lines, whereas blockading a grain-exporting country was hardly likely to cause widespread starvation. These facts were fairly clear to Pompey's army, and they continued to make the point that they were meant to be fighting Mithridates even when they were far to the south campaigning around Petra. Even Cicero, generally an enthusiast for Pompey, commented that no-one would regard Roman possession of Asia Minor as secure until it was certain that Mithridates was not going to rise from defeat yet again.[7]

There was, however, a certain logic to Pompey's actions. By blockading the ports open to Mithridates he prevented both the import of war materiel and the export of grain which could be used to turn a profit for the kingdom. At the same time, he had been given a sharp lesson in the difficulties of campaigning in the north. With support from sympathetic Scythian kings, Mithridates was quite capable of retreating deep into the hinterland where Pompey would find it difficult to follow and where Scythian horsemen would make life very difficult for foragers or supply convoys. Given that Mithridates was in his late sixties and in poor health, Pompey took the position that the Mithridatic issue would resolve itself in due course. Time was an enemy even more relentless than Rome.

The Grand Plan

Mithridates might indeed have considered it excusable to retire in the sanctuary he had won for himself and spend his last years in peace. Probably this was the gist of an embassy he sent to Pompey. With a certain degree of brazenness, his messengers announced that Mithridates was prepared to let bygones be bygones, and would even pay tribute to the Romans if he was allowed to return to ruling his ancestral kingdom of Pontus. Pompey appeared to take the offer at face value and replied that Mithridates had the same opportunity as Tigranes had been offered – he should make his submission in person, and trust to the mercy of the conqueror.

Against the example of Tigranes, Mithridates would have set the treatment offered to Gnaeus Papirius Carbo, who had been brought before Pompey in chains at the end of the civil wars of the 80s BC. He had received only the mercy of a summary execution – and if this was the treatment meted out to a former consul of Rome, then the killer of 80,000 Romans and Italians might well have reservations about an unconditional surrender. Furthermore, the king had an eye on how he would be viewed by posterity, and replied that such a surrender was unthinkable 'as long as he was Mithridates'.[8] However, sons (whom Mithridates generally considered expendable), or other ambassadors, were available to make the king's submission on his behalf, should Pompey so require.

The degree of sincerity which both sides brought to the negotiating table was probably best illustrated by the fact that even as negotiations dragged on (Pompey was now in Syria), Pontus was being integrated into the Roman empire, and Mithridates was energetically preparing for war.

According to Appian, Mithridates had decided that as Pontus was in Roman hands, he no longer needed to defend his kingdom, and so might as well go to the source of the problem and invade Italy. For an old, sick, semi-refugee this was a breathtakingly audacious plan, but Mithridates always liked to think big. The man who had recently come through the trackless wilds of Scythia was hardly to be daunted by the thought of doing the same through the much better-charted tribes of the upper Danube, which, far from being an obstacle, Mithridates probably considered a potential recruiting ground.

Basically Operation Invade Italy would have run along something like the following lines. First an army was to be raised by the recruiting of freed slaves and mercenaries paid for by a heavy programme of taxation. At the same time, ambassadors would approach the tribes of the Danube basin with an eye to recruiting these men for a march through the eastern approaches to the Alps and from there a surprise descent into plunder-rich Italy. Mithridates calculated that the Italians would rise again if presented with a credible saviour. If Spartacus, an escaped slave, could rampage up and down the country for two years unchecked due to the support he had received from the Italian dispossessed, how much more eagerly would they support a man with credentials which included twenty years (and counting) of opposition to Rome, a king who was bringing his own army to the event?[9]

Buoyed by a wave of discontent with Rome, Mithridates and his Danubian allies would sweep down Italy, plundering all who resisted, and finally kill the Roman wolf in its lair. With Italy aflame, Spain would rise (it was already half-risen, with Rome's garrisons there occupied with fierce Spanish guerrilla resistance), Africa would opt for the independence it had only recently lost, and the Macedonians would rebel for a final time. In short, the Roman empire would collapse like a house of cards.

The theory that Mithridates was contemplating such a plan is made more credible by the fact that he did not treat the Bosporan kingdom as a long-term base. His tax regime was fierce and unsustainable. Also he ordered the killing of plough-oxen for their sinews. This move had obvious economic implications for future crop yields, but Mithridates evidently regarded this as less important than that these sinews were one of the few elastic substances known in the ancient world (women's hair was another) and important in building catapults for siege warfare. Significantly, neither Hannibal nor Spartacus had possessed the wherewithal to mount a serious siege of Rome.

Some modern historians are sceptical that the 'grand plan' was anything other than a Roman propaganda exercise. The logistic and financial difficulties were immense. Various routes between the Bosporus and Rome have been proposed by historians ancient and modern, but the most practical (or least impractical) was through Thrace, then across eastern Macedonia, and up the Danube valley to the Alps. Of course, this meant overcoming Roman resistance in Macedonia, presumably with the help of the Macedonian people, and giving the Romans due warning of his arrival. One of the alternatives involved a huge loop which brushes the borders of modern Ukraine, and would certainly have killed off the ageing king if his army did not mutiny first, and even Mithridates must have ruled such an odyssey out of consideration.[10]

The End

The army was already more than somewhat unhappy, as Mithridates was now 68 years old and increasingly unwell. Access to the royal person was limited to three eunuchs, who, it was rumoured, were enriching themselves by making the exactions of Mithridates' tax men even more ferocious than necessary. On the other hand, it is quite possible that Mithridates was using the dodge, ancient even in his day, of getting someone else to carry out vital but unpopular actions, and then later repudiating the doer, but not the deed. If so, he received early warning that all was not well when the trading town of Phanagoria revolted and Trypho, one of the unpopular eunuchs, was killed.

Three of Mithridates sons and one daughter were captured in the rising. Though the rebels set fire to the citadel, the garrison there held out, inspired by the resistance of another royal daughter called Cleopatra (a common Hellenic girl's name). Eventually, this gallant girl and the rest of the garrison were evacuated by ship, since Phanagoria was on the shores of the Black Sea.

This rebellion caused several other local strongpoints to join the rebellion. Mithridates feared that the army – which at this point was mainly conscripts – was no longer to be trusted. Accordingly he arranged to marry some of his apparently-inexhaustible supply of daughters to more Scythian princes in return for military support. The princesses set off with an escort of 500 men under the command of the surviving royal eunuchs, but as soon as the escort considered itself out of Mithridates' reach, the men killed the eunuchs and defected to the Romans, taking the princesses with them.

That he should so badly have misjudged his men is a sign that Mithridates was losing his usually sure grip on the political situation. Certainly he had made misjudgements in the past, and others had conspired to betray him. But earlier disloyalty was swiftly rooted out, and none of the earlier mistakes were fatal, simply because until now Mithridates had got the fundamentals right.

However, as Appian remarks, 'there was nothing mean or contemptible about him, even in misfortune'.[11] Whilst he had been ill, his generals had been conquering outlying parts of the Chersonese and Bosporus, and the royal army was an impressive, though brittle, force of 36,000 men. With this force he was (allegedly) determined to press on with his plan to invade Italy. Amongst those who had grave reservations about the plan was Mithridates' son and heir apparent, Pharnarces. By any standard, an invasion of Italy was a huge gamble against massive odds, and Pharnarces had little interest in going for death or glory. Rather Pharnarces reckoned that Pompey was showing so little interest in the Pontic remnant in the north that he had every chance of inheriting a tidy little kingdom on the death of his father. But this required that his father did not insist on ruining the place in pursuit of his doomed vendetta with Rome.

It is probable that the discontent of Pharnarces had not progressed far beyond the point of grumbling, because inevitably word of what was afoot reached Mithridates. Ever quick to scent a conspiracy, Mithridates rounded up the 'ringleaders' – that is, those whom he suspected were positioning themselves to best benefit from his death or deposition from power. However, he did not include his son amongst those condemned to death or exile. Possibly Mithridates felt that Pharnarces was genuinely guilty of no more than honest disagreement with his father's policy, or maybe, as Appian suggests, he was dissuaded from violent action by genuine fondness for his son.[12] If so, this was the first time Mithridates had turned from drastic action out of family considerations. This was after all, the man who had killed his mother (probably), brother (almost certainly), sister and sundry offspring (without doubt), and often on a very slight pretext.

Pharnarces did not intend to take the risk that his father's uncharacteristic mercy was merely a passing moment of weakness. In this, as with his commitment to decisive action, Pharnarces was certainly his father's son. He went first to Mithridates' hardest core of supporters, the Roman exiles. Either these exiles, being better informed than most about the dangers of invading Italy, welcomed a leader who offered an alternative, or they simply understood that Mithridates was ageing fast and decided to transfer their allegiance to a younger man who could offer them decades of protection. In either case, the exiles were won over and with their support the tide turned in favour of

Pharnarces' coup. Through the night, messengers were sent speedily to other units of the army, which generally welcomed the news that the current oppressive regime was at an end.

The collapse of Mithridates power came quickly. Even those loyal to him saw that they were in a rapidly decreasing minority and realized that their chances of survival depended on how swiftly and convincingly they changed sides. By early in the morning, when Mithridates was eventually awakened by the tumult, it was already over. He sent servants to find out what was going on and these brought the reply that the army had turned against him. Appian has them say 'We want your son as king. We prefer a young king to an old one who rules through and is ruled by eunuchs, a man who has killed so many of his sons, generals and friends'.[13]

Undaunted, Mithridates went to rally his men, perhaps believing that even now the force of his personality combined with a few well-timed concessions might be enough to stop the revolt in its tracks. If so, he would have been shaken when his soldiers fled from him and tried to join the ranks of the advancing rebels. The rebels refused to accept these latest defectors, pointing to Mithridates and telling them to prove their worth. To avoid death or capture, Mithridates retreated to one of the towers of his fortress, and there, from one of the upper galleries he watched as his son was crowned king in a makeshift ceremony.

Even now Mithridates was scheming for a way out. He sent messengers to his son saying that he would not oppose the usurpation of his kingdom if he was given only the chance to flee with his life. None of the messengers returned. Mithridates must have known that they probably would not. The dearest ambition of Pharnarces was to be confirmed by the Romans in possession of the Bosporan kingdom; there was no surer way of gaining Roman goodwill than handing Mithridates over in chains. That at least Mithridates had in his power to prevent.

He sent his bodyguard, ostensibly to surrender themselves to the new regime. However, Pharnarces knew his father, and at the sight of Mithridates' loyalists approaching him in a group he did not pause to reflect on their motives. The men were immediately cut down. This last desperate throw of the dice, if it had been that, failed. The kingdom of Mithridates consisted now of a few rooms and the battlements of his tower, and his subjects were two of his daughters and Bituitis, an officer in the Gallic bodyguard who had remained with his master.

Even the indomitable Mithridates could see that his long war was over. For years he had carried in the sheath of his sword the potions with which to meet such an eventuality. As he mixed the concoction which would bring his life to a swift and painless end, his daughters insisted that they be allowed to share their father's fate. Either they believed that Pharnarces had planned for them a fate literally worse than death, or they were driven by the powerful loyalty which Mithridates seems to have been capable of inspiring. In either case, they physically prevented Mithridates from taking the poison until they were allowed their share.

The poison slew the girls as quickly and easily as intended, but not the stubborn body of Mithridates. Years of taking antidotes had hardened his system to the extent where he could withstand potions which would kill three normal men, and he had already given a fatal dose to each of his daughters. Not enough remained to kill, or even seriously inconvenience him. Mithridates took a brisk walk about the borders of what remained of his kingdom in the hope that exercise would encourage the poison to work, but he finally had to accept that more direct action would be required.

It is highly probable that the eloquent farewell speech preserved in Appian is the historian's own invention, but it would be remarkable if Mithridates did not comment bitterly on the irony of his precautions being so thorough that he was unable to kill himself even when he wanted to. He might well have included a few choice remarks on ungrateful sons, but the only witness was the faithful Bituitis, of whom Mithridates asked one last service. He, who had been monarch with absolute power over a great kingdom, now needed the help of his bodyguard to die and be saved from the disgrace of appearing as a captive in a Roman triumph. Bituitis did his king the service he requested.

Cassius Dio offers an alternative ending to the story, which is that Mithridates was not killed by the poison, but seriously incapacitated. Consequently he was helpless when followers of his son finally broke into his rooms, and killed him. Whichever version is correct, it seems certain that at the end Mithridates, the warrior king, died by the sword.

Epilogue

The news of the death of Mithridates reached Pompey in 62 BC, whilst he was campaigning in Judea. His troops welcomed the occasion with rejoicing and sacrifices, for they were well aware that no-one would consider their campaign over whilst their inveterate enemy still lived. As it was, Pompey was now able to begin closing down military operations and preparing to return home in the secure expectation of a Roman triumph for a mission well accomplished.

As Mithridates had no doubt expected, his corpse was pressed into service by his son as a peace-offering to the Romans. Pharnarces, now ruling as Pharnarces II, was eager to be confirmed as ruler of the Bosporan kingdom, and enthusiastically surrendered himself, his kingdom and the mortal remains of Mithridates to the mercy of Pompey.

The embalmed body of Mithridates was conveyed to Sinope by trireme. Pompey was aware that although his battles in Asia Minor were finished, he had still other battles to fight in the political arena of Rome. Therefore, the better to show his accomplishment in bringing about the downfall of Mithridates, he ordered that his former opponent should receive funeral honours appropriate for a great king. Mithridates was given a royal burial, his remains being interred among the tombs of his ancestors.

Only now, as word of his death spread to the far corners of Mithridates' former kingdom, did those holding the last Pontic castles and strongholds finally contact the Romans and make arrangements for their surrender. Pontus did not survive as an independent kingdom, but was annexed to Bithynia and administered as a joint province. Pharnarces was allowed to reign in his Bosporan kingdom (with the exception of the town of Phanagoria, which was made independent as a reward for being the first to rebel against Mithridates). Asia Minor itself was now firmly under Roman control.

It is fascinating, though fruitless, to speculate whether a different person in Mithridates' place might have succeeded where Mithridates failed. The Roman political and military systems were at their weakest in decades, with political misgovernment leading to military overstretch and the constant danger of civil war. Nor should we forget how close Mithridates had come to success at Orchomenos in Greece, when a crushing victory over Sulla might indeed have united Rome's enemies under the Pontic banner. Could a Pontic Alexander, with greater charisma and generalship have swept Sulla aside in Greece, re-ignited the embers of the Italian revolt and crushed Rome?

Or did Mithridates never have a chance? Certainly he always acted as if he did. Nothing in his conduct suggests that he saw himself as a plucky hero fighting a doomed battle against overwhelming odds. Mithridates regarded himself as a rival of Rome, not a victim. No-one now can know how firmly he believed that Rome had over-reached itself, and was about to be brought crashing down, undermined from within by rebellious subjects and seditious generals, and attacked from outside by kings such as himself and Tigranes. Mithridates' best hope was that Rome had become as rotten as the Seleucid empire in its final days, and he worked tirelessly for himself and his kingdom to take maximum advantage should Rome begin to crumble, as for a while in the early 80s BC it looked as though it might.

The bumbling foreign policy of the senate, combined with the greed of its individual members, certainly showed Rome at its worst. Despite the experience of the Seleucid wars, Rome was still not fully capable of fighting overseas campaigns, and it was Rome's flawed political system as much as Mithridates' ability which allowed him to survive as long as he did. Nevertheless, the durability of Mithridates, in what could be mildly understated as trying circumstances, was truly remarkable. The fact that he was militarily defeated time and again meant that his political credibility was immensely damaged. Yet, right until the end, he remained firmly master of whatever dominions he controlled. At the same time, his constant probing for Roman weaknesses, be they military or political, meant that he was able to make the most of the few opportunities which he found. And even when down, he was never out, but was constantly seeking means – such as by subsidizing the pirates – of making his Roman enemies share his pain. It is quite possible that as the final levies went east to join the Pompeian army, some of the younger recruits were sped on their way by grandfathers reminiscing how they too had fought Mithridates when they were that age.

Also it was Mithridates' misfortune that he was matched against some of the best generals of his day. Pompey, Lucullus and Sulla were generals of the first class – and they, like the soldiers under their command, had been hardened in combat against the finest troops in the world in the course of fighting civil wars against their own armies. Yet, when Mithridates fought these same troops under lesser generals such as Murena or Triarius, he defeated them handily. Also of course, it goes without saying, that in fighting the Roman army of the late republic, the forces of Pontus were comprehensively outmatched in terms of training, experience and (usually) morale.

Under these circumstances, the performance and tenacity of the Pontic troops was admirable, and certainly superior to that offered by the levies of Tigranes of Armenia. However, the Pontic infantry lacked both the ferocity and the staying power, not to mention the battle-hardened experience of the Roman legionaries; it was this, particularly in the crucial battles in Greece, which eventually turned the tide. Had Mithridates succeeded in his later idea of creating a force of pseudo-legionaries to match against the Romans, the results would have been interesting, though perhaps not in a way which the Romans would have appreciated.

It is difficult to evaluate Mithridates as a general. As a strategist he seems to have had both the vision to conceive of plans on a regional, or even Mediterranean-wide scale, and he had both the daring and the decisiveness to carry these plans out. This, and his characteristic ruthlessness, was seen in his order for the murder of tens of thousands of Romans and Italians in the First Mithridatic War. The massacre was intended to commit the cities of Asia firmly to enmity with Rome, but in the end the perpetrators made their peace with Rome, while Mithridates, the planner, committed himself to a lifelong war against an enemy which seldom forgave, and never forgot. Again we will never know if Mithridates ever regretted this.

During the same war, the king's foresight in developing a navy gave him a major advantage over the Romans who had not done so, and who, indeed, only realized that one was necessary because of the use Mithridates made of his. Mithridates certainly botched the siege of Rhodes, but to be fair, this was his first experience of direct command of military operations. He learned fast, and by the time of the Armenian campaign against Lucullus, though his men were outnumbered and outclassed, Mithridates hardly put a foot wrong.

Strategically, Mithridates might be condemned for undertaking his Greek adventure and losing armies at Chaeronea and Orchomenos. But Mithridates was a gambler, and when he saw the tide turning against Rome he could hardly be expected not to see how far his luck would ride. Less excusable was his refusal to cut his losses at Cyzicus during his final push into Bithynia, when he should have abandoned the siege as soon as it became plain that his supply lines were endangered.

But abandoning the siege would have been totally contrary to the stubbornness which was ingrained into Mithridates' character. Mithridates never gave up. At Cyzicus this was a fatal failing, but without his indomitable will, he would not have been Mithridates, and he would not have been great.

As for Pontus, Pompey was only really interested in the seaboard between Heraclea and Amisus. This was annexed to Bithynia to become the province of Bithynia et Pontus, though by and large the Romans referred to the entire province simply as 'Pontus'. A *lex Pompeia* provided a basic constitution by which the province was governed, and this, lasting for centuries, proved more durable than another of Pompey's city foundations. This was called Neapolis, which shortly afterwards vanished without trace from history. Presumably the new city was in a district called Pompeopolis in coastal Paphlagonia, which was also made part of the new combined province. The founding of new cities, and the raising of towns or even villages to city status was needed to create new administrative districts in the Roman style. The devolved form of government favoured by the Romans contrasted sharply with the former centralization of power by the Mithridatid kings and was probably the main difference which the local people discovered in the change to Roman rule.

Deiotarus of Galatia gratefully received back those parts of his people's former lands which Mithridates had annexed. Cappadocia, so long a victim of Pontic expansionism was also able to expand somewhat at Pontus' expense. Ariobarzanes enjoyed his fifth and final restoration to the Cappadocian throne in 63 BC. Thereafter Cappadocia maintained a precarious independence by constantly switching sides to whoever looked as though he might come out on top in the next bout of Rome's civil wars. Eventually Cappadocia was subsumed into the Roman empire in AD 17. Much of the remainder of what had been Pontus was lumped into an autonomous area called Pontus Galaticus, which was finally absorbed into the Roman empire when Galatia too became a province in 2 BC.

Nevertheless, to a large extent these changes in borders were purely nominal. Rome was now the unchallenged hegemonic power in the entire region, whether its rule was direct or indirect. Furthermore, for majority of the people of Mithridates' kingdom life continued as it had before, under the rule of local dynasts, and changed little because these dynasts answered to a different authority.[1]

As for Pharnarces, he remained quietly in his Bosporan realm. As soon as he decided that the Romans were sufficiently distracted by their increasing political strife, he overran and reabsorbed Phanagoria into his domains. After a reign of sixteen years, he eventually proved too much a son of Mithridates to sit quietly in the north while his ancestral kingdom remained under Roman control just across the Black Sea. During the great Roman civil war of 49-45

BC he pushed his luck further and took control of Colchis and Armenia Minor. The latter was now part of the kingdom of Deiotarus, and the Galatian king appealed to the local Roman authority, a Caesarian general called Domitius Calvinus. Mithridatid and Roman armies met once again in 48 BC, near Nicopolis, where Pompey had driven Mithridates from his kingdom. This time the result went the other way, not least because the Galatian forces fled after a mere show of resistance. On the strength of this victory Pharnarces was able to reconquer all of Pontus at least as far as his father's former capital of Amisus.

This brought none other than Julius Caesar himself to the region where he had last campaigned as a callow ex-student who had gleefully dropped his scrolls to help organise the defence of Asia against the second attack of Mithridates in 74 BC. The final confrontation came on 2 August 47 BC. Pharnarces was distracted by rebellion in his new conquests and had Caesar approaching with his usual disconcerting speed from the south. In an effort to outstrip even Caesar's alacrity, Pharnarces launched an all-out attack on the Romans as they were entrenching their camp. This unexpected manoeuvre might have worked with the unskilled levies of Calvinus, but the startled veterans of Caesar's army simply closed ranks and began to drive the Pontic army from the disadvantageous position on the hillside in which their attack had left them.

The Pontic army collapsed and dissolved, leaving Pharnarces to struggle back to the Bosporus. Like his father, Pharnarces was killed when even that last refuge revolted against him. Caesar disparagingly remarked that Pompey had been lucky to make his reputation by fighting against such poor stuff, and reported his victory to Rome with the famously laconic quote 'veni, vidi, vici' (I came, I saw, I conquered).[2]

It took over a century for the region to recover from the devastation of the Mithridatic wars and the exactions of the Roman taxmen. Even after the final Roman conquest, Roman aristocrats continued to bleed the eastern provinces dry to support their massive expenses. Relief only came when the Republican *publicani* were replaced in their tax-gathering by more responsible imperial officials. We have a comprehensive report of Pontus as a province of Rome's empire at its peak. This comes from Pliny the Younger, who corresponded frequently with the Emperor Trajan whilst he was governor from AD 109-111. Pliny was sent to sort out a financial crisis, but his letters show that much of his time was spent in the un-dramatic minutiae of civil administration. Ironically, the complete integration of his former kingdom into the Roman empire shows the fatal flaw in Mithridates' assumption about the nature of Roman power. Rome did not just rule her conquests, but made them Roman, and the edifice of Rome's empire was far more stable than Mithridates imagined.

On his death, Mithridates passed into legend. The Romans remembered him for his indomitable stubbornness but also for his pharmaceutical skills. These became exaggerated with the passing centuries until, by the Middle Ages, there was a whole catalogue of potions allegedly drawn from his pharmacological researches.

Mithridates, who had loved music, found fame almost two millennia after his birth in an opera, *Mithridate,* written in 1770 by the young Austrian musical prodigy, Mozart. Undoubtedly, Mithridates would have been delighted so see himself on stage (sung by a tenor) and defeating the scheming Roman tribune Marzio (tenor). He might have winced slightly as his character tries to poison his fiancée Aspasia (soprano) and at his final theatrical reconciliation with his son Farnace, though he would have been grimly delighted that the latter's role was written for *alto castrato*. Something about the combination of warrior king and poison specialist has constantly intrigued later generations, and it is somehow appropriate that the legend of Mithridates, like the man himself, refuses to die quietly.

> He gathered all the springs to birth
> From the many-venomed earth;
> First a little, thence to more,
> He sampled all her killing store;
> And easy, smiling, seasoned sound,
> Sate the king when healths went round.
> They put arsenic in his meat
> And stared aghast to watch him eat;
> They poured strychnine in his cup
> And shook to see him drink it up:
> They shook, they stared as white's their shirt:
> Them it was their poison hurt.
>
> I tell the tale that I heard told.
> Mithridates, he died old.
>
> > A E Houseman (1896)

Finis.

Notes and References

Chapter 1

1. Bosworth, Wheatley, 'The Origins of the Pontic House', in *The Journal of Hellenic Studies*, vol 118 (1998), pp 155-164.
2. Diodorus Siculus, 20.111.4.
3. Plutarch, *Life of Demetrius*, 4.
4. Polybios, *Histories*, 5.43
5. Strabo, *Geography*, 12.3.11
6. This theory (still controversial) is mentioned in Francois Hinard, Sylla (Paris, 1985), pp 21-22 and discussed by John A Madden & Arthur Keaveney in 'Sulla Père and Mithridates (Notes and Discussions)', in *Classical Philology*, vol 88, No 2 (1993), pp 138-141.
7. Pliny, *Natural History*, 23.149 and Celsus, *De Medicina*, 5.23.3; cf 'Mithridates' Antidote – A Pharmacological Ghost', in *Early Science and Medicine*, Issue Volume 9, Number 1 (2004).
8. Justin, *Epitome*, 37.1.2.
9. Ibid, 38.4.7.
10. Strabo, 12.3.32; cf Deniz Burcu Erciyas, 'Comana Pontica: A City or a Sanctuary?', in *The Danish National Research Foundation's Centre for Black Sea Studies*, University of Aarhus.

Chapter 2

1. Eva Matthews, 'Roman Avarice in Asia', in *Sanford Journal of Near Eastern Studies* (1950), gives a detailed account of Roman financial activity with regard to Asia and Pontus in this period.
2. Eutropius, *Epitome*, 4.5.
3. Cf. Saprykin Sergey, 'The Policy of Mithridates Eupator and the North Coast of the Black Sea', in *Danish National Research Foundation's Centre for Black Sea Studies*, University of Aarhus.
4. Strabo, *Geography*, 7.4.3.
5. Justin, *Epitome*, 37.3.4ff.
6. Ibid, 38.1.1ff.
7. Strabo, *Geography*, 12.5.2.
8. Diodorus Siculus, 36.15.1.
9. Justin, *Epitome*, 38.1; Memnon, FgrH434 (22).
10. Plutarch, *Life of Marius*, 31.

11. Justin, *Epitome*, 38.3.1-4.

Chapter 3

1. Plutarch, *Life of Sulla*, 5.
2. Cf. Brian C McGing, *The Foreign Policy of Mithridates VI Eupator, King of Pontus* (Leiden, 1986), pp 84-85 for references to many of these.
3. An overview of Roman policy to date is to be found in A N Sherwin-White, 'Roman Involvement in Anatolia, 167-88 B.C.', in *The Journal of Roman Studies*, (1977).
4. Appian, *Mithridatica*, 3.17, is clear that at this point Aquillius was not following orders from the senate but making up policy as he went along. We should also note that later Roman historiography was probably influenced by the anti-Marian, and therefore anti-Aquillius, historian Rutilius Rufus, who was living in Asia at that time.
5. Ibid, 2.14.
6. Dio, fr 97.2, is certainly wrong to state the Mithridates was dealing directly with the senate at this time. Cf Cicero, pro Flacco, 98, for Aquillius' greed.
7. Troop numbers are largely based on Appian, *Mithridatica*, 3.17.
8. Ibid, 3.18.
9. J Munro, 'Roads in Pontus, Royal and Roman', in *The Journal of Hellenic Studies*, (1901), remains one of the best sources for the contemporary geography.
10. Kenan T Erim and Joyce Reynolds, *Aphrodisias and Rome: Documents from the Excavation of the Theatre at Aphrodisias Conducted by Professor Kenan T. Erim, together with Some Related Texts by Joyce Reynolds*, published by the Society for the Promotion of Roman Studies (London, 1982).
11. R K Sherk, *Roman Documents from the Greek East* (RDGE), 260, no 48.
12. Pliny, *Natural History*, 33.14.

Chapter 4

1. Appian, *Mithridatica*, 22.
2. The exact date of the deed is uncertain. The best guide is Cicero, *De imp. Pomp*, 7, which says it was twenty-three years before 66 BC, so early 88 BC or thereabouts, at the time when Mithridates was awaiting the Roman onslaught which never came.
3. Appian, *Mithridatica*, 23ff, for the gory details.
4. Ibid, 25.
5. This siege merits almost a small bibliography of its own, of which the most informative and entertaining works are: L Sprague de Camp, 'Master Gunner Apollonios' , in *Technology and Culture*, (1961); William Ledyard Rodgers, *Greek and Roman Naval Warfare* (Annapolis, 1984); and Duncan B Campbell, *Ancient Siege Warfare* (Oxford, 2005).
6. Sporting tries at disentangling Athenian politics of the period include: Glenn Richard Bugh, 'Athenion and Aristion of Athens', in *Phoenix*, (1992); and Sterling Dow, 'A Leader of the Anti-Roman Party in Athens in 88 B.C', in *Classical*

Philology, (1942).
7. Plutarch, *Life of Sulla*, 10ff, for details of this early campaign

Chapter 5
1. Plutarch, *Life of Sulla*, 11.
2. Ibid, 2.
3. Appian, *Mithridatica*, 38.
4. Plutarch, *Life of Sulla*, 14.
5. What follows is largely a synthesis of the accounts of Appian, Plutarch and others, though precedence has been given to Plutarch as Charonea was, after all, his home town and he had merely to take an afternoon stroll to see the battleground for himself.
6. W. Kendrick Pritchett, 'Observations on Chaironeia', in *American Journal of Archaeology*, Volume 62, No 3 (July, 1958), pp 307-311, is mainly interested in the earlier battle of 338 but still has some useful observations on topology.
7. Plutarch, *Life of Sulla*, 18. It was thanks to the downhill slope that Roman light artillery was able to participate in the battle – an unusual occurrence on ancient battlefields.

Chapter 6
1. Appian, *Mithridatica*, 47.
2. Plutarch, *Life of Sulla*, 21.
3. Memnon, 33.
4. Frontinus, *Strategems*, 2.3.17.
5. See E Badian, 'Waiting for Sulla', in *The Journal of Roman Studies*, (1962), for the situation in Italy at this time
6. Cf: J Madden and A Keaveney, 'Sulla Pere and Mithridates', in *Classical Philology*, Vol 88, No 2 (1993).
7. Plutarch, *Life of Lucullus*, 3.

Chapter 7
1. Plutarch, *Life of Sulla*, 22.9, says Pontus had to pay 2,000 talents as well. Memnon, 35.2, puts the figure at 3,000 talents.
2. Modern discussions of this settlement are surprisingly rare. Perhaps the best is Sherwin-White, *Roman Foreign Policy in the East, 168 BC to AD 1* (Norman, Oklahoma, 1983), pp143-149.
3. For a full treatment of what this term entailed, see 'Rex Socius to Rex Datus', in *Maurice Sartre, The Middle East under Rome* (Cambridge, Massachusetts, 2005), pp 71-90.
4. Plutarch, *Life of Lucullus*, 7.
5. Memnon, 26.3. Information for the period between the first and third Mithridatic wars is scanty and often contradictory. The description of this campaign is a

synthesis drawn largely from the work of Plutarch, Appian and Memnon.

6. Appian, *Mithridatica*, 65.
7. Ibid, 66.
8. Suetonius, *The Life of Caesar*, 2.
9. Tigranes is another character whose life has been sadly under-chronicled. The most comprehensive modern work, Herant K Armen, *Tigranes the Great* (Detroit, 1940), is a somewhat flawed and haphazard text.
10. No-one is quite sure exactly where. Cf: T Rice Holmes, 'Tigranocerta', in *The Journal of Roman Studies* (1917).
11. Figures, as ever, courtesy of Appian, *Mithridatica*, 70.

Chapter 8

1. Justin, 38.4–7. Justin explicitly states he is passing on the speech unaltered as he received it from Trogus, a historian contemporary with Mithridates.
2. As Vellius Paterculus adds, Mithridates was the last king in the region, apart from that of the Parthians, who was totally independent of Rome. Vellius Paterculus, 2.40.1.
3. For a fuller discussion of this complex question, see B C McGing, 'The Date of the Outbreak of the Third Mithridatic War', in *Phoenix*, Volume 38, No 1 (1984), pp 12–18.
4. Memnon, 37.
5. Plutarch, *Life of Lucullus*, 8.
6. Appian, *Mithridatica*, 69. Strabo, 12.8.11, puts the numbers at 150,000.
7. Cicero, in *Pro Murena*, 33, calls Cyzicus the key to Asia: *'eamque urbem sibi Mithridates Asiae ianuam fore putasset qua effracta et revolsa tota pateret provincia'*.
8. The description of Cyzicus in antiquity is drawn from Robert de Rustafjaell, 'Cyzicus', in *The Journal of Hellenic Studies* (1902).
9. The siege is mainly from Appian, *Mithridatica*, 74, with Plutarch, *Life of Lucullus*, 9–12.
10. Eutropius, 6.6.
11. Assuming these are the 100 described in Florus 3.5.18.

Chapter 9

1. Much of the geography of military action in Pontus is based on the work of J Munro over a century ago: J Munro, 'Roads in Pontus, Royal and Roman', in *Journal of Hellenic Studies* (1901).
2. Plutarch, *Life of Lucullus*, 14.
3. Appian, *Mithridatica*, 78.
4. Plutarch, *Life of Lucullus*, 15; Appian, *Mithridatica*, 79, gives the same story, but dates the event later, probably in 71 BC.
5. Memnon, 45.
6. Plutarch, *Life of Lucullus*, 15.

7. Two articles which make valuable reading in conjunction with this account are: C
    Konrad, 'Reges Armenii Patricios Resalutare Non Solent?', in The *American
    Journal of Philology* (1983); and a sceptical reading of Plutarch and Appian by D
    Mulroy, 'The Early Career of P. Clodius Pulcher: A Re-Examination of the
    Charges of Mutiny and Sacrilege', in *Transactions of the American Philological
    Association* (1974-1988), which is also sympathetic toward the Fimbrian legions.
8. Cicero, in his speech On the Command of Pompey, 23, shows this was indeed the
    reaction in Rome.
9. Strabo, 12.2.1.
10. Appian, *Mithridatica*, 85.
11. Plutarch, *Life of Lucullus*, 26.
12. Phlegon, fr12.
13. Plutarch, *Life of Lucullus*, 27, is the main source for this reconstruction, with help
    from Appian, *Mithridatica*, 85; Frontinus, *Strategems*, 2.1.14; and Memnon, 57M.
    Valuable geographical detail is to be found in T Rice Holmes, 'Tigranocerta', in *The
    Journal of Roman Studies*, 1917.

Chapter 10

1. Sallust, *Letter of Mithridates*, 1.1.
2. Ibid, 20.
3. Appian, *Mithridatica*, 87. Most modern historians agree this figure is too high for
    the population available, and is in any case not borne out by the kings' conduct in
    the subsequent campaign.
4. Dio, 36.5.
5. Alternatively spelled 'Mush', in the Taron region of modern Armenia.
6. Appian, *Mithridatica*, 89. Further help on reconstructing the battle is found in Dio,
    36.12.
7. Plutarch, *Life of Lucullus*, 35.
8. Cicero, On the command of Pompey, 3; cf W Loader, 'Pompey's Command under
    the Lex Gabinia', in *The Classical Review* (1940) for discussion of what this
    command entailed.
9. Plutarch, *Life of Crassus*, 9.
10. Cicero, On the command of Pompey, 12.
11. Plutarch, *Life of Pompey*, 31.
12. Army numbers based on the work of Sherwin-White (1983) and *Cambridge Ancient
    History* (1951)
13. Plutarch, *Life of Pompey*, 32.
14. The main sources for this reconstruction of events are Appian, *Mithridatica*, 100;
    Plutarch, *Life of Pompey*, 32; Cassius Dio, 36.48; and Livy, *Epitome*, 101, with
    geographical assistance from Strabo, 12.3.28.

Chapter 11
1. Plutarch, *Life of Pompey*, 32.
2. Cassius Dio, 36.50.
3. For details of this and other Pompeian foundations in Pontus see W Fletcher, 'The Pontic Cities of Pompey the Great', in *Transactions and Proceedings of the American Philological Association*, volume 70 (1939).
4. Strabo, 11.13.1.
5. J Thorley, 'The Development of Trade between the Roman Empire and the East under Augustus', in *Greece & Rome* (1969), p.215.
6. Site of the modern city of Kertsch.
7. Cicero, *Pro Murena*, 30-33.
8. Appian, *Mithridatica*, 107.
9. Ibid, 109.
10. Florus, 1.40.25; Strabo, 7.5.1.
11. Appian, *Mithridatica*, 109.
12. Ibid, 110.
13. Ibid
14. The last hours of Mithridates are recorded in Appian, *Mithridatica*, 111, and Cassius Dio, 38.12-14.

Chapter 12
1. J C G Anderson, 'Pontica', in *The Journal of Hellenic Studies*, volume 20 (1900), pp 151-158; A J Marshall, 'Pompey's Organization of Bithynia-Pontus: Two Neglected Texts', in *The Journal of Roman Studies*, volume 58, parts 1 and 2 (1968).
2. Adrian Goldsworthy, *Caesar: Life of a Colossus* (London, 2006) pp 446-447.

Bibliography

Anderson, J, 'Pontica', in *The Journal of Hellenic Studies*, Vol 20 (1900), pp 151-158.

Armen, H, *Tigranes the Great* (Detroit, 1940).

Badian, E, 'Waiting for Sulla', in *The Journal of Roman Studies* (1962).

Bosworth, W, 'The Origins of the Pontic House', in *The Journal of Hellenic Studies*, Vol 118 (1998) pp 155-164.

Bugh, G, 'Athenion and Aristion of Athens', in *Phoenix* (1992).

Campbell, D, *Ancient Siege Warfare* (Oxford, 2005).

Darbyshire, et al, 'The Galatian Settlement in Asia Minor', *Anatolian Studies* (2000)

Deniz Burcu Erciyas, 'Comana Pontica: A City or a Sanctuary?', in *The Danish National Research Foundation's Centre for Black Sea Studies* (Aarhus).

de Rustafjaell, R, 'Cyzicus', in *The Journal of Hellenic Studies* (1902).

de Souza, P, *Piracy in the Graeco-Roman World* (Cambridge, 1999).

Dow, S, 'A Leader of the Anti-Roman Party in Athens in 88 B.C.', *Classical Philology* (1942)

Fletcher, W, 'The Pontic Cities of Pompey the Great', in *Transactions and Proceedings of the American Philological Association*, Vol 70 (1939)

Goldsworthy, A, *Caesar: Life of a Colossus* (Orion, 2006).

Gruen, E, *The Hellenistic World and the Coming of Rome* (Berkeley, 1984).

Hildinger, E, *Warriors of the Steppe: A Military History of Central Asia, 500 B.C. to A.D. 1700* (Staplehurst, 1997).

Hinard, F, *Sylla* (Paris, 1985).

Kendrick Pritchett, W, 'Observations on Chaironeia', in *American Journal of Archaeology*, Vol 62, No 3 (1958), pp 307-311.

Konrad, C, 'Reges Armenii Patricios Resalutare Non Solent?', in *The American Journal of Philology* (1983).

Loader, W, 'Pompey's Command under the *Lex Gabinia*', in *The Classical Review* (1940)

Madden, J & Keaveney, A, 'Sulla Père and Mithridates' (Notes and Discussions), in *Classical Philology*, Vol 88, No 2, (April 1993), pp 138-141.

Marshall, A, 'Pompey's Organization of Bithynia-Pontus: Two Neglected Texts', in *The Journal of Roman Studies*, Vol 58, Parts 1 and 2 (1968)

Matthews, E, 'Roman Avarice in Asia', in *Sanford Journal of Near Eastern Studies* (1950).

Matthews, R, 'Hittites and "barbarians" in the Late Bronze Age: regional survey in northern Turkey', in *Archaeology International*, 3 (2000) pp 32-5.

Matyszak, P, *Enemies of Rome from Hannibal to Atilla the Hun* (London, 2004).

McGing, B, 'The Date of the Outbreak of the Third Mithridatic War', in *Phoenix*, Vol 38, No 1 (1984), pp 12-18.

McGing, B, *The Foreign Policy of Mithridates Eupator* (Leiden, 1986).

Mulroy, D, 'The Early Career of P. Clodius Pulcher: A Re-Examination of the Charges of Mutiny and Sacrilege', in *Transactions of the American Philological Association* (1974).

Munro, J, 'Roads in Pontus, Royal and Roman', in *The Journal of Hellenic Studies* (1901).

Reynolds, J, *Aphrodisias and Rome: Documents from the Excavation of the Theatre at Aphrodisias Conducted by Professor Kenan T. Erim, together with Some Related Texts*, published by the Society for the Promotion of Roman Studies (London, 1982).

Rice Holmes, T, 'Tigranocerta', in *The Journal of Roman Studies* (1917).

Rodgers, W, *Greek and Roman Naval Warfare* (Annapolis, 1984).

Rostovtzeff, M, et al, *The Roman Republic 133-44 BC* (Cambridge,1951)

Saprykin, S, 'The Policy of Mithridates Eupator and the North Coast of the Black Sea', in *Danish National Research Foundation's Centre for Black Sea Studies* (Aarhus)

Sartre, M, *The Middle East underRome* (Cambridge, Massachusetts, 2005).

Sherwin-White, A N, 'Roman Involvement in Anatolia, 167-88 B.C.', in *The Journal of Roman Studies* (1977).

Sherwin-White, A N, *Roman Foreign Policy in the East 168 BC To AD 1* (Norman, 1983).

Sprague de Camp, L, 'Master Gunner Apollonios', in *Technology and Culture* (1961).

Thorley, J, 'The Development of Trade between the Roman Empire and the East under Augustus', in *Greece & Rome* (1969).

Thorley, J, 'The Silk Trade between China and the Roman Empire at Its Height, Circa A.D. 90-130', in *Greece & Rome* (1971).

Totelin, L, 'Mithradates' Antidote – A Pharmacological Ghost', in *Early Science and Medicine* Vol 9, Number 1 (February, 2004).

Ünsal Yalçın, 'Early Iron Metallurgy in Anatolia', in *Anatolian Studies* (1999).

Wilcox, P, *Rome's Enemies: Parthians & Sassanid Persians* (Oxford, 1986).

Index